A Prophetic History of the Church Since WW2

PAUL DAVIES

Ark House Press
PO Box 1722, Port Orchard, WA 98366 USA
PO Box 1321, Mona Vale NSW 1660 Australia
PO Box 318 334, West Harbour, Auckland 0661 New Zealand
arkhousepress.com

© Paul Davies 2021

Scripture quotations taken from The Holy Bible, New International Version®
NIV®. Copyright © 1973 1978 1984 2011 by Biblica, Inc. TM
Used by permission. All rights reserved worldwide.

Cataloguing in Publication Data:
Title: A Prophetic History of the Church
ISBN: 978-0-6451031-1-3 (pbk)
Subjects: Christian Resource; Prophesy; Prophets; History;
Other Authors/Contributors: Davies, Paul

Design by initiateagency.com

Dedication

To my Dad, Rev. J. E. Davies, who faithfully laid the foundations in me for the Lord to build upon, and encouraged me to keep going.

To my friend, spiritual father, and overseer, Raf Shaw, who brought out the Pente-Rascal, and forced me to learn to hear for myself.

To Dan Reisc, Paul Cain's former assistant and President of Paul Cain Ministries, who gave hours of his time via Skype to share stories, correct errors, and encourage me.

Petra—Beyond Belief 1990

> We're content to pitch our tent when the glory's evident
> Seldom do we know the glory came and went
> Moving can seem dangerous in this stranger's pilgrimage
> Knowing that you can't stand still you cross the bridge
>
> (chorus)
> There's a higher place to go beyond belief, beyond belief
> Where we reach the next plateau beyond belief, beyond belief
> And from faith to faith we grow towards the center of the flow
> Where He beckons us to go beyond belief, beyond belief

Lyrics by Bob Hartman

Foreword

This book began as a Keynote presentation to accompany a message given at One Accord Fellowship, Middleton, South Australia on 4th October, 2020. My intention was to tell the stories of the work of the Holy Spirit over the post-war period. Spectacular miracles and events have been almost completely suppressed by the cessationist Churches (those who teach God 'ceased' working in the Supernatural anymore), so that most Christians don't even know these things occurred. This robs the Lord of Glory and FAILS to "honour the fathers" who went before us, many of whom set a level in the Spirit that few have touched since.

This book could be sub-titled: **"The Acts of the Holy Spirit through fallible servants who were available for Him to use."** It is important to note that like all of us, these ministers were sinners, redeemed by Grace and the Blood of Jesus through His death and Resurrection. Their sins are forgiven, not necessarily absent, and many who were used powerfully fell into sin at some point. The Church is the only Army that shoots its own wounded (Paul Cain used to say "we're the only army on earth that buries their wounded alive"), and the lack of forgiveness and grace from the wider body when such high-profile ministers fall is appalling. Many leave NO room for repentance and restoration for such men and women—confessing Christians even though this is the foundation of our Gospel message. "Brothers, if someone is caught in a sin, you who are spiritual should restore him gently" (Galatians 6:1). Few understand the demonic opposition that walking so closely with Jesus can bring—a little step away from Him towards the flesh nature can bring a demonic response that is way out of the experience of most believers. Some ministers have even been physically assaulted by demons during the night, and bear the marks of such assaults on their bodies.

When you read these stories, ask the Holy Spirit for "wisdom and revelation". There are lessons in the successes AND the failures for our time.

Paul warned: *"He who thinks he stands take heed lest he fall"* (1 Cor 10:12). God is about to bring another Wave of the Holy Spirit that will dwarf anything the Church has yet seen, because "God saves the best till last"—the 'moral' of the Water-into-Wine story at the Wedding Feast (John 2:10).

Men such as William Branham, Oral Roberts and A. A. Allen were household names in their day. Others such as prophetic ministers Bob Jones and Paul Cain were well-known in certain circles, and ignored by others. Recent leaders such as John Wimber, Mike Bickle and Bill Johnson have all played a part in preparing the church for God's purposes.

My reading of research done by various ministers shows that many of the popular stories told about these men and women are **incorrect** or have been deliberately **falsified** by their opponents. Though seemingly difficult to believe, there have been those professing Christ who have done despicable things to oppose the work of the Spirit, because their theology, personal preferences, financial greed or jealousy caused them to hate the events they witnessed. Today, we also have the "Internet Pharisees"—the self-appointed "defenders of orthodoxy" whose web pages loudly and boldly denounce those who move in the Spirit as "false". Most of these people have little if any experience with healings or miracles (if they deign to accept them as valid at all) and certainly don't have "eyes to see or ears to hear". Like the Pharisees, we have become experts in knowing a lot about God, but are woefully lacking in *knowing him* intimately, especially in regards to hearing his voice. As Bobby Conner likes to say, many of us "are way too familiar with a God we barely know."

Knowledge is easily gained in our information age, wisdom far less so, yet the Bible says "*wisdom is supreme, therefore get wisdom*" (Proverbs 4:7). Knowledge costs you little but your time, whereas seeking the Lord for wisdom goes against all worldly training. **My purpose is to give you the opportunity to hear the tales and investigate them yourself.** Many of these stories come from audio tapes, video interviews and books, most of which are publicly available or searchable on the Internet. I will try and list some sources in each case so that you can check things out.

As a Science teacher in High School, I always tried to teach my students to think for themselves. I would encourage them to investigate and dig on their own, and learn to evaluate for themselves, rather than simply believe what they were expected to believe. I believe that if you have the Holy Spirit, He will "*guide you into all truth*" (John 16:13)—that is His role! We have been taught to blindly accept the theologies, practices and preferred Scriptural interpretations of our home churches without question, and with any challenge to the current status quo vigorously persecuted. We need to become better at asking the "awkward questions", and seeking the Lord for His perspective.

You can investigate these stories yourself. There are over 1000 recorded sermons from William Branham, for example, easily available over the Internet, where you can check what he believed for yourself, rather than simply accept the claims made by others. Similarly, many recordings, books and magazines are available about others mentioned here. Go carefully, and pray "*without ceasing*". Even those reports favourable to the men and women concerned didn't always get it right. Take care to humbly ask the Lord to give you "eyes to see, ears to hear and a heart to understand", and be patient. Sometimes He takes decades to bring you around to His way of thinking.

Also, some are always concerned about ANY focus on people rather than Christ. I don't know if you noticed, but the only part of Jesus the world will see at the moment is what we Christians allow him to reveal through US! We are His hands and feet, and we need to step up. Jesus gave us a package deal as our Mission Statement:

1. **Preach the gospel (of the Kingdom),**
2. **Heal the sick,**
3. **Raise the dead,**
4. **Cleanse the lepers,**
5. **Cast out demons,**
6. **Do it for free!** (Matt 10:7,8).

God does not shy away from promoting His faithful servants. He said to Joshua: "*This day I will begin to exalt you in the sight of all Israel, that they may know that just as I have been with Moses, I will be with you*" (Joshua 3:7). I am NOT trying to put these men on a pedestal—**we follow Jesus, not men**—but to honour their faithfulness to the Lord and their willingness to obey, often at great cost to themselves.

Finally, we are called to follow our Master. He said clearly on several occasions that "*…the miracles I do in My Father's name, these testify of Me*" (Jn 10:25); "*…believe the miracles, that you may know and understand that the Father is in me, and I am in the Father*" (John 10:38). There WILL be false signs, false teachers and false prophets in the end times—"*by their fruit you will recognise them…*" (Matthew 7:16). Fruit takes time to mature.

FOREWORD

Don't be hasty to judge things that are weird (have you READ Ezekiel??) or different—<u>take it to the prayer closet and seek the Lord</u>.

Pray Psalm 139:23-24 often: "*Search me, O God and know my heart; test me and know my anxious thoughts. See if there is any offensive way in me, and lead me in the way everlasting.*" Be careful of criticising the "*speck of sawdust*" in a brother's eye when you may be ignorant of the "*plank in your own eye*" (Matt 7:3).

Finally, be VERY slow to criticise a brother or sister you feel is in error, or even in sin. Isaiah 58 warns against "…*the pointing finger and malicious talk*" and promises numerous blessings for those who overcome and "*clothe the naked*"—cover their brother's sin or error by NOT publicising it. Take it to the Lord in prayer, NEVER gossip to others, regardless of how convinced you are of your accuracy.

God has been telling His Prophets that He is about to "do it again" – there is a major Wave of the Holy Spirit coming that will usher in the "Billion-Soul Harvest," of which so many have been told by the Lord in recent decades. My prayer is that this book will open your eyes to what the Lord has already done, so that you can have faith for what He is about to do, in which you are called to play a part.

Blessings, PaulD.

<u>NB: Warning!</u> The reader should not assume that the stories I relate are the ONLY things the Holy Spirit is doing. He is working all over the place through all sorts of wonderful people, and has prophetic servants everywhere. I continue to hear amazing testimonies of miraculous lives walked by people I had never heard about while they were alive. I DO believe that the men and women I have focused on were used by the Lord to "raise the bar", both in what many of us were seeing, and in what we had faith to believe God would do.

CONTENTS

Dedication		iii
Foreword		v
1	The End Of The War	1
2	The Angel And The Cave	9
3	The First Healing Campaign	21
4	Branham Meetings Explode	28
5	The Re-Establishment Of Israel	36
6	The Voice Of Healing Revival	40
7	The Healing Of Congressman Upshaw	55
8	The Boy Who Sees With A Plastic Eye	61
9	Little Brother—The Boy Prophet	66
10	Branham Prophesies The End Of The Revival	81
11	The Second Wave—The Charismatic Movement	88
12	The Death Of William Branham	97
13	The Death Of A.A. Allen	104
14	The Jesus People	109
15	The First Death Of Seer Bob Jones	115
16	The Death Of Kathryn Kuhlman	127
17	The Sands Of Time Vision	132
18	John Wimber's Progress To The Vineyard	135
19	Angels Visit Roland Buck	143

20	Mike Bickle And Kansas City Fellowship	147
21	The Third Wave—The Vineyard Movement	159
22	Rick Joyner'S Vision Of The Harvest	171
23	Paul Cain'S Re-Emergence	175
24	The Prophetic History Of The Toronto Blessing	181
25	The Toronto Blessing	186
26	The Final Quest Visions	198
27	The Brownsville Pensacola Revival	202
28	Heidi Baker Visits Toronto	208
29	24/7 Prayer Begins At IHOP-KC	212
30	Bethel Church And Jesus Culture	216
31	The Millennium	221
32	The Postman's Letter	224
33	Todd Bentley And The Florida Healing Outpouring	228
34	Bob Jones Dies On Valentine's Day	234
35	John Paul Jackson Dies	238
36	The Attack On The Prophets	242
37	Kim Clement Dies	246
38	Paul Cain Dies	250
39	The Significance Of February	255
40	Neville Johnson Dies	259
41	Where Are We Now?	262
42	Who Is Still Around?	265
43	There Are Not Enough Lifeboats	268
44	Abiding In Him	282
45	Prophets And Prophecy	289
46	Further Reading And Sources	298

Afterword   **301**

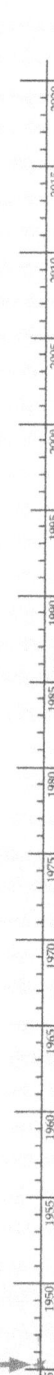

1945

8 May 1945

VE Day

- WW2 finally ends:
  - Allies (esp. US) determine to rebuild former enemies rather than repeat errors of Versailles Treaty
  - Rape/devastation of Berlin, determination of German people to rebuild
  - Nuremburg Trials - Justice
  - Jewish refugees flee Europe after the holocaust - fulfilment of Biblical Prophecy
    - Deut 30:1-5
    - Isa 11:11-12
    - Jer 29:14
    - Eze 20:41-42

The End of the War

On the 8th of May, 1945 the War in Europe came to an end, and the true horror of what had been done by the Nazis began to be revealed. The appalling genocide of the Holocaust—Hitler's "final solution" to the "Jewish problem", meant that many people felt justified in taking revenge on the German people.

One of the lesser-known events of the final days of the war was the "**Rape of Berlin**". As the Russian armies approached the German Capital, Stalin promised that the first army to reach the capital would have three days to do whatever they wished with the populace. The Russians had lost more men taking Berlin than the United States did in the entire war. In the aftermath of the fighting, and aware of the rape of many Russian women by German soldiers after the previous years the Russian soldiers went wild, and the officers totally lost control of them. The plunder, rape and murder went on for two weeks, with estimates from Hospital records of over 100,000 rapes in that period. Finally, the Russian officers began to shoot their own men who refused to return to barracks.

One of the first Allied officers to enter the Russian-controlled city was Colonel Eugene Bird, later to become the U.S. Commander of the Spandau prison, where Rudolf Hess was detained. He testified of his hatred for Germans after the years of war, and the smell of death that lingered 30 miles away from the city. The Allied commanders were so appalled at the destruction of the city they decided it would be easier to rebuild elsewhere. One estimate was a hundred boxcars a day for 30 years just to remove the rubble.

What impressed Col. Bird was the determination of the German women to rebuild. After months of starvation, constant bombing, and finally the rapes, they refused to allow the Allies to deport them, and were out in the streets with buckets collecting rubble. Bird's hatred turned to awe, then respect and finally love. Eventually the Allied leaders decided, whatever the cost, to honour their determination, and rebuild the city.

This decision to rebuild the cities of their enemy was arguably one of History's great moments. Determined not to repeat the errors of the Treaty of Versailles after The Great War (World War One—WW1) where Germany was crippled by massive reparations, embarrassed, and blamed for all that had occurred, the rebuilding turned their enemies into staunch Allies.

Another major move was the decision to try Nazi leaders accused of planning or involvement in war crimes. Both Stalin and Roosevelt had made public comments in favour of the summary execution of Nazi leaders, though Churchill was vigorously opposed to execution for political purposes. Roosevelt continued to support the concept, and only abandoned it in the face of severe public disapproval. When he died, President Harry S. Truman pushed for a judicial process suggested by the U.S. War Department, and negotiations began on the format for the Nuremburg Trials.

It is always important that true justice be seen to be done. For the Allies to repeat the mistakes of Versailles and abandon the fundamental principles of law they espoused would have had catastrophic consequences for the restoration of Europe. Agreeing to what has been described as "the greatest trial in history" by Sir Norman Birkett, one of the British judges, meant that the defeated German people could be walked through the horrors perpetrated by their countrymen piece by piece. The truth had to be brought into the light, and faced, before true healing could begin.

Ensuring that trials under International Law were held publicly for all the major Nazi War Criminals was a very important step towards re-building the devastated lands of Europe. Executions were carried out at the dictates of the Court, NOT summarily based on unfounded accusations of victims.

The MOST significant event of the immediate post-war years was the fulfilment of a Biblical Prophecy about the return of the Jewish people to their historic homeland. Some of the passages are:

> *Even if you have been banished to the most distant land under the heavens, from there the LORD your God will gather you and bring you back. He will bring you to the land that belonged to your fathers, and you will take possession of it. He will make you more prosperous and numerous than your fathers.* (Dt 30:3-5)
>
> *He will raise a banner for the nations and gather the exiles of Israel; he will assemble the scattered people of Judah from the four quarters of the earth.* (Isa 11:12)
>
> *I will be found by you, declares the LORD, and will bring you back from captivity. I will gather you from all the nations and places where I have banished you, declares the LORD,*

> *and will bring you back to the place from which I carried you into exile.* (Je 29:14)
>
> *I will accept you as fragrant incense when I bring you out from the nations and gather you from the countries where you have been scattered, and I will show myself holy among you in the sight of the nations. Then you will know that I am the LORD, when I bring you into the land of Israel, the land I had sworn with uplifted hand to give to your fathers.* (Ezekiel 20:41-42)

Since the Diaspora (the dispersal of the Jewish people from the land of Israel) of A.D. 70, when Roman Emperor Titus destroyed the Temple and the city of Jerusalem, the Jews had been scattered and oppressed throughout the world. Josephus records that the Romans killed over a million Jews, and on the same day that the previous Temple had been destroyed by the Babylonians in 586 B.C.

For nearly 2000 years the Jews lived as refugees in foreign lands—their strong sense of identity as "God's Chosen People" and adherence to different religious and social customs kept them apart from the societies in which they lived, and led to regular outbreaks of persecution. In much of Europe, Jews were banned from holding posts in government and excluded from membership of the guilds and professions. Religious prejudice, which saw Jews blamed for the Crucifixion of Jesus (incorrectly—He died for each and every person ever created. All of us sin, and we ALL deserve Hell. It is ONLY Jesus' death in our place that allows our restoration to the Father), and the success of Jews in trade and moneylending, led to the periodic expulsion of Jews from most lands in Western Europe, and many Jews settled in Russia, Turkey and Poland.

Interestingly, many of the most famous generals in history had played a part in attempting to free the Holy Land from foreign governance. Several of these were well aware of the Biblical prophecies and were trying to restore the Jewish homeland. Napoleon, for example, passed laws to protect Jews in every country he conquered, and a major reason for his attempt to invade the Middle East was to provide a refuge for the Jews of Europe. Ironically, in this he was thwarted by the British.

In 1897, an Austro-Hungarian Jew called Theodor Herzl proclaimed the modern political movement of Zionism, and encouraged Jews to flee Europe and migrate to Ottoman Palestine. This gained in popularity after the pogroms in Russia and rising anti-Semitism in several other European countries, and had the stated objective of establishing a Jewish homeland and sovereign state in Palestine.

In 1917, the Palestine Campaign of WW1 saw the liberation of Jerusalem from Ottoman Turkish governance, spearheaded by the Australian Light Horse, who were crucial to every facet of the campaign after their incredible victory at Beersheba. By November, the British government had begun to look favourably on the Zionist goals, and the famous Balfour Declaration was issued, as the first political recognition of Zionist aims by a Great Power.

```
Foreign Office
November 2nd, 1917
Dear Lord Rothschild,

  I have much pleasure in conveying
to you, on behalf of His Majesty's
Government, the following declaration
of sympathy with Jewish Zionist aspi-
rations which has been submitted to,
and approved by, the Cabinet.
```

> "His Majesty's Government view with favour the establishment in Palestine of a national home for the Jewish people, and will use their best endeavours to facilitate the achievement of this object, it being clearly understood that nothing shall be done which may prejudice the civil and religious rights of existing non-Jewish communities in Palestine, or the rights and political status enjoyed by Jews in any other country."
>
> I should be grateful if you would bring this declaration to the knowledge of the Zionist Federation.
>
> Yours sincerely,
Arthur James Balfour

This position was internationally recognised in the mandate of the post-war League of Nations, which recognised the historic connection between the Jewish people and their ancestral home, and recognised their right to re-settle. Several waves of migration occurred in the between-wars years, though many Jews preferred to remain where they were established. The British established immigration quotas for the region, but as persecution increased in Nazi-controlled areas greater numbers of illegal immigrants began to flood Palestine. After the genocide of the Holocaust, with over 6 million Jews having been exterminated throughout Europe, increasing support for Jewish immigration, and Jewish emphasis on 'Making Aliyah' (a pilgrimage to Jerusalem) placed pressure on the British to withdraw from the region.

Initial attempts to give equal status to both Arab and Jewish residents led to a UN plan to Partition the region into separate states, which was summarily rejected by the Zionists. The Civil War of 1947-48 erupted between the two groups, and on 15th May, 1948, the British formally terminated the Palestinian Mandate. Over 500,000 Jews were now resident in the Holy Land, and they were determined to stay.

1946

7 May 1946 *Jefferson, Indiana*

The Angel & the Cave

- Frustrated by the visions he was receiving which were coming true, but which he was told by senior ministers were 'demonic', William Branham went to his cave to seek the Lord.
- After hours begging God for deliverance, he was reminded of various scriptures that supported his experiences, and asked for forgiveness for rejecting them.
- An Angel appeared, and commissioned him to take Divine Healing to the 'peoples of the world':
  - *"If you will be sincere when you pray and can get the people to believe you, nothing shall stand before your prayer, not even cancer."* (Jorgensen, 1994, Book 2 p.168)
- Two Signs:
  - *Vibrations in the hand*
  - *Tell by vision the very secrets of their hearts*

2

The Angel and the Cave

It is interesting to realise that the spiritual shifts at the end of World War Two (WW2), released all sorts of other activity in God's purposes. Since the Reformation, and the translation of the Bible into English, the Christians of Great Britain had spearheaded the Evangelistic Age of Christianity—a direct result of the influence of the 100-year prayer movement of Count Zinzendorf and the Moravian community at Herrnhut. Moravian missionaries impacted both John Wesley and George Whitefield, who sparked the Wesleyan revival and the First Great Awakening. In the early 1700s, a great wave of evangelical missionaries began to travel around the world, spreading the gospel of salvation *"I know your deeds. See, I have placed before you an open door that no one can shut. I know that you have little strength, yet you have kept my word and have not denied my name"* (Rev 3:8). The years leading up to the early 1900s were marked by incredible missionary exploits of men such as David Livingstone in Africa, original Ashes test cricketer C.T. Studd, Chariots of Fire Olympian Eric Liddell and Hudson Taylor in China, and Anthony Norris Groves in Baghdad, Iraq, many of whom were household names of the period. The famous meeting between Livingstone and Henry Morton Stanley on the shores of Lake Tanganyika in 1871 spawned the well-known phrase "Dr Livingstone, I presume."

By the early 1900s, the spread of the British Empire under the godly Queen Victoria had peaked, and had been responsible for spreading Christianity all over the world. But in Britain itself, society had fallen into a legalistic modernism, where the form of religion had replaced true pursuit of holiness. The fateful sinking of the Titanic on 15 April, 1912, symbolised the end of the British 'leadership' of Christendom. The arrogance exemplified by the popularised claim "God himself couldn't sink this ship" (which cannot be correctly attributed to an individual) has heralded the progressive decline of British influence in every way since that time.

America, however, had been quite the opposite. Since the rise of the early proponents of Divine Healing from the mid 1800s- Australian John Alexander Dowie, Mariah Woodworth-Etter, John G. Lake and Englishman Smith Wigglesworth, knowledge of God's continued providence had spread. In 1906, the Pentecostal Outpouring and Azusa Street revival saw the beginnings of what has been called the "First Wave" of the Holy Spirit in the 1900s. [This is **not** to imply that the Holy Spirit had not been at work in the Welsh Revival of 1904-5, but rather a recognition that from Azusa Street onwards the restoration of the Charismatic power-gifts to the Church became a priority in the work of the Holy Spirit.] Numbers of believers began to seek the Lord for a fuller experience of Himself, expressed through the "gifts of the Spirit" outlined in 1 Cor 12, particularly the expression of 'speaking in tongues'.

One of the most interesting stories of the day was that of teenage evangelist, Uldine Utley. Uldine had been saved at age nine, at a meeting with Aimee Semple McPherson in Fresno, California in 1921. Soon after her conversion, she was filled with the Holy Spirit and had an encounter with

Jesus. She became a famous girl preacher, ministering in Madison Square Garden to 14,000 people in 1925, aged 14. She taught at tent revivals and churches on the Baptism of the Holy Spirit and the gift of tongues, and often the Spirit fell on the audience in power at her meetings.

Utley had a genuine walk with the Lord, and the fruit of her ministry was well-known, but she nurtured in her heart a desire for Hollywood fame. In 1938, aged 24, she married a travelling salesman who promised her he could get her into movies, and walked away from her ministry. Within a short time, she succumbed to a spirit of insanity, and spent the next 57 years in mental institutions. Many people asked famous healers to go and deliver her, particularly Paul Cain and William Branham, but the Lord would not allow them to go. Eventually, just before she died in 1995, Paul Cain was given permission to visit Uldine. As he walked into the room, the spirit left her, and he spent time reminiscing with her over the 'glory days' before she passed away. Paul said the Jealousy of God for His servants is not well understood, and woe betide those who turn their backs on Him to pursue selfish interests.

By the end of WW2, various Pentecostal denominations had arisen, which had little fellowship with the traditional denominations or each other, and a lot of heated theological controversy ensued about whether the "gifts" were for today. There was little practical co-operation between the different streams of the Church who all claimed to be followers of Jesus.

By 1946, a poor Baptist pastor in Jeffersonville, Indiana had come to a crisis in his spiritual walk. After a ball of fire had flown into the cabin and rested above his cot when he was 15 minutes old (witnessed by all present), William Marrion Branham had grown up in extreme poverty and only achieved a Grade 7 education. He was working in the Public Service and as a game warden and struggling to lead his tiny Baptist fellowship, while navigating some of the major theological issues of the day. He led a disciplined life of prayer, often retreating to a cave he'd found in the mountains to spend time with the Lord, and had seen remarkable answers to prayers over several years. He had on several occasions since age 7 in 1916 experienced open visions of events that occurred soon after, and had seen a number of miraculous healings as a result when he prayed for those he had seen in his visions.

In June, 1933, he had been baptising converts from his first Revival meeting in the Ohio River before a crowd of around 1,000 people. He heard a voice say "Look up," three times, and a ball of swirling fire fell out of heaven and hovered above his head. All the crowd witnessed the event, and it was reported in the newspapers.

Through various encounters with godly men from Pentecostal churches in 1935, the Lord showed him He was still working today. Branham saw the fruit of the operation of tongues, prophecy and prayer for healing, and could not reconcile the Godly character and joy of the Pentecostal Christians he witnessed displaying the gifts with the claims of his educated denominational leaders that such things were not God, but 'demonic deception'.

In 1936, Branham was drawn to visit a "Jesus Only" meeting in Mishawaka, Indiana. He found out later it was a National Pentecostal Convention, with people from all over the country. Although living in his car, with no change of clothes, he was called up to the podium and invited to preach. He gave a fiery evangelistic message about the Rich Man and Lazarus. Branham was aware that these Pentecostals had a zeal he himself did not, and was quick to confess to them he did not speak in tongues. His strange gift allowed him to discern that some of the people ministering were genuine, and others hypocrites, hiding gross sin in their lives. Branham was given invitations by several leaders from around the country to "Come hold a revival", and believed that God was calling him to step out among these "holy rollers".

His wife Hope wasn't so sure about leaving the little they had to go on the road, and convinced him to discuss the matter with her own mother. Bill was excited about the happiness he had observed amongst the Pentecostals, but Mrs. Brumbach was adamant: "William, I'll give you to understand that I'll never give my daughter permission to go out with a bunch of holy-roller trash like that." It is important to note that most Pentecostal believers at the time were from the poorer elements of society, and there was definitely an element of class condescension from members of traditional 'proper' churches. Although Hope was willing to follow her husband despite her mother's objections, Branham decided to "put it off for awhile."

Scared by the vehement denials of leaders he trusted, the manipulative threats of his mother-in-law, and confused by the hypocrites he also witnessed amongst the Pentecostals, he refused invitations to speak in Pentecostal churches. This was a major turning point in his life that he came to regret. He believed later he had ignored God's call and opened his family to judgement, and it cost him dearly. His beloved wife Hope died of tubercular pneumonia, and none of Bill's prayers for her were answered. He arrived at her deathbed when she was unconscious, and asked God to let him speak to her on last time.

Hope opened her eyes and asked "Why did you call me back?" She had been in heaven "going home", with "two people dressed in white" either side of her, when she heard her husband calling in the distance. She asked him, "You know why I'm going, don't you? … We should never have listened to Mother… Those Pentecostal people are right."

Hope passed away in July, 1937, and the day after her burial, Branham's baby daughter Sharon Rose died as well. When he had prayed for his wife and child, he had seen a vision of a black sheet falling down. Shattered by his loss and his failure, he went through his darkest time, even at one point trying to kill himself, but God prevented the gun from firing. In the depths of his despair, God gave him an experience of seeing his wife and daughter in heaven, which helped him turn the corner. God took time restoring him and encouraging him.

In particular, Branham's recurring visions were causing him a lot of heartache. In the spring of 1940, he had an encounter during the night where an angel walked him through two healings. The angel took him to a cabin where he saw the scene in detail—the furniture, positions of the parents, and a baby boy with legs twisted up behind his back. The angel asked him "Can that baby live?", and he answered "Sir, I do not know." The angel instructed him "Have the father bring the baby to you and place your hands upon its stomach." Branham obeyed, and prayed, and the father dropped the baby. While he watched the child its legs straightened, and the boy walked to the corner and back to Branham. "Brother Branham, I am well now," the 'baby' said in the vision. The angel asked "Did you consider that?"

Then the angel transported him to a graveyard beside the road telling him to remember the names and dates he saw on the tombstones. He took him again to a crossroad with a few houses and a store, where an old man wearing overalls with a white moustache and a yellow corduroy cap walked out. "He will direct you," the angel said. A third time they shifted, and he was entering a house, again seeing the detail of the chunk stove, the yellow wallpaper with red figures, the "God Bless Our Home" sign on the wall and a brass bed with a another badly crippled girl—both right leg and arm were twisted. "Can this girl live?" the angel asked again, and again he answered "Sir, I do not know." "Put your hand on her and pray," the angel instructed. As he obeyed, he heard someone exclaim "Praise the Lord!" and watched the girl straighten out.

He awoke from the vision to someone calling his name—a young father he had baptised previously. The man asked him to come and pray for his son, who was on the point of death. The father had backslidden during the war, and already lost his other child, and begged Branham for help. The man also asked his cousin to come, who had just been converted. On the way, Branham asked the man about his house, describing the scene from the vision, and what the boy was wearing. The man exclaimed: "That's him exactly. Have you ever been to my house?" The man repented on the spot, begging God for mercy.

When they arrived at the house, the baby's lungs were full and it was almost dead (details of the story imply that the term 'baby' referred to a young child). Branham asked the father to bring him the boy, and prayed, but nothing happened. He then realised that some of the people he had seen in the vision were not present, and others not in the places he had seen, so he waited—over an hour and a half, refusing to explain. He was repenting himself, worried that he had spoiled things by "running ahead of the vision" in his ignorance. Around 6 o'clock, as the men got up to leave, he saw the child's grandmother approaching the door—one of the missing attendees from his vision. Realising he was sitting in the place where one of the other men needed to be, he got up. The mother, grandmother and cousin all moved to the places he had seen, and he asked the father again to bring him the baby. When he prayed, the boy screamed "Daddy, Daddy," awoke to consciousness and threw his hands around his father's neck. The Holy Spirit moved him to say: "Lay the child on the bed. It will take three days for his legs to straighten out."

Encouraged by this result, he told his congregation about the second girl. About two weeks later he received a letter from the girl's mother, asking him to come and pray. A deacon in his church and Brother Brace and his wife wanted to go and see the vision fulfilled. After driving a while, he began to feel an intense sensation in his chest, and Sister Brace thought he was unwell, but he knew was a sign the angel of the Lord was nearby. He got out and rested his foot on the rear bumper. To his right was a graveyard and he recognised the gravestones from his vision. When he told the others Sister Brace began to cry. Soon after they came to the crossroad, and out came the man with the moustache and cap, who told them how to get to the house they needed. Mrs Brace fainted. At the house, he recognised the stove, wallpaper, sign and bed. Mrs. Brace fainted a second time. He walked to the crippled girl on the bed and prayed, and immediately her hand and leg straightened out. Mr Brace had just aroused his wife in time to see the girl raised up, and she fainted in his arms a third time.

The more that incidents like this occurred the more troubled Branham became. Although the Godly fruit of the healings was clear for all to see, he was the subject of intense criticism by almost every minister in the area. Some denounced him as a demon-possessed deceiver, others as an unscrupulous charlatan—but all agreed that the visions he saw and the miracles that followed were demonic deceptions. God simply didn't do those things anymore. He prayed for God to "take this thing away from me," and almost immediately had another series of revelatory experiences, which left him perplexed.

He had no desire to re-marry, but gossips were beginning to talk about his young housekeeper, Meda Broy, whom he had hired to look after his young son. Branham tried to distance himself from her to protect her, but after Meda began to pray, the Lord spoke audibly to him and said, "Go get Meda Broy and marry her this coming October the twenty-third."

In May, 1946, determined to "have it out with God" concerning his visions and the miracles that resulted, he went off to his cave, and spent hours praying and reading his Bible, begging the Lord to deliver him from demonic influences that were leading others astray. Late into the night, he felt the presence of the Lord enter the cave. Immediately a thought struck him: What if all those other ministers were wrong? In his humility and embarrassment in his lack of education he had never considered such a possibility. He was reminded of the persecution of Jesus by the religious leaders, who accused the son of God of having a demon, whereas the demons identified Jesus correctly. As more and more scripture ran through his mind, he began to repent for resisting the visions.

As soon as he had framed the words, a ball of amber light began to manifest in the cave, getting bigger until a huge angel walked out of it. With the amber light flickering around him he walked toward Bill, who was terrified but had nowhere to run. The man stopped a few feet away and looked down at him in kindness, saying "Do not fear…", and Bill's fear vanished. It was the same voice he had heard speaking to him in all the visions over the years.

The angel said: "I am sent from the presence of Almighty God to tell you that your peculiar birth and misunderstood life had been to indicate that you are to take the gift of Divine Healing to the peoples of the world. If you will be sincere when you pray and can get the people to believe you, nothing shall stand before your prayer, not even cancer…." The angel told him the Lord would give him two signs to prove he was sent from God. First, he would take a person's right hand in his left, and a series of vibrations or bumps would manifest on his hand that would allow him to detect the presence of any germ-caused disease. If the bumps disappeared when he prayed, the person was healed. Secondly, "if you stay humble" he would see by vision the very secrets of their hearts.

There was more, but the angel finished with the promise that "I will be with you." Branham was greatly encouraged and told his wife Meda, and immediately went to see his former pastor, now Bishop of the Missionary Baptist Churches in that area. He told the tale, but was interrupted by the question "Billy, what did you eat for supper that night? You obviously had a nightmare.... It's just another of those hallucinations you see. You've got an overactive imagination…"

Determined to be obedient (he had by now learned his lesson), but unsure of how to go about it, he went back home. A few days later he went to the store to cash his pay check and noticed a man looking around as though lost, but who stared at Branham like he knew him. When he came back out the man was still there, so he went over to see if he could help him. He had come 200 miles in response to an angelic visitation, telling him to go to Jeffersonville, Indiana, and ask for somebody named Branham to pray for his healing. Bill prayed for him in the street, greatly encouraged that God was truly sending him.

Over the next week, several more incidents occurred which stirred the community, including a Mrs. Morgan who was healed of intestinal cancer, and an invitation arrived asking him to pray for a pastor's daughter, Betty Daugherty, in St Louis. The little girl had been shaking in great pain for 3 months, and had the doctors stumped. Branham's congregation had raised the money for a train ticket. When he walked in, and took the little girl's hand, there were no vibrations, which left him puzzled. Then he remembered the angel had said specifically that the sign would only work for "germ-related" diseases, so he reasoned that the girl had something else wrong.

He went down to the church to wait on the Lord for about three hours, and eventually promised the Lord that if He would heal the little girl, he would "move out into the ministry you called me to… as long as You provide my needs, because I don't want to ever beg the people for money." Back at the house they waited several more hours, praying quietly, as different people came and went. Branham began to experience a vision, but it was interrupted by the child's grandfather. He went outside for a bit and sat in Brother Dougherty's car, asking the Lord to let the vision return. Eventually the swirling ball of fire appeared, swirling around the bonnet (hood) of the car. Branham's eyes were opened and he had a vision of the girl's accident. He went back inside, and instructed those present to stand where he had seen them in the vision. He explained the problem he had been shown—she had a displaced vertebra in her back. Her father pushed it back into place and she was healed!

1946

14 June 1946 *St Louis Missouri*

First Healing Campaign

- Not knowing how to proceed, Branham went to visit his former pastor, now Bishop of the Missionary Baptist churches of Indiana. He was told that he was being foolish, that no-one would listen to a man with a seventh-grade education, and he should 'take a nap'.
- Almost immediately he had a divine encounter with a man who had been told in a dream to go to Jefferson and find a man called Branham to pray for his healing. This led to others seeking him out, and his first healing campaign in June.
- Cripples, Blind and Deaf were all healed. The next day he prayed for an insane woman in the hospital. Cancers, paralysis, and a woman who rejected healing, suffered a heart attack on her way home, was raised from the dead.
- Crowds came despite foul weather.

3

The First Healing Campaign

What is important to note is that William Branham did not instigate his ministry, or set out to promote himself—even after such clear angelic visitation and commissioning. God confirmed it to him, God brought others to him, and then God opened the door for him to start healing meetings on a larger scale. This is a very important principle that need to be better taught in our churches and Bible Colleges. It is best exemplified by David in the Bible, who, though anointed as King, would not lift a finger to make it happen - even when King Saul repeatedly tried to kill him, but waited for the Lord to establish him in His own time.

Several weeks after the healing of Betty Daugherty, her father Robert drove to see Branham, and asked him to hold a week-long Healing Revival in St Louis. Branham felt he had to accept in order to be obedient to the promise he had made to God. He resigned from both his jobs—Public Service Indiana and State game warden. He told his church about his promise to God and his desire not to have to ask for money, preached his last sermon at home for several months, and set off for St Louis. Mrs. Morgan went along with Bill and his wife Meda to share her testimony.

Robert Daugherty had rented a large Circus Tent and advertised the meetings around the city. On the opening night only a few dozen people attended. Branham shared his testimony of the angelic visitation, and Mrs. Morgan shared about her own healing, followed by local girl Betty Daugherty telling her own tale. After a short sermon encouraging people to trust God, eighteen people came to the front for prayer.

A 70-year-old woman came forward with a bandaged head and a large lump on her nose. Branham's hand turned an angry red and began to swell with the vibrations. He looked at the pattern of white bumps that formed, which were the same as Mrs. Morgan's a few weeks before. "It's cancer, isn't it?" he said, and the woman agreed. He prayed for her in the Name of Jesus Christ, and pronounced her healed when the bumps faded, even though the lump was still present on her nose.

An old man who had been crippled for many years was next, limping with a cane. After prayer, he threw the cane away and walked away with no difficulty. In addition, two deaf people began to hear and a blind man received his sight. Not every healing was visibly dramatic, but everyone who received prayer claimed that something changed when Bill had prayed for them.

The next morning Branham was asked to make a sick call to an insane lady in the psychopathic ward of the St Louis Hospital, who was restored and released. A drive to nearby Granite City saw a lady healed of cancer, and another home visited where a lady paralysed on her right side was set free and her voice restored. Word of the healings had spread, and the tent was packed on the second night. Many stood outside in the rain all night, and the Lord continued to do miracles. When the people had diseases, Branham identified them by the sign in his hand, and he began to recognise the patterns of the bumps and what they meant. Years after, men who travelled regularly with Branham testified that they became so familiar with the patterns they could look at Brother Branham's hand and know the disease before he called it out.

Some Christians have real difficulties with God using His servant in this unusual way. There are many scriptures where the Lord says He is DIFFERENT to us—His thoughts and His ways are NOT like ours. Isaiah 55:8 says: "*For my thoughts are not your thoughts, neither are your ways my ways, declares the LORD.*" This is why we are to judge by FRUIT, not by what we think God would do. Many are quick to label people as "False" prophets, ignoring the implication that there must also be "real".

> "*Watch out for false prophets. They come to you in sheep's clothing, but inwardly they are ferocious wolves. By their fruit you will recognise them. Do people pick grapes from thorn bushes, or figs from thistles? Likewise, every good tree bears good fruit, but a bad tree bears bad fruit. A good tree cannot bear bad fruit, and a bad tree cannot bear good fruit. Every tree that does not bear good fruit is cut down and thrown into the fire. Thus, by their fruit you will recognise them*" (Mt 7:15-20).

A cursory reading of Ezekiel and Revelation will reveal that Heaven is MUCH stranger than what most people would be comfortable with, and there are "living creatures" "covered with eyes", and so on. Thousands of people were set free from "the devil's work" (1 John 3:8) and many salvations occurred as a fruit of Branham's ministry.

Other notable healings during the St Louis campaign were a 93-year-old man with a peg leg and glass eye, who wanted his hearing restored, and received it. A well-known local coloured pastor who had been totally blind for 20 years received his sight. Another woman rejected the call of the Spirit, left the Tent, and suffered a heart attack. Branham went out and prayed for her, after which she rose up and confessed how she had rejected the Lord.

On the Monday morning a group of local pastors came to his hotel and asked him to continue the meetings. Bill asked for time to pray, and his wife opened her Bible to Isaiah 42:1-7 (KJV):

> *"Behold my servant, whom I uphold; mine elect, in whom my soul delighteth; I have put my spirit upon him: he shall bring forth judgment to the Gentiles.... I the LORD have called thee in righteousness, and will hold thine hand, and will keep thee, and give thee for a covenant of the people, for a light of the Gentiles; To open the blind eyes, to bring out the prisoners from the prison, and them that sit in darkness out of the prison house."*

Branham felt this was confirmation of what they had been seeing all week, and agreed to continue. To a packed tent every night he preached, and stayed praying for the sick until the early hours of each morning, seeing people set free from sinus trouble, gallstones, glandular diseases, defective vision, high blood pressure, arthritis and cancers. The lady from the first night with the cancer on her nose came back to show it had gone—it dropped off later the same night she was ministered to. A man whose arm had been paralysed for 29 years could swing it above his head; a crippled woman walked under her own strength; a man with tuberculosis in the bones of his foot had all pain vanish; and a baby who had never opened its eyes was healed. Several deaf children were set free—one had been driven all day from Northern Illinois by her father. By the final nights of the Crusade, so many people were crowding the platform for prayer that Branham had difficulty moving around to pray for them. He was staying till the early hours of the morning ministering, and then during the day making house calls with Rev Daugherty to people who were too sick to attend the meetings.

Unfortunately, Branham's compassion for the sick almost led to his eventual undoing. He failed to seek the Lord for wisdom about how to manage his time, assuming that the Lord would give him the necessary strength, and the combination of late nights and busy days eventually took its toll on his health. He allowed the needs of the people to dictate his time, and this first campaign set up unhealthy patterns which continued over the next few years.

Like Jesus at the Pool of Bethesda, we need to be careful to "only do what we see the Father doing" (John 5:19), and not simply respond to the need that is expressed. The Bible says: "… *for God's gifts and his call are irrevocable*" (Ro 11:29), and it is clear He will continue to back up His Word even when we go beyond what He is calling us to do. As we will see, many ministers were still operating in great spiritual power even with gross sin in their personal lives (which was NOT at all true of Branham).

Psalm 68:18 says, "*Thou hast ascended on high, thou hast led captivity captive: thou hast received* **gifts for men; yea, for the rebellious also,** *that the LORD God might dwell among them.*" God continued to use even the rebellious while He gave them time and grace to repent. We cannot assume that just because a servant is being used by the Lord to bring good fruit that they are sinless. None of us are! Our sin is covered by the Blood of Jesus, our status is changed to Righteous, and we operate in that grace. Our Christian walk should be progressively overcoming "the world, the flesh and the devil" (to quote the Book of Common Prayer) as we "*…deny (ourselves) and take up his cross and follow me*" (Mt 16:24).

Also, over the years many people have claimed to have "heard the call" to ministry, and have quit their jobs to "live by faith", and it led to disaster. The Bible says *"For many are called, but few are chosen"* (Mt 22:14). The calling is not the release to minister—after that comes the training, and God trains his people in deserts (Is 40:3). Wait for His commissioning, then you'll know what you're called to do and how, and you won't go ahead of Him in presumption. Additionally, *"…. faith comes from hearing, and hearing by the word of Christ"* (Ro 10:17). True faith is from HEARING the voice of the Holy Spirit clearly—not vague impressions or strange coincidences. Wait in the prayer closet until know you have heard!

King David, who was "a man after God's own heart", understood that premature inheritance will get you killed by the enemy. If you get ahead of the Lord you are NOT guaranteed His protection. Presumption is Dangerous! Even though David was called, and even anointed as King, he would not lift a finger to establish himself, waiting for the Lord to move in His time. Far less damage would have been done to the Body over the last few decades if this message had been better taught.

William Branham was a man steeped in humility. He treated others with respect, and did not consider himself "better" than them, though he had been given a most spectacular spiritual gift. He did not move until he was clear that the Lord had "opened the door" for him, and had confirmed his calling and commission. Only then did he quit his job and move into ministry full-time.

He also never took a big salary. In the mid-50s, when the IRS went after the leading Revivalists, his annual salary was $7000, whereas his manager paid himself $80,000. He refused to "flog the till" for money, trusting that God would do what He said he would do. Other Revivalists of the day were being paid $15000 annually. If only other ministers over the years had walked in such integrity.

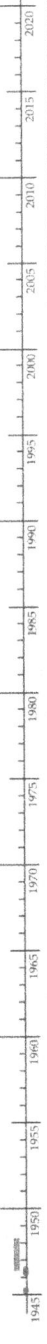

1946–48

Branham Healing meetings explode

- Word of the miraculous healings spreads
- Some come to Jefferson as a results of dreams and visions asking for Branham
- Divine encounters even outside meetings - blind coloured lady ran into him after losing her father.
- T.L. Osborn encouraged to go to a meeting by his wife after a public deliverance of a antagonist - God speaks to him
- Gordon Lindsay hears about the meetings and meets Branham in Sacramento. Lindsay opened doors into the major Pentecostal groups. Ern Baxter and Jack Moore join the team.
- Early 1948 a young evangelist called Oral Roberts visited a Branham campaign and started praying for healing in his own meetings.
- Kathryn Kuhlman's healing ministry takes off with very different focus on honouring the Holy Spirit

4

Branham Meetings Explode

News of the healings in St Louis spread by word of mouth throughout the southern states, and invitations began to flood in. Over three short months campaigns were held across Arkansas, with Branham keeping to his busy personal schedule. He didn't own a suit, and was given a second-hand one that needed mending. His own poor effort fixing the right-hand pocket led him to shake hands with his left—too embarrassed to expose the torn coat.

In Camden, Arkansas, he felt he was struggling to get the crowd to trust God over an atmosphere of caution and suspicion. Suddenly, he felt the presence of the angel, and said "I won't have to speak anymore about it, for here it comes now." The "whirling circle of fire" came through the back doors of the gymnasium and up the aisle, to the gasps of the crowd. When it passed over a crippled Baptist pastor he jumped to his feet and started pushing his own wheelchair around the building. A photographer snapped a photo of the supernatural light as it rested above Branham, and then it disappeared. Hundreds of people flocked to the prayer line, and miracles took place in hundreds of lives. Branham prayed till after midnight and found his hand had become numb.

In the morning, the reporter showed up at his hotel with the photograph he had taken. The hotel manager joined them, asking to be born again, and Bill was only too happy to pray with them both on the spot. A boy arrived with a telegram inviting Branham to Little Rock, Arkansas, and he asked to "know Jesus too", as his father had been healed the night before. This went on all week, and by Saturday night, he was exhausted. He managed to preach Sunday morning, but wasn't feeling strong enough to pray for all those who had gathered. As he was being escorted by police to the car to go on to Little Rock, he felt the Holy Spirit prompting him to respond to an elderly black man among those crying for mercy. The policemen warned him it could start a race riot, but he insisted, and the blind man was healed.

The crowds were even larger in Little Rock, and the power of God flowed. Every diagnosis was correct (in fact several people who travelled with Branham over the years all testify they never saw him "miss it"). He was always careful to point people to Jesus "I can't heal nobody, only He can." Some problems were obvious, such as the man with a huge goiter on his neck. As soon as Branham prayed for him, the goiter turned white and dropped off onto the floor. A reporter nearby took a picture which made the front page the next day.

At times the Lord would warn him NOT to visit a sick person, saying "his time has come." He tried to be obedient to whatever the Lord was calling him to do. He told one supplicant that he wouldn't go, but would continue to pray. Several days later, he had a vision of the man being healed, and the Lord gave him the passage from Isaiah where King Hezekiah was granted 15 more years of life after fervent prayer. He caught the next plane to Memphis to pray for the man, who was instantly healed. Night after night he would minister till about three in the morning, and then collapse into his hotel bed. One night he was asked downstairs "for a break" to be faced with a husband and his wife, who was manifesting a demonic spirit. The woman was covered in blood from the damage the demons had done to her as she struggled against those who were trying to restrain her. Bill took authority over the screaming spirits and the woman fell silent.

The constant demands were taking a toll on Branham, despite his fitness from years spent as a game warden. He rarely was given the chance to recover, and would be woken by the next urgent need. He found it very difficult to refuse calls for help, even when he'd only snatched a few hours of sleep. One call from a Mr. Morgan, whose 12-year-old daughter was dying of pneumonia with only hours to live, saw the party driving 70 miles so that Branham could pray for her. She was at school 3 days later.

By the Jonesboro, Arkansas, campaign, Branham was recognising his own need for rest. The largest building in the town couldn't hold the crowds who had come from all around—one estimate was 28,000 people. One lady sitting near the front with her husband and children was the insane woman from Little Rock—she had been completely delivered.

Knowing that he was about to take time off to recover, Branham declared he would pray for every sick person in the prayer line. He kept going through the night, taking meals at the pulpit. After a short nap on the stage, he awoke to find the prayer line still in place, patiently waiting for him. Very few wanted to leave, and the meeting went on all week. People would keep their seats and telephone friends, and the numbers just kept growing, and a huge line of people formed of those waiting to get inside the auditorium, eagerly listening to the testimonies of the few who were leaving.

Just before the final night, Branham took a short break to leave the building to meet his wife at the station. On the way back, they had to park many blocks away, because of the huge numbers of people. On the way in he was recognised by an ambulance driver, and agreed to pray for a lady he was sure was dead. The shouting when she was raised attracted attention, and he had to sneak out the side and head back for the auditorium. On the way he bumped into a blind, coloured girl who was crying for her daddy. She had cataracts over both eyes, and no-one was willing to help her because of the Jim Crow laws that enforced segregation. The 17-year-old explained that she had heard on the radio about the healings and had hope for her sight, but couldn't get close to the building and had lost her father, so she couldn't even get back to the bus. Branham prayed for her right there and she was healed. Immediately a crowd surged in his direction, and ushers tried to hurry him away. A crippled man nearby cried out, and his twisted leg was straightened.

After eight straight days with almost no sleep, Branham was so tired he was so jittery he couldn't sleep, and drove straight home to Jeffersonville. When he got home, after a near miss on the road, he was stunned to find 200 people lined up outside his house. He was there till 2 am praying for them, before he finally collapsed into bed. In his sleep, he was mumbling "only believe—The angel said if I could get them to believe…" Almost immediately a car pulled up with a sick baby, and he ministered healing in his pyjamas. Before he had time to crawl back into bed, another emergency drove up, asking him to drive 35 miles to pray for a girl with appendicitis. After praying for her, he fell asleep in a chair, and finally got some rest.

Rev. Jack Moore, who became a keen supporter of Branham and co-editor of the Voice of Healing Magazine, wrote the following comment about the things he observed in the meetings of those early days:

"Yes, Bible days were here again. Here was a man who practiced what we preached.

I say this, not to exalt any human, but only to emphasise that our deep appreciation for our brother stemmed from the fact that his ministry seemed to bring our Lover Lord closer to us, and to better acquaint us with His living works, His personality, and His deity than anything had before…"

Jack Moore testified to "diseases to be accursed, broken homes to be reunited, drunken fathers to repent, prodigal sons to return, feuding churches to…make peace, and lukewarm Christians to be rekindled by the fire of their first love."

Branham travelled to Texas, Arizona, California, Canada and Florida over the next few years. Several future evangelists were inspired by their experiences in the meetings and launched out in their own ministries. O.L. Jaggers and Gayle Jackson attended the early meetings in Arkansas. In Florida, Branham met well-known Pentecostal healing evangelist F. F. Bosworth, who himself later joined the Branham party, often preaching in afternoon meetings. In 1948, in Kansas City, he met fellow evangelist Oral Roberts, and encouraged Roberts in his own efforts to pray for the sick.

In March, 1947, Jack Moore wrote to his friend Rev Gordon Lindsay about what he was seeing and hearing, and suggested he meet them at the Sacramento Campaign. Lindsay opened the door for the Branham party to meet ministers from the Full Gospel circle. Lindsay attended several other Branham campaigns in 1947, and was able to observe events up close by assisting in the prayer line. He began to plan a series of campaigns from Vancouver down into the US, where city-wide meetings would be preceded by corporate prayer meetings and backed by churches from all across the host city.

Rev. Ern Baxter wrote concerning the 4-day Vancouver meetings: "…the largest available auditoriums were inadequate to accommodate the teeming multitudes that waited on the ministry of our brother. Surrounding towns and villages seemed to literally empty…until the whole city was conscious of the spiritual impact of thousands of praying, believing people."

Lindsay also commented on Branham's compassion for people, and the lengths he would go to, to try and minister to as many as he was able. "The results of these meetings were all the more remarkable when we consider how the evangelist was ministering beyond his strength… In the future we were careful to see that he should not get involved in more services than could be properly handled."

One particular event from May 1947 is of particular interest. Branham had begun to challenge the audience on the first night of his campaigns "bring me the worst case you can find and give me enough time to pray for that person, and I'll guarantee that Jesus Christ heals that person before he leaves the platform." His motivation was to exalt the Lord and bring the audience quickly into a place of faith where God could work. That night they brought forward a boy who had been born blind. Branham prayed for over an hour-and-a-half with no result, and the audience were becoming restless. At about one hour forty-five minutes, the boy began to quiver and jerk. He stepped back into his mother's arms and started to point at the lights and different objects around him.

That night the angel visited Branham in his room. When he felt the presence of the spirit he knelt and began to pray, having been attacked by demons before. As it came close, he recognised the presence as that of the Lord, but the angel remained silent. Branham waited for over five minutes, before the voice spoke a rebuke:

"Your commission was to pray for the sick. You are confining too much of the gift of healing to the performance of miracles. If you keep this up, it will come to pass that people will not believe you unless they see a miracle."

He repented immediately, and as the angel turned to leave, asked if his son was allowed to witness the visitation. His eldest had been consumed by fear whenever his father left to travel, and Branham wanted Billy Paul to understand that the Lord was in charge. The angel didn't answer, but remained, and Bill shook his son and brother Donny" awake. They both screamed when they saw the fire burning in the air, but Bill hugged them and they saw the figure of the angel, who then disappeared into the light and vanished. God cared enough for the fears of a small boy that he tarried.

Since we are trying to detail the Acts of the Holy Spirit, not just particular people, it is interesting to note that it was 1946 when Kathryn Kuhlman began to focus on divine healing more regularly in her preaching. As she was preaching one night in 1947 in Franklin, Pennsylvania, a woman in the crowd was spontaneously healed of a tumour. As more and more people began to experience healing and deliverance in her meetings, crowds blossomed as lines formed for ministry.

Although the broad flow of events tended to revolve around William Branham during these years, the Holy Spirit is never limited, and many evangelistic and healing ministries were launched during this period, as the Spirit called them forth.

1948

May 14 1948 *Washington*

President Truman recognises the modern State of Israel

- Truman was the first world leader to recognise the new state, over the opposition from his own Secretary of State
- Truman was ambivalent about the move at first, weighing personal, political and strategic concerns.
- A blessing was released on Truman's home town, Kansas City, because of his actions

5

The Re-Establishment of Israel

On May 14, 1948, the British Mandate over Palestine came to an end, and David Ben-Gurion proclaimed the creation of the State of Israel, and became its first Prime Minister. President Harry Truman of the United States chose to officially recognise the new State on May 15, becoming the first World leader to do so, and surprisingly to many, followed three days later by the Soviet Union.

The Soviet regime had been particularly negative towards Zionism for years, and had taken a pro-Arab line during the riots of 1929 and 1936. Most historians note that Stalin's attitude towards Zionist goals shifted after the German invasion of Russia in 1942. It is believed that he sought to maximise support for Russia's war effort, and recognised the doorways into the West that the worldwide Jewish Community represented. At least part of the Russian declaration in 1948 was due to the distrust of the West after the War and a desire to maintain a measure of Soviet influence in the region.

This is undoubtably one of the greatest fulfillments of Bible prophecy in modern times. Many Christians believe that this event marks the beginning of the Biblical "End-Times".

> "*However, the days are coming, declares the LORD, when men will no longer say, 'As surely as the LORD lives, who brought the Israelites up out of Egypt,' but they will say, 'As surely as the LORD lives, who brought the Israelites up out of the land of the north and out of all the countries where he had banished them.' For I will restore them to the land I gave their forefathers*" (Je 16:14-15).

As I will detail in the next chapter, this single event marked a period of great increase for the work of the Holy Spirit, and several notable events occurred in the months around this date.

One of the more interesting stories from a prophetic perspective was not to unfold until the 1980s, during the time of growth at Kansas City Fellowship, where God supernaturally gathered many of the major prophetically gifted ministers in the US at the time into the same congregation. When Pastor Mike Bickle wondered why they had been so favoured, Bob Jones told him "It's because of Harry S. Truman."

Because Truman had taken a stand for Israel in 1948, Bob explained, a blessing was released on his home town, Kansas City. In addition, one of Bob's first words to Mike was "…you'll be over in Grandview next to Harry S. Truman…" Some years later they ended up obtaining the building next to the Truman family farm, and in the course of time they were given the Truman property for the Lord's work.

The old hymn says "God moves in many mysterious ways His wonders to perform." God Himself declares: "For my thoughts are not your thoughts, neither are your ways my ways, declares the LORD" (Isa 55:8). We need to be careful not to scoff at such claims by prophetic people, and at very least "take it to the Lord in prayer."

1948 – 57

April '48 – Jan '57

The Voice of Healing Revival

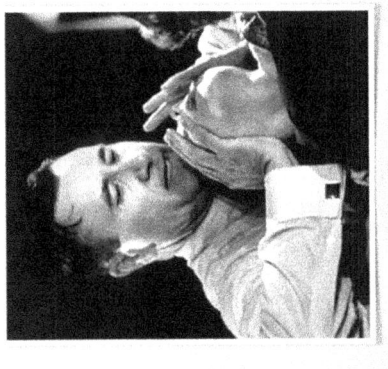
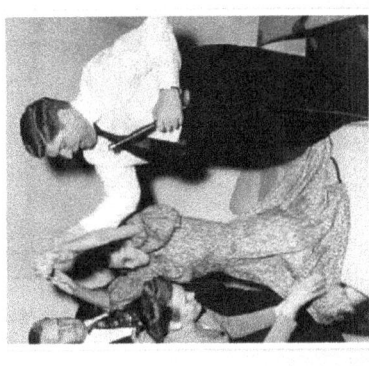

- In April 1948, the first issue of Gordon Lindsay's *The Voice of Healing Magazine* was published, to publicise the great things God was doing through the Branham Crusades. In May, Branham was exhausted and took time to recover, so the new magazine started to report on other leader's meetings.
- Names like A.A. Allen, Jack Coe and Oral Roberts became well-known. About 100 ministers were doing revival tent meetings around the country - about 80% fell into sin - Girls, Gold or Glory…….
- Many ministers entered into a competitive rivalry to have the biggest meetings, greatest miracles and so on.
- Free PDF book *"The Acts of the Holy Spirit in the Voice of Healing Revival"*

6

The Voice of Healing Revival

The success of the city-wide inter-evangelical campaigns had pleased William Branham, who always had a heart for the whole Body of Christ, and opposed any who tried to tell him to focus on a particular denominational group. He asked Gordon Lindsay to assist Jack Moore in the organisation of his campaigns in the future, from an inter-church foundation, convinced that this was God's will.

Lindsay was conflicted at the idea of leaving his church, but the Lord "spoke directly" to him in prayer, and told him He would lead Lindsay "step-by-step" in his part of the "great work He was beginning to do over the land." Early in 1948 they gathered together with Branham to discuss several practical issues. One of these was that the campaigns to date had been chronicled by a denominational magazine in Texas. They felt that the meetings should not be tied to a particular group, and asked the Brother who was the editor whether he would allow his magazine to become inter-denominational. When he declined, the Voice of Healing Magazine was born, with Lindsay as the Editor.

It was agreed at the start that the magazine would not allow discussion of divisive matters of doctrine, but was "to proclaim the message of the Great Commission, the sounding of God's last call to the unsaved, the healing of God's people, to the end of uniting them in spirit, and preparing them for Christ's coming."

The first issue was published in April 1948, and was initially created to document the events of Brother Branham's meetings. In just a few months the magazine grew to over 30,000 subscriber's, and featured teaching articles, revival reports and testimonies of some of the healings that occurred (Look for the free PDF-book "The Acts of the Holy Spirit in the Voice of Healing Revival", which is simply healing testimonies taken direct from the pages of the magazine).

As 1948 went on, Branham was becoming more and more weak. In Phoenix, Arizona, he prayed for a woman with arthritis, who stood in place as though frozen when he'd finished. A few nights later the woman's husband came up to speak to him, saying his wife kept asking about the "other man" who had ministered to her on the podium. Thinking there was something else wrong with his wife, he wanted assurance. Realising the woman had seen the angel of the Lord, Branham inquired further. The man fidgeted and shared what the angel had said: "Don't worry… You will be healed," he told her, then looked back at Branham. "Doesn't Brother Branham look thin and frail? But he'll be strong again after a while." Bill was greatly encouraged that he would eventually be all right.

After Phoenix, Branham held campaigns in Florida, Kansas, Missouri and Illinois, and despite the healings and miracles that were occurring, his health kept getting worse. He had difficulty keeping his balance while ministering, and was plagued by difficulty falling asleep, and then waking up. On 13th May, 1948, (the Day before the restoration of Israel), he tottered backwards from the prayer line and was caught by two men. The next day he summoned his team and told them he would have to cancel all other commitments until further notice.

This was a terrible blow to Gordon Lindsay in particular, as he had resigned as church pastor in Ashland, and put a lot of energy and time into the Voice of Healing Magazine, which suddenly had no purpose. Many other ministers had begun holding their own healing meetings by this time, and Lindsay felt that the magazine needed to report on a broader range of healing ministries than a single individual.

Branham returned home, where he struggled to eat, plagued by reflux and a churning stomach. Doctors labelled his illness as "nervous exhaustion" brought on by overwork, but after two months of rest, Branham was still deathly ill. He felt as though the Lord was ignoring his pleas for healing, even though he had been faithful to the call himself. Eventually, he began to understand the lesson the Lord was trying to impart—he had pushed himself way beyond the bounds of sense, allowing his compassion, and the need of the people, to dictate his habits. He came to understand that just as Moses needed to spread the load and rely on others, so too did he himself. The latest issues of the Voice of Healing carried reports of Oral Roberts, T.L. Osborn and others who were now preaching Divine Healing and seeing the Lord respond.

It was during this time of illness before August, that the Voice of Healing Magazine moved on from being "An Inter-Evangelical publication of the Branham Healing Campaigns", to "An Inter-Evangelical publication of the Last-Day Sign-Gift Ministries". Not knowing when, or even if, William Branham would return to campaigning, Lindsay moved to broaden the scope of the magazine's focus, though to some in the Branham party, it felt like a betrayal. Rev. Peary Green told of the visit where Gordon Lindsay and associates "took his magazine away" from Branham, intending to form the Voice of Healing into a wider organisation. Green was in the room in

Jeffersonville when the documents were presented and signed. They could not take it away without Branham signing away his rights, as Branham was part-owner. Branham already knew from the Lord what would happen, and had told his associates beforehand what would occur, and that he would allow it. Once the signing was done, Lindsay and his party tried to leave "We've got a flight to catch…" Branham insisted they stay and preach for him that night. His love for people and his character was such that even though he knew what they were up to, he still asked them to preach in his church, and he kept Lindsay as his manager.

Whatever the heart motives of those involved at that time, the Lord used the expansion of the Voice of Healing Magazine for His purposes, and it catalysed the Healing revival into a broad movement of evangelists holding meetings across the United States and internationally. It was really from this time that the Voice of Healing Revival began. Branham was moved from publisher of the Magazine to "senior editor" until August 1949, when he was listed as an "associate editor".

After a six-month rest, Branham had a vision that gave him hope for his own healing. He rang Gordon Lindsay about new campaigns, and Lindsay suggested he make Ern Baxter his manager, as he was personally busy with the magazine. Baxter and elderly F. F. Bosworth were careful to analyse their earlier mistakes, and protect Branham from wearing himself out again. They also decided to use "prayer cards" to limit the prayer line on any given night. Bill would randomly call out a card number and minister to that person.

Branham began to return to limited meetings, but it was a full 10 months before he felt well enough to return to full-time preaching. In July of 1949, he was going through central Canada, and, as biographer Owen Jorgensen wrote: "It was on this trip that the course of Christian history changed forever." One night as a lady approached on the stage for prayer,

Branham had a vision of exactly what was wrong with her, and she had been blinded when she was 12 years old by a pencil hitting her in the eye.

This was the second sign the angel had foretold in the cave in 1946, and was something very new in the healing ministry. It was to define Branham's ministry from that moment on, and set him personally apart from most other evangelists of the day. Only the youngest of the Voice of Healing ministers, the then teenage Paul Cain, was operating in that type of prophetic discernment on a regular basis.

After Branham, the three most recognisable ministers of the Voice of Healing revival were Oral Roberts, A. A. Allen and Jack Coe, all of whom had numerous testimonies of notable miracles God performed when they prayed. All had difficult childhoods, and had to overcome many struggles, before the Lord began to use them publicly.

Oral Roberts was dedicated to God in the womb, but left home at 16, and turned away from God. He had a bad stutter, and his mother had always told him "one day God will heal your tongue and you'll preach to millions." He began living a wild life and contracted tuberculosis a year later, before returning home and recommitting his life to God. He was coughing up blood and had little hope of medical help, but God spoke to his sister Jewel promising to heal her brother. He was doubtful, but agreed to go with his older brother Elmer to a healing Revival in Ada, Oklahoma not long afterwards. On the way to the meeting, he heard the Lord speak into his heart: "Son, I'm going to heal you and you are going to take the message of my healing power to your generation."

Roberts was too sick to stand in the prayer line, and had to wait for Evangelist George Moncey to come over to him at the end of the service. Around 11pm his parents had to lift him up so Moncey could pray for him. He was instantly healed, breathing freely for the first time in months, and his tongue was loosed—his stutter was also gone. Over the years from

1935—1947 he pastored churches, travelled as an evangelist, taught in Bible school and wrote various books and articles, though he didn't feel he was fulfilling the call God had on his life.

In 1947, while pastoring in Enid, Arizona, the Lord challenged him to a period of prayer and fasting, and he began to read and re-read the gospels and Acts on his knees for 30 days. He began to see the ministry of Jesus, healing the sick with compassion, and was having a regular dream from the Lord where he heard the cries of suffering people crying for someone to bring deliverance to them.

He decided to test the water, and asked God for three confirmations that he was to pursue a ministry in healing: 1. That 1000 people would attend (a seeming impossibility to a pastor who regularly preached to 200), 2. God would help him pay the rent on the building he'd hired for the meeting ($160), and 3. God would give him a miracle to confirm his call. On the night of the meeting, he had a crowd of 1200, the offering was $163.03, and a German lady with a crippled hand was healed.

Roberts resigned his church and began an itinerant ministry, seeing several notable healings occur. He noticed that his meetings "seemed to be blotting out denominational barriers, colour lines and disunity," in a time where segregation was law in many States, Roberts was willing to be criticised for holding inter-racial meetings. In Tulsa, Oklahoma, he was ministering one night when a man fired a gun at his head, missing him by inches. The event brought national attention and rapidly grew his ministry. He began publishing a magazine called "Healing Waters" in November 1947 that rapidly grew in circulation.

Early in 1948, Roberts met William Branham in Kansas City, and was greatly encouraged by the miracles he witnessed. He asked Branham "Brother Branham, do you think God would answer my prayers for the sick?" Branham replied, "He answers anybody's prayers for the sick." Roberts bought a tent, established the Oral Roberts Evangelistic Association, and began travelling full-time as a healing evangelist. His first tent seated 3000, which he quickly changed for one that held 12,500 people.

Roberts was one of the first evangelists to embrace and use media for the gospel. In 1954, he began to film his crusades, play his sermons on the radio and having crusades aired on television. Thousands began to write to his ministry headquarters with testimonies of salvation after they watched someone healed on the television. By 1957, the Roberts ministry was receiving over 1000 letters a day, and he established a full-time prayer team to minister to those who contacted the ministry.

Asa Alonso Allen was a charismatic preacher known as "God's man of faith and power," and was the most severely criticised of the Voice of Healing evangelists. Growing up with an alcoholic father and unfaithful mother, he ran away at age 14, surviving by doing odd jobs. In 1934, he drove by the Onward Methodist Church in Miller, Missouri, and was drawn in by the sound of joyous singing. The message from the lady evangelist touched his heart, and the next night he committed his life to Christ. The change in his life was immediate—he abandoned his life of bootlegging and dances, and began to obsessively read a Bible his sister had won in a contest. Soon after he heard a Pentecostal preacher at a house meeting and began seeking after the gifts of the Holy Spirit. At a Pentecostal Camp Meeting in Oklahoma, he received the gift of tongues, and was overcome by the presence of God. He began to hold his own revival meetings, basing his sermons on his heroes, Dwight L. Moody and Charles Finney. He saw many saved, relying totally on the Lord for supplying the needs of his family. In Holly Colorado, he was asked to pastor the Tower Hill Memorial Assembly, being ordained as an Assemblies of God preacher in 1936.

Allen was determined to see more of the power of God in his life and ministry, and began to fast, desperate to hear from God. He freely confessed his failures during that time, being seduced from the prayer closet by the smell of his wife's cooking. He finally overcame his flesh, and determined to win through, had his wife lock him inside the prayer closet until he had heard from God. After a long period, where he set his heart not to leave even if he died in there, a light began to fill the closet, and he heard the Lord speaking to him about 13 issues in his life that were preventing the Lord from using him in power (detailed in The Price of God's Miracle Working Power by A. A. Allen).

Soon after, the Allens resigned and set out as itinerant evangelists again. An invitation to Missouri challenged their faith when a totally blind former coal miner came forward for healing. Many were healed of headaches colds and deafness, but they kept putting off the blind man. Eventually Allen cried out "There's unbelief in this room. I can feel it." A man near the back got up and left, and the blind man was healed.

In 1947, Allen was asked to pastor an Assembly in Corpus Christi, Texas, and was very excited to embrace the stability this would provide for his family. He threw himself into preaching and training his flock, dreaming of a church that would operate in evangelism with the gifts of the Holy Spirit. He was excited by the idea of preaching over the radio, but his plans were shut down by the church board, who complained he was wearing them out. Allen was gutted, and went through an emotional breakdown, being tormented by a spirit of depression, until he asked his wife to pray for him and was delivered.

By 1949, the Allens began to hear reports of the Healing Revival meetings that were exploding around the country, and the uncountable miracles that were being experienced. Allen struggled to believe the reports, even from his own flock. He saw an early copy of The Voice of Healing Magazine but dismissed the reports as "fanaticism." He was eventually persuaded to attend an Oral Roberts Campaign in Dallas, Texas, and witnessed the power he had so desperately sought years before being manifested before his eyes. As he watched the prayer line, he heard the Lord speak into his heart: "My son, eleven years ago you sought My face...Eleven years ago I called you into the same ministry...but you failed to pay the price and make the consecration..." Allen repented, resigned his pastorate, and began to study the 13 requirements the Lord had given him, being encouraged that 11 had been marked through on his list. He set his heart to deal with the final two.

In May 1950, Allen sent his first report to The Voice of Healing Magazine, after a campaign in Oakland, California. "Night after night, the waves of Divine Glory so sweep over the congregation that many testify of being healed while sitting in their seats." In 1951, Allen took a leap of faith and purchased a tent, using his last money as a down-payment. On July 4th, 1951, the A.A. Allen Revival Tent went up in Yakima, Washington. By November, 1953, Allen saw his radio dream fulfilled, and began the Allen Revival Hour, which rapidly spread and opened the door for him to Cuba and Mexico.

In 1955, after butting heads with the Assemblies leadership for his refusal to operate inside their churches (where the church would receive a tithe of the offering), accusations began surfacing against Allen, particularly that he was an uncontrollable alcoholic. While in Knoxville, Tennessee, in the fall of 1955, Allen was driving to the auditorium where the meetings were held, and habitually stopped at a local cafe for a glass of milk. Commenting to his manager, H. Kent Rogers, "Rog, that milk tasted funny," he set off for the meeting. Feeling woozy after a few blocks, he pulled over to let someone else drive, and was immediately surrounded by the media, several denominational pastors, and the local police, who arrested him for "drunk driving". (In 2006, an elderly pastor from that denomination publicly confessed and repented of being part of the spiking of Allen's drink, having been led astray by men he trusted).

R.W. Shambach was in the car with Allen and also testified that he was NOT drunk. Allen refused to stop his meetings at the demand of the Assemblies leadership, and turned in his accreditation, continuing as an independent evangelist.

Jack Coe was a giant of a man, and known as "the man of reckless faith". Paul Cain described him in 1990 as "the most similar to Smith Wigglesworth," of all the Voice of Healing Revivalists. Also born into great poverty and a broken home, Coe and his brother were eventually abandoned to an orphanage, as their mother couldn't keep them. He fell into a life of sin, and his health was devastated by alcoholism. He developed severe ulcers, and was told by a doctor that the next drink could kill him. None of his resolve could help him, nor his re-connection with his mother and siblings. Finally, after yet another binge, noticing his heart fluttering, he heard a voice: "This is your last chance. I've called you several times, and I'm calling you now for the last time." He fell to his knees, begging God to "…give me until Sunday, I'll get right with you." He was gloriously born again in a local Nazarene Church, and was there until 4am praying and praising God. The change in his life was so dramatic that it led to his mother being saved as well.

Coe eventually encountered Pentecostals when he attended a "holy roller" meeting with his sister. Challenged by the minister to read the Bible about tongues, he was warned off by his Nazarene pastor. He kept being drawn to the meetings, and after turning down several opportunities to receive prayer, the Lord spoke into his heart: "You know it's for you: you know it's real." The next night he ran forward for prayer. As the group prayed for him, he saw a bright light growing in intensity. A hand reached out of the light and took his hand, and he spent some time walking and talking together with Jesus. When he came to, he was lying in sawdust and speaking in tongues, which continued for three days—he had to write English words down to communicate with his family.

After Pearl Harbor he joined the Army, preaching whenever he could. He would go 45 miles each Sunday to church, walking and hitchhiking, which saw him committed to the army psychiatric ward. He was determined to fast and pray, which only convinced the doctors he was crazy. After nine days, the ward boy knocked on his door and confessed he was a backslidden pastor's son, "I'm going to lose my mind if I don't get what you've got." He was born again on the spot.

Coe felt a burning desire to preach, and asked the local pastor for an opportunity, saying he would do anything. He was asked to be the janitor, and refused, though after a sleepless night of wrestling with God, agreed. In time he was invited to teach Sunday School beginners, then song leader, youth minister and associate pastor, eventually marrying a girl he had first met years before.

He began to seek the Lord about Divine Healing, having heard testimonies of people who had been healed after prayer. One day he fell asleep and had a vivid dream of his sister being healed in a hospital room. He found out that his sister was dying of double pneumonia, and got leave to see her. She was miraculously healed. In 1944, he was stricken with malaria, and his liver and spleen swelled to twice their normal size. He had an experience where the Lord began to show him sins in his life, and he repented each time, feeling more and more free. Eventually, he said "Lord I'm ready to go now." A voice spoke in his heart "You don't have to." He felt warm oil washing him from head to toe as the Lord said "You're healed now." He went straight out on the street and led three people to the Lord.

In 1945, he held his first healing meeting, but his faith was shaken when a blind woman entered the prayer line. The Lord challenged him to be faithful to pray: "Do what you are supposed to do, and I will do what I am supposed to do." He repented, and anointed the woman with oil. Her eyes were opened and she began to cry out "I can see."

In 1947, Coe bought a tent, truck and caravan, and hit the road as a travelling healing evangelist. There are some claims that he was co-editor of the Voice of Healing Magazine in 1946, which are patently false, as the Magazine didn't exist until 1948 and Coe is not listed as editor in any edition (I checked up to 1950). Coe describes his first encounter with William Branham, which he (incorrectly) remembered as 1945, though Branham was not ministering in this way before late 1946. It was most probably during 1947.

"I was having a tent revival in San Antonio in 1945 (almost certainly an error, since Branham's healing ministry didn't really begin till late 1946), when I heard that a man called William Branham was discerning people's hearts and praying for sick. Sometimes we think we are the only one doing something for God. When I heard about discernment, I thought that was fortune telling. So, I decided to go find for myself what it was all about since he was in the same town I was. I tried to get in the healing line but failed. He was discerning people and declaring them healed. One man that he prayed for had no eyeballs at all and he told him that eyeballs will be formed in three days. I thought anybody could say that! So as William Branham finished praying for the people, they led him out using the door to where I was sitting nearby. As he reached close to me, he stopped instantly and laid his hands on me as he prayed silently. After that, he told me that I was not sick but that my body was just tired. Then he softly said 'You were doubting whether this is of God or not, I want to tell you that this is of God and we are both fighting the same devil. Go on and continue in your revival for you were also called to pray for the sick.' When I left that meeting it was like I was walking on clouds! After three days I decided to find out about that man without eyeballs. When I saw him, he was still blind but eyeballs had formed. It was now noon. And that night, after he fell asleep, he awoke around 7 pm and started running around shouting praises to the Lord because he was now seeing. From then on, I knew that Rev. Branham was no ordinary preacher but was called for a dispensational purpose".

Coe was a bold and boisterous man who seemed to love a challenge. Like Smith Wigglesworth, he was criticised for slapping, hitting or jerking people who came for prayer, but they walked away healed. He was very competitive with other evangelists, even measuring Oral Roberts' tent so he could order one marginally bigger. He had a heart for orphans, and started his own children's home in Dallas. He started his own magazine, The Herald of Healing, was preaching on radio by 1952, and was seeing huge crowds of up to 30,000 people by July 1954. His Pittsburgh campaign saw 75 per cent of those on stretchers rise up and walk.

Unfortunately, Coe had ignored doctor's advice to monitor his health. He was overweight and like Branham in the early years, would stay praying for people till the early hours of the morning. He would often do three meetings a day for 6 weeks straight. Early in 1957, he was hospitalised with Polio, and, according to his wife, the Lord spoke to him and told him he was going to take him home. Not long after that he passed away.

Some prominent evangelists scolded Juanita Coe for not allowing them to pray for her husband, but Gordon Lindsay suggested that "his ministry had simply been fulfilled." As we will see, there were a lot of other things going on in the Spirit in 1957.

A brief mention of the Latter Rain Movement is necessary, as many confuse it with the Voice of Healing Revival, from which it was inspired and they ran concurrently. The Latter Rain was mostly focused on the Pacific Northwest and Canada. Those involved in the beginnings of the Latter Rain were inspired to seek the Lord after attending a Branham meeting in

Vancouver, Canada, 1947, where 5 thousand people were jammed into the Exhibition Garden to witness the healings that were occurring. A group of students from the Sharon Bible College in Saskatchewan began to pray and fast to seek more of the presence of God. On February 12th, 1948, after persistent prayer and fasting since October, there was a visitation of the Holy Spirit among the student body. On Easter weekend, 1948, they held special services, which led to their first Camp Meeting in July. Large crowds came to attend, seeking a renewal of Pentecost Power amongst the spiritually dry Pentecostal churches. Naturally, some of the established denominations denounced the move as "extreme", and denounced the "Latter Rain" theology as divisive and exclusive. Many different groups were inspired by this move, some went off-track due to immaturity, some went overboard and became controlling in their pursuit of holiness. Many became part of the Charismatic movement of the 60s, where some of the theological extremes were mitigated. Many orthodox groups remain critical of their theological ideas, such as Joel's Army or the Manifest Sons of God (Rom 8). Most of these criticisms which I have encountered are unfairly condemning—few of the people involved in the movement believed they had already attained such a standard. Most believed it was a Call for the whole church to seek in unity. As Paul Cain said: "It started pure… This time we'll get it right…"

1951

Feb 8, 1951   Calvary Temple, Los Angeles

The Healing of Congressman Upshaw

- In 1884, age 18, William Upshaw fell on the crosspiece of a hay wagon and was paralysed. He sought Divine Healing his whole life.
- He was elected to Congress 1918 - 1924, campaigning to eliminate teaching of Evolution from schools. 1933-52 he was Chairman of a National Christian organisation, and was ordained a Baptist minister in 1938 at age 72.
- At age 84, in 1951, he attended a Branham meeting. By this time Branham would only pray for about 100 people / night using prayer cards. He stopped and related a vision:

"A young man falling from a hay stack and braking his back. A doctor with a white mustache and glasses that sit low on his nose, working on the young man, but to no avail. The youngster grows to become a famous person who writes books. People are applauding him."

- Upshaw was instantly healed, and spent the rest of his life testifying to what Jesus had done.
- Shortly before this death in Nov 1952, he published his testimony in a tract which he sent to every Senator and member of the House of Representatives, President Truman, Winston Churchill, and King George of England.

7

The Healing of Congressman Upshaw

One of the most dramatic healings during the Revival period was the healing of well-known political figure, Congressman William Upshaw. In 1884, the eighteen-year-old Upshaw fell from a haystack onto the crosspiece of a wagon and fractured his spine. He spent 7 years bedridden, and through sheer determination learned to walk again using crutches, which he called his "little buddies". He maintained his whole life that "Jesus will heal me one day—it's just not the right time."

He was vice-president of the Georgia Anti-Saloon League in the early 1900s that played a major role in that state adopting prohibition in 1907, and was known as "the driest of the dry's". He was elected to Congress as a Democrat in 1919 and served four terms, where he was known as "the Billie Sunday of Congress" for his work as an evangelist. He campaigned against the teaching of evolution in schools, and even ran for President in 1932 on the Prohibition Party ticket.

At age 84, on February 8th, 1951, he attended a William Branham revival service, after having been healed of a cancer on his face two years earlier after the prayers of Wilbur Ogilvie. Branham had been ministering for a while, and was being carried away from the pulpit from exhaustion, when he saw a vision. He later described it as:

> "A young man falling from a haystack and braking his back. A doctor with a white moustache and glasses that sit low on his nose, working on the young man, but to no avail. The youngster grows to be a famous person who writes books. People are applauding him."

Branham also saw where in the building the Congressman had been sitting.

He did NOT relate the vision publicly at the time, but told the pastor, LeRoy Kopp, "Tell the Congressman he is healed," so Kopp returned to the microphone and relayed the message.

Upshaw wrote: "*My heart leaped. I said in my battling soul, "Branham knows the mind of God ... I will step out and accept the Lord as my Healer." I laid aside my crutches and started toward the startled LeRoy Kopp and my happy, shouting wife ... and the bottom of heaven fell out! And now at 84, with no gray hairs, and without my boon companions for 59 years (my crutches) I began a new life, joyously testifying that Christ the Great Physician who said, "I am the Resurrection and the Life," can not only save the souls of wicked men and women, but He can and does heal the bodies of the sick the maimed, the deaf, the dumb, and blind, bringing Heaven down to this sinning, staggering world. My crutches are still on the Calvary Temple pulpit, and I am "Happy on the way ... Leaning on the Everlasting Arms." Praise God!*

William David Upshaw 2524 24th Street, Santa Monica, Calif. (*The Voice of Healing*, April-May, 1951, p. 2-3).

Paul Cain was an eyewitness to this miracle. He was sitting immediately behind Upshaw when the power of God fell on him. As the Congressman got to his feet the crowd went into pandemonium, unable to believe what they were seeing.

A number of "internet pharisees" have tried to discredit this testimony based on rather frivolous discrepancies in the relating of the story over the years. At the time, audio recordings of meetings were rare, television happened during the course of the revival, and nit-picking fact-checkers were unknown. I do not find it at all surprising that sometimes the details of exactly what happened in what order got muddled—we all do it. Implying that there was intent to mislead in the erroneous reporting years later is rather a big stretch, given the many testimonies of the miraculous that so many claimed "were too numerous to recount."

One such testimony from Branham's South African visit in 1951 came from Fred and Nellie Roberts, reported by Rev. Jerrell H. Miller:

DURBAN, SOUTH AFRICA -- Two of the most respected pastors in all of South Africa are Fred and Nellie Roberts. Coming to this country and looking at its Pentecostal History, I questioned several people who were in the city before I met the Roberts and asked them if they had been in the great miracle service with William Branham at the race track. As we came in from the airport, we could see the old track from the road and once I had seen it, it brought back total recall of what happened there in 1951.

Sitting in a room at the Durban Christian Center just before Rodney Howard-Browne preached I began to speak with the pastor's wife Nellie Rogers. I asked her if she was at the meeting and she said, "Yes, Fred and I had just been married for three years when we saw one of the most awesome displays of God's power. If you go to the race course there you can still see the stands where it happened. Fred and I were sitting in the choir, he took a man's hand and said, 'Oh you have cancer.' The demons are crying out to demons of the people who have cancer in the audience that you have cancer. As Branham touched the man's hand, Branham's hand turned red and when it went back to normal, the man was totally healed of cancer. That one meeting put the hunger inside of us for the supernatural power of God. William Branham was the best we have ever seen.'"

Fred Roberts gave his account of the meeting, "In those days we were segregated, the Indians on one side, the blacks and several other ethnic and tribal sectors divided off from each other."

"When William Branham walked on to the field going up to the podium he passed by a row of people in wheelchairs as they reached out to touch him each one came out of their chairs and started running. My brother had been suffering as an acute asthmatic, he was miraculously healed along with many others."

"He was the most unique man I have ever witnessed in the healing gifts because he did it with prophecy. He was a prophetic healer. Very often before he prayed for the sick, he would tell them their names, the name of their doctors, and then tell them what was wrong with them. Some of the revelation and knowledge was absolutely powerful. I remember one night in praying for a man who had ulcers, he stopped and said, 'You've got ulcers' and then he pointed to a man in the front row and said, 'You've got ulcers too, the demons in this man are calling out to the demons in this man for help.' He then paused and pointed to the upper gallery and said, 'That man right up there in third balcony you've got ulcers, is that right?' The man said yes. 'I have driven them out of these two men and now they are trying to go into you.' All three men received their healing that night. These meetings had a tremendous influence on my life and gave Nellie and

I a hunger for the things of the supernatural. We were in the choir and had been married for about three years."

"They brought a woman in a complete body cast from an ambulance with a broken back, it had been broken in three places. She was totally incapable of moving at all. The women was instantly healed. The plaster cast was put up against the wall and she walked out of the meeting perfectly made whole. One night he went right down the row and told a woman that she had touched him when he saw her today and that God had healed her baby. 'Your baby is healed tonight, the man next to you is your husband.' Branham named her husband, and them went right down the row like that naming people by name and calling out their illnesses. With Branham, what-ever God revealed to him was healed. In Johannesburg two men brought a man in saying that he was blind, they thought they would expose the man of God up as a deceiver and hoax. Branham recognised it immediately and called them out and said, 'Those two men bringing that man down the aisle, he's not blind, you came here tonight to show up the servant of God. Because you have dishonoured God you will be blinded for three days.' Immediately the man screamed, he was instantly made blind." (quoted from theremnant.com, written by Rev. Jerrell H. Miller).

1952

Mid 1951   Sapulpa, Oklahoma

The Boy Who Sees With A Plastic Eye

- August, 1950 - Ronnie Coyne was playing with his brother when a piece of wire was pushed into his right eye. It became infected, and was removed, being replaced by a plastic shell.
- In July, 1952, he went to a Vacation Bible School, and gave his hear to the Lord.
- About two weeks later, the family attended a revival in Sapulpa. Ronnie went into the prayer line to avoid having his infected tonsils removed. Sister Gillock (sister of T.L. Osborn) noticed something was wrong with his right eye and asked him if he believed he could be healed, not realising the eyeball was missing.
- When Ronnie said he believed, she prayed for him to see, and he began to see from the plastic eye, and even the empty socket.
- To the day he died in 1994, Ronnie Coyne was able to see from the empty socket, and would testify in churches of the miracle God had done for him.

8

The Boy Who Sees With A Plastic Eye

My favourite of all the testimonies in the Voice of Healing Magazines is the story of Ronnie Coyne, told in *The Voice of Healing*, Feb, 1954, p6-7.

In May, 1950, the Coyne family moved to Sapulpa, Oklahoma. In August, Ronnie was playing outside with his brother when had managed to get a piece of wire penetrating his right eye. Late in the afternoon his mother noticed a white spot on the eyeball, and took the boy first to his local doctor, then an eye specialist, who rushed him to hospital.

A few days later the family were notified the eye would have to come out, but his mother refused. On later examination she realised the eye was totally white and the sight was gone. Surgery was attempted to try and save the eye but an abscess was discovered that couldn't be drained. In this pre-penicillin world, the options were remove the eye or risk losing both eyes and his life. A plastic shell was fitted to cover the empty socket and Ronnie came home four days later.

After ten months of total blindness in his right eye Ronnie became worried about his soul, and was saved in July 1951 at a Vacation Bible School. Two weeks later the family attended a Revival meeting in Sapulpa organised by T.L. Osborn's brother Lonnie. His sister Mrs. Gillock was ministering that night, and Ronnie's mother told him to join the prayer line, as he had a throat infection and was facing having his tonsils out.

Sister Gillock prayed for him and then noticed there was something wrong with hie eye. "Yes, I'm blind in my right eye," the boy told her—she had no idea the eyeball was missing. She asked Ronnie if he believed God could heal him, and when he agreed prayed for his sight. Immediately, Ronnie began to see the steps, the microphone and was able to count fingers, with his remaining natural eye covered. The family and others tested him for four days, after which God spoke to Ronnie's mother and told her to "Go and tell the people." Ronnie testified and demonstrated his ability to see before thousands at the Voice of Healing Convention in. Dallas in December, 1952. He was tested by numerous doctors and eye specialists. They noted that if a "rank sceptic" tried to test the boys he would temporarily go blind, just like Jesus was unable to do miracles in Nazareth because of their unbelief.

The Chattanooga News ran a story on the miracle, including testimony from an optometrist, Dr N.R. Morris, who attended the service on request to privately examine Ronald. He was quoted as saying:

"With no receptive organ and with eye completely removed, his ability to read was demonstrated with foreign reading material. It was read as satisfactorily as could be expected from a child his age under normal circumstances.

There is absolutely no scientific explanation for this marvellous phenomenon. This can only be a spiritual gift."

Gordon Lindsay wanted more, and took the boy to other eye specialists, often without warning them beforehand. One unbelieving doctor did not notice the plastic eye and had his nurse run the tests. When she gave him a rating of 20/20 vision, they queried her competence, and the doctor noticed the eye was plastic. He shouted at the nurse to make the test again, with the same result.

To the day he died in 1994, Ronnie Coyne could see perfectly out of his empty eye socket. There is even a video clip (YouTube) of him demonstrating his ability to read messages scribbled on church newsletters from the empty socket.

Pastor John Hamel, of John Hamel Ministries, came to know Ronnie Coyne personally during the later years of his life. He wrote: "This was a true miracle of God which I came to witness firsthand.

"I personally covered his existing left eye with my own handkerchief, not some transparent prop provided from Rev. Coyne's bag of unholy "tricks". (I covered his other eye with) a handkerchief which I folded six or eight times over. I then held it in place with approximately one-half roll of adhesive tape, similar to what you will see below, only better. I taped it so tightly to Rev. Coyne's nose and cheekbone that he later told me, "You hurt me when you did that. If I didn't like you so much, Pastor John, I would have been angry with you for that." He was correct in his analysis of my eye covering tape job. I was determined that he would not be able to see out of his existing eye.

"Brother Coyne removed his plastic eyeball and placed it on my pulpit. He then read everything brought to him by our congregation, from the Bible to drivers' licenses, birth certificates, newspaper articles, etc., WITHOUT ONE SINGLE MISTAKE. Forty-one people handed him something to read in that service. One woman shrieked when she realised her maiden name was still on her nursing license. She did not realise it until Rev. Coyne read it aloud. Brother Coyne flawlessly demonstrated this miracle of God not only in our morning service but during our evening service as well! Many tears were shed as people realised they were in the presence of a miracle working God!" (http://www.johnhamelministries.org/index2.htm).

There is a video clip on YouTube of Paul Cain ministering in the 50s. After about 15 minutes he gets young Ronnie Coyne up to demonstrate his ability. Search for "paul cain only believe 1953?" Paul told his assistant, Dan Reise, that he believed Ronnie wasn't actually "seeing", but was operating in the "purest word of knowledge gift" he'd ever seen.

I have often been asked by people when I tell this story, why wouldn't God recreate the eyeball? Why do something weird like that? Personally, I'd rather have a new eye. But all I hear from the Lord whenever I ask is: "Because I CAN!"

1948 - 57

Paul Cain - The Youngest of the Revivalists

- Miracle birth, Garland Texas, 1929.
- Salvation and Angelic Visitation age 8, sparks his public ministry
- 1947 (Age 18), Paul began to hold large meeting in tents, auditoriums and churches.
- He became friends with Branham despite their age differences because of their similar gifts.
- 1952 - began to film his meetings, 1954 - brought the World's largest tent from Jack Coe
- 1957 - Lord began to speak to him about the excesses of the revivalists. Promised he would meet "a new breed" if he would lay down his ministry. He wrote a public letter, cancelled his magazine and tv show, and spent 25 years waiting on the Lord.

9

Little Brother—The Boy Prophet

The youngest of the Voice of Healing Revivalists was Paul Cain—a teenager when the Revival began. His family heritage held a great spiritual lineage. Paul's great-grandmother would regularly see open visions. Others around would wonder what she was seeing, so she would place her hand on a person's shoulder, and immediately they would see the same thing in the Spirit. The anointing passed down to his grandmother and mother, who both moved in the Spirit, and were very faithful followers of Jesus.

In 1929, his Jewish father, William Henry Cain (56), managed to sustain the family by working odd jobs on the railroad. His 45-year-old mother, Anner, had lost 3 of her 5 daughters before they were a year old, and was currently very ill. She had terminal heart condition, terminal tuberculosis, had both breasts eaten away by cancer and three malignant tumour blocking the birth canal. At the university hospital in Dallas, Texas, she was a test case for a new cancer treatment, but was pronounced 'incurable' and sent home. The St Louis doctor told her when she was 8 months pregnant:

"neither you nor the baby will live, and he cannot be born because of the tumours blocking the birth canal."

Being a very devout woman, she began to seek the Lord back home in Garland, Texas. At the "hour past midnight", which afterwards became her favourite time, the Angel of the Lord walked into the room, laid his right hand on her shoulder and told her: "Daughter, be of good cheer. Fear not. You will live and not die. The fruit of your womb is a male child and he will be born in perfect health. You shall name him Troaz Paul, because he will preach the gospel like My apostle of old." She was instantly healed. Her breasts were restored and Paul was a breast-fed baby. Two weeks after his birth the doctors did a series of tests, having never seen a restorative miracle before. She was written up in hospital records as a "miracle woman". One cancer doctor told Anner "only God can do this." Paul used to joke about the phrase "you will live and not die", as his mother lived to over 105.

Dan Reise, Paul's assistant in his final years, explained that his birth certificate actually states his name as 'William Paul Cain'. Paul's father filled out the certificate, and he wanted his son named after himself. Paul didn't find this out till much later, when he needed to apply for a passport.

Anner had the wisdom not to tell Paul the details of his birth, leaving it to the Lord to call his servant. She had many chores to do in the household, and the young Paul spent a lot of time with his grandmother. This wonderful woman of God had read the whole Bible three times before she turned 13, and never stopped till she died at 87. Paul said "she knew the Bible almost… from cover-to-cover… we called her a 'walking bible'… all the genealogies… it'd drive you up the wall just to be around her." The Jehovah's Witnesses blacklisted the family home because they could not contend with his grandmother's knowledge of Scripture. Paul said "she never wore glasses, never had false teeth… never walked with a cane (other than me), … she trusted the Lord…"

Paul told of his grandmother looking out the window, and seeing open visions—she saw the attack on Pearl Harbour, and a number of dangerous tornados, several days before the newsboys would be announcing the "extra". Like her own mother, she would lay her hand on Paul's shoulder and he would also "see just enough to terrify me all over again…" The church of her day rejected her and refused to allow this sort of activity—they were so afraid of the supernatural realm, but were happy to allow her to settle theological debates, though Paul said the Baptists "always had a problem with speaking in tongues."

Paul told of how his grandmother and mother would 'tag-team' as they would have corresponding visions of great accuracy. Paul recounted a time in Mulberry, Texas, where both women had a vision of the town being destroyed by a tornado. They went from door-to-door warning the people of the time the storm would hit. The women were known and credible because of the accuracy of previous words (lost cows found, people healed), and no lives were lost, though the town was completely destroyed—"wiped off the map".

Anner would have accurate warnings for the young Paul which helped him avoid some major pitfalls. She would see people who were trying to use him (after he began ministering) and warn him against accepting their promises. Paul said: "I was so busy trying to become famous that she was spending more time with the Lord than I was and was hearing much more clearly." Several promoters came along who promised to "buy the biggest tent" of "make him the greatest prophet", but Anner warned her son "they will destroy you and the purposes of God for you will be lost". She would also know who was trustworthy and faithful.

When he was eight years old Paul and his fourteen-year-old sister Mildred (who had herself been supernaturally healed as a two-year-old) were returning home from a prayer meeting at the local Baptist Church.

There had been a strong sense of the Lord's presence which remained on Paul as he headed home, increasing in strength to a frightening level. When they reached the room they shared, he heard the Lord call his name, and ran in terror, hiding under the bedclothes. The light of the Angel of the Lord filled the room as Paul hid his face under the blankets. Mildred boldly asked the Lord to speak to her instead "I'm here too." The Angel recounted the story of Paul's miraculous birth (which Anner had not told him) and both children heard every word. Paul has always told of his great fear every time an angel would appear, carrying the holy presence of the Lord. He said "I never wanted to do the will of God… I resented being different. I think that's why I would have such great fear whenever the Lord would manifest himself in any way because I knew what he might be up to and I knew I wasn't up to what He might be up to."

Paul began to experience visions himself, and didn't fit in at school. He was baptised in the Spirit at age 9, and "fell in love with the Lord." he said "after that, I wasn't much good for anything." He would slip out in the early hours of the morning to go into a field and spent time with the presence of the Lord. He begged the Lord not to speak to him privately, because it was such a frightening experience. Paul remembers a wonderful young teacher called Mrs. Strange, who made him her class chaplain, and he would read from the New Testament every day. He was ostracised by other children, and nicknamed "Droopy Eyes", because he was shy and not interested in the sports and activities they were. They could not relate to this boy who was always praying and reading the Bible, even if he couldn't yet understand it, and who knew things before they happened. Paul resented the loneliness that his revelatory gift brought—he wanted to be like everybody else, and didn't want to be different.

Paul and his sister began a children's church in their yard. They would worship and pray, and Paul would read from the Bible. Paul remembers "there was even the falling in the Spirit" when children prayed for each other. He remembers one girl he didn't particularly like because she was the popular white blonde hair "beauty queen", and knew it. He prayed for her one night and she was "slain in the Spirit". Her head knocked over the coal bucket when she fell and the handle fell under her chin. She ended up with a metal helmet, coal-black hair and face, and a lot more humility. Paul joked "I didn't push her either... I didn't help her."

The children constructed a small outhouse building out of scrap lumber for their services (Paul said they pinched the shingled roof of the family wood shed, and got a whipping). Paul was embarrassed if his grandmother came because she would dance in front of the Presbyterian visitors, so he often waited until she had gone to bed before beginning services.

One regular vision Paul has had over the years was "Joel's Army". Paul saw, around age 10, a powerful angel with drawn sword pointing to a building with an illuminated sign out the front saying "Joel's Army, Now in Training", which he has seen many times over the years. The First Baptist Church pastor, Dr Paris, had a love for the supernatural, and recognised the anointing that had run through Paul's family line. He would take young Paul with him on sick calls, and ask him what he was seeing. Paul would have detailed information by revelation that would prove accurate, describing the scene they would encounter in detail—what people were wearing, names, where they would be when they entered, and what the problem was. Paul cannot remember anyone actually being healed. He said Dr Paris was one of those "if it be thy will" people, and he remembers asking the Lord at the time "Lord, if I ever get sick, don't let those people come pray for me."

Paul didn't often have visions and audible voice manifestations. He said most often people would ask him a question and he would suddenly just know the answer and speak it out. Just before WW2 his grandmother had seen the coming conflict, and Paul had started gathering up all the used tyres that rich people had discarded. He filled the barn with these tyres, which turned into a source of supply when rationing started. His gifting would also enable to see the unconfessed sin in people's life, which really impressed the pastors, and he said they did him a disservice, because as a young boy he didn't know that calling out sin wasn't the Lord's preferred way to operate. He was talked about as the Boy Prophet who could see sin, and it caused him problems later on. The Baptist church didn't have a place for the strange boy, and the local Pentecostals invited him to speak around age 17. Paul used to practise preaching as a boy by setting up spikes from the railroad as a congregation.

Paul's first public meeting was in Memorial Assembly of God in Dallas. He had been promoted as "The Boy Prophet", "He knows all, sees all." They didn't know he'd never preached before and had spent hour practicing the motions he had seen other pastors use—especially the shaking hand movements. When he got up before the crowd, he was overcome with stage fright and was shaking violently. He struggled to open his Bible and was about to try and speak when his hand fell down in exhaustion. It happened to be pointing at a man several rows back. He leaped to his feet, and called out "That's enough Little Brother. Stop right there," and he ran to the front and fell on his face. Paul continued to shake in fear, and every time his hand pointed in a direction, others would run to the front. Another man stood and gave a prophetic warning, and general repentance broke out—Paul hadn't said a word.

He had a lot of invitations after that, but didn't feel that he was to take them. He got to participate in some meetings with others and grew in confidence. He felt the Lord telling him to go to Tulsa, Oklahoma, where Raymond T. Richie had seen great healings in the past. He came to the Bethel Temple (AG), where Dr William Ward was pastoring. Paul boldly told him Jesus had sent him there and if he'd have him for a meeting the Lord would fill the building and heal and save many. Dr Ward tearfully agreed, though the board turned him down. Paul went instead to the Revival Tabernacle, where he said the Lord would do twice as much. The pastor agreed and started to promote the meetings on radio, while Paul went to fast in preparation. He stayed day and night in his hotel waiting till Sunday without food or water, and was "loaded with revelation" by the time the meeting started. He said the Lord "honoured his ignorance." He said "I had no wisdom but plenty of revelation."

Paul would describe the "amber light" of the Lord that would move around the room and settle over particular people. When he looked at the light over the person he would "know" details about them and their situation. That night it moved to a little old lady in a green-and-white polka dot dress. Paul instantly knew her details, and said: "Lady, you're from San Antonio, Texas. You're badly crippled with Arthritis. The Lord says for you to get up, walk out to that aisle and run. You're completely healed." She shot to her feet and was instantly healed and restored and ran along the aisles. Paul spent hours praying for people in the prayer line. Another lady came up "with the sweetest little nose." The angel of the Lord told Paul she had colitis, which he mis-heard as "cold-itis". Thinking she had a cold, he grabbed hold of her nose, commanded her to be healed, which she was, despite his ignorance. Paul would also see the sins in the congregation—he called out those who were "messing around"—even though he didn't really know what that meant. At the end of the meeting Paul looked around for the pastor, but couldn't see him anywhere. He dismissed the crowd and went back to his hotel. The next morning the pastor rang him and said: "I have a radio show at eleven. You need to listen in." When he came on air, the pastor said "Well folks, we're having a genuine revival down at the Tabernacle. But I just want to warn you folks: don't come with any unconfessed sin in your heart, 'cause this young prophet will call it out. And just in case you're wondering where I was at the close last night—I was under the grand piano repenting of everything I could think of." The pastor eventually spoke to Paul and said "Little Brother, your expertise is healing and discerning the sick. God didn't call you to call sins out." Paul didn't understand what the problem was: the Lord was showing him these things. He confesses to some "prophetic arrogance" as well—"I can't disobey God." A few nights later he again disclosed the sins of the congregation, including deacons, city officials and so on. Finally, the pastor was so disturbed he called up a friend in Sacramento and recommended he invite Paul to speak. He told Paul "They need you there. There's more sin there in California."

Paul said he was quite cocky when he arrived in Sacramento, believing that he had been called to be a trouble-shooter to clean up the church. The opening night he was looking for just that, and saw a 6-foot usher piously holding the collection bag. The Lord showed him the man's wife and children sitting in the meeting, and what he was planning. He shot to his feet "You old hypocrite. Thus sayeth the Lord. You see this lady. Sitting over here… that's your wife. Shame on you brother. See that woman sitting over there in that rust-coloured dress. That's the woman you're running off with after these meetings." He dropped his offering bag and ran toward the podium. All the other ushers ran forward to restrain him and Paul said (arrogantly) "Leave him alone. He can't hurt the man of God." The man fell to his knees and looked up at Paul with tears in his eyes, "Oh Little Brother. It's all true. What on earth am I gonna do?" The self-righteous 18-year-old replied, "Well I don't know. I don't move in that area."

A similar situation arose some years later in Phoenix, Arizona around 1957. Paul had visited the church a year previously and given a salvation message. A woman stood up suddenly and gave a message in tongues and an interpretation, which cut across the anointing. Paul thought it very strange. In this second meeting, Paul noticed the woman fidgeting, about to interrupt again, and called her out. "Please don't do that."

The pastor came up after the first night and told Paul they would have to cancel the rest of the meetings, mumbling a feeble excuse. Paul knew instantly what was going on and said "No that's not the reason. The real reason is that lady I exposed—her husband has offered a million dollars if you close me down." The pastor sheepishly admitted the truth, but was firm in his decision. Paul told him "you will live to see the new building but not to preach in it." Some months later, as the man was walking up to the pulpit in the opening service, he dropped dead of a heart attack.

Gradually, Paul did learn both wisdom and humility. The meetings were full of healings and miracles, with incredibly detailed revelation that built faith. Paul explains now that he had no understanding at the time of the difference between the revelation, the interpretation and the application. Eventually the Lord began to deal with him about telling the people things they already knew. The revelations were to edify the body and help people.

In 1950 (age 21), Paul was driving late at night through Santa Maria California, engaged to be married, heading for his quiet prayer place—a cabin owned by a friendly police captain. The Lord appeared next to him in the front seat of his car dressed as a monk, and told him he was jealous of his companions and he had a special work for him to do. "You have too many friends… I created you for a purpose, and I'm jealous for that purpose."

Paul was surprised because he didn't feel like he had many friends at all, and those he had were godly young people. He was even more surprised when he was pulled over by a policeman, who was looking carefully around the car for the other man he had seen through the windscreen.

"I'm a minister," Paul told him. "That was the Lord."

"Well, are you aware that you and the Lord just ran through a series of red lights in downtown Santa Maria?" the cop asked. Paul had been so distracted he hadn't had a clue.

"Well, I can't give the Lord a ticket," the policeman said, and let him off with a warning. Paul drove on to the cabin, and when he arrived, found Jesus standing inside, waiting for him. Paul was aware that the Lord was unhappy.

"Lord, I'm engaged to be married. Do you want me to marry or not?" he asked.

The Lord looked at him for a while, but didn't answer directly. He wanted Paul's free will agreement. "I walked alone," was all He said.

"Lord, I want what You want," Paul said, "but you'll need to take this desire from me."

The Lord touched him on his chest and "changed his body chemistry".

Many years later, Paul was told by Jack Deere that the Monk's robe was his call to celibacy. Paul broke off the engagement, which brought him a lot of persecution from the Assemblies of God—his fiancée was the daughter of the General Presbyter of the AoG. Funnily enough, the naive Paul was engaged to the "wrong" sister. He had seen the younger girl's picture in a yearbook, and phoned the house, unaware that it was her older sister who answered.

"Do you know who I am?" he asked, after he had introduced himself. Of course, she had heard of the young minister.

"I think the Lord wants us to marry," Paul said. The girl agreed and it was arranged, and announced. The family were none too pleased when Paul broke off the engagement, but the Lord provided a godly husband for the girl.

Paul's father remained an agnostic, despite the miracles that had occurred. He believed the reality of his wife's healing, and if someone made a snide comment about the angelic appearance he would "hit them in the nose"; but he wasn't sure of the truth of the gospel. He had formerly been a member of the First Methodist Church, and they called him up the front to lead in prayer. He never went back, saying "If they don't have enough discernment to ask someone like me to lead in prayer, then if there is a God, they don't know him." Paul tried for years to lead his father to the Lord, but was always brushed off. In the early 1950s he attended on of Paul's Revival meetings in Dallas, and had an open vision of two large angels standing wither side of his smaller son. He told Paul "it was all I could do not to run down the front immediately and give my heart to the Lord right then, but I waited until you gave the call." Not long after he died in 1952.

In 1948, Paul met William Branham, and they became quite good friends, despite their dissimilar ages, because they were so similarly gifted. Paul had attended a Branham meeting, and Branham had discerned his gifting, and asked to meet. Paul told of how they would call each other up from different parts of the country and 'practise' over the phone.

"Well, Paulie, you're real good today. How am I?" Branham would ask, and Paul would tell him. [Many years later, Mike Bickle, after hearing this story, rang Paul up one day from Kansas City. Paul was in Texas. Mike said jokingly "Paul, you sound really good today. How am I?" Paul replied: "Well Mike, your hair is wet and you've got a towel wrapped around your middle 'cause you've just got out of the shower." Mike hung up in shock].

Paul is quite clear that he never shared the platform with Branham—they never "ministered together" in that sense, though there were several occasions where Branham couldn't continue and would call Paul to go on the next week. In 1957, Paul had a dream in Seattle, Washington of ministering to a mass of people in Europe. He understood he was supposed to go to Europe soon, but had no idea how to make it happened. He planned all day to take an offering that night to raise the money to do what he had seen. As he was about to leave, his mother told him she'd had a visitation from the Lord "and He told me to tell you not to take that offering tonight." Paul protested "you don't understand", but she held firm. "The Lord also told me you're going to Europe right away, but you won't need a penny. Your way is going to be paid around the world."

That night he totally forgot to pass the plate. Late that night he received a call from Brother Branham in Jeffersonville, Indiana. "Brother Paul… how would you like to go to Europe?"

"Europe?" Paul asked in surprise. "Did I hear you right?"

"Yes. How would you like to go to Europe?"

Paul told him about the dream he'd had, which Paul thought didn't seem to impress Branham (who had them himself all the time). Branham told him the Angel of the Lord had told him not to go to Europe but to send Paul instead, as people were waiting to arrest Branham with trumped-up charges to try and discredit the ministry. "If I send you they can't do anything to you. You won't need a penny. Your way will be paid around the world." Paul ended up preaching to 30,000 people in Karlsruhe, Germany, including some from behind the Iron Curtain, and thousands were saved. Over 180,000 people in total attended those meetings.

Throughout the 50s, notable miracles occurred in Paul's meetings. In Stuttgart, many police were in attendance. A lady came up in the healing line with a grapefruit-sized goiter on her neck. Paul told her, by revelation, "Sister the goiter on your throat is going to disappear in 15 seconds." Paul was worried he would be "tarred and feathered" before the interpreter could finish, but he felt the goiter disintegrate under his hand. Many were saved and healed as faith grew amongst the crowd.

One lady at a meeting had been told by numerous doctors that she was pregnant—one even told her she had twins. Paul said "the Lord allowed me to see a number of things… She had a 15-pound 'water-tumour' and she would pass that tumour that night. The tumour burst that night and she came back to the meeting completely delivered."

Another night Anner told Paul before the meeting not to overlook a lady in a blue dress in a wheelchair. "She has faith to be healed tonight if you call her out. And that man over there, it's his wife's birthday and it would be a wonderful birthday present if the Lord were to heal her husband from cancer of the tongue." Paul said he didn't get to preach that night, as the man was saved, healed, called to preach and started preaching himself.

Another night she warned Paul "don't overlook that lady in the front row with breast cancer." Paul said he "didn't have an ounce of faith for that lady.... The stench of that cancer. I don't know how people could stand to be around her. And here she was night after night and I never had the faith to call her out." He obeyed, and the woman was healed and was still living in the late 80s.

Raymond T. Richie, a famous healing evangelist from the late 30s and 40s, who was Paul's boyhood hero, flew to Europe to attend the meetings there. Paul used to listen to Ritchie on the radio and prayed that he might carry his bags. He was a great encouragement to Paul, and wept to see what the Lord was doing through the younger man. He was one of the few who walked in power for a time who didn't go to his grave in infamy. In humility, he carried Paul's bags around Europe.

Paul maintained that the Revival started in purity, and was pure for the first few years. He said the competitive spirit entered around 1952 as promoters began to pursue the speakers to make them famous. He jokes about the silliness of the claims: who had the biggest tent, the biggest tumour healed and so on. He said if you lowered the centre poles of the tent you could stretch it a few extra feet to be bigger.

In 1957, the Lord began to speak to Paul about the excesses of many of the Voice of Healing Evangelists. He said: "Paul, you're in a rat race, and even if you win, you're still a rat." By that time Paul had his own magazine, and was negotiating to go on television. The Lord said to him: "If you will spend your time from now on waiting on me and studying my Word, I'll bring you to stand before a New Breed of leader who will never be corrupted by Girls, Gold or Glory." Paul wrote an open letter explaining why he was stepping away from public ministry that cost him a lot of friends.

He laid down everything and retired to a little house in Texas with his mother, who was adamant he hadn't yet done what the Lord had told her he was called to do. Paul thought it would only be a few years, and went from over 300 speaking engagements a year to 3-5. Every time he would minister during the "silent years" the power would break out, and he would start to think "this is it," but the Lord would say "I still can't trust you," and send him back.

1956

Church of Philadelphia,
Chicago, Illinois

Jan 16, 1956

Branham Prophesies the End of the Revival

- "America, America", "you have turned down your opportunity", "40 years in the desert" - didn't recognise the time of her visitation
- Branham prophesied the Lord was taking away the Healing Revival, because the nation had not put aside their denominational differences and come into unity
- Despite all the Revivals, and the publicity surrounding the miracles, little had changed outside the meetings themselves.
- 40 years later, Rick Joyner hosted a meeting in Moravian Falls on Jan 16th on the Anniversary of Branham's prophecy.
- Two other men
- Ray 'Kurschke' (77) - last disciple of John G Lake. The day before they had been emptying out hospital wings.

10

Branham Prophesies the End of the Revival

On January 16, 1956, the spirit of prophecy came on William Branham in a meeting in Chicago, Illinois.

The WilliamBranhamHomepage.org has the following unreferenced quote, which is consistent with the reports of what Branham prophesied:

> "But, O, America, America, how oft would God have taken thee; thou which killest the prophets, and stonest them that are sent unto thee; how often would I have gathered thy children together, as a hen [doth gather] her brood under [her] wings, and ye would not! Behold, your house is left unto you desolate—spiritually desolate… (a paraphrase of Luke 13:34-35).
>
> "Saying, if thou hadst known, even thou, at least in this thy day, the things [which belong] unto thy peace! but now

they are hid from thine eyes. For the days shall come upon thee, that thine enemies shall cast a trench about thee, and compass thee round, and keep thee in on every side, And shall lay thee even with the ground, and thy children within thee; and they shall not leave in thee one stone upon another; because thou knewest not the time of thy visitation," (Luke 19:42-44).

America had been visited with the greatest outpouring of Signs, Wonders and Prophecy since the first century, yet the Institutional churches opposed the move, refusing to work together, and put aside their political and theological differences for the sake of what God was doing among them.

I have been unable to find a direct source for that prophetic word, though the Billy Graham Center Archives confirm that meeting took place, as does the reference in "Footprints in the Sands of Time", the out-of-print biography of Branham. Branham said that America had not "discerned the time of her visitation", and had rejected the Lord. He said that they would have one more year to return to the Lord, and that the Revival was being taken away because of the Church's refusal to come into unity. Branham himself referred to the meeting and the prophecy on several occasions:

Visions And Prophecy, April 8, 1956: "I predict that America this year, the United States this year, will either receive Christ or she will start falling, from this year, ... something's holding me to America. All the others seems to be the same way, and I believe that America is going to get her last call this year [1956]..."

God Keeps His Word—04/07 1957: "And I say this, with the reverent heart to God, "The testing time has come for America, and she's failed."

The Gospel has been preached from the east to west, from north to south; they've combed every little place and crack and corner. Great revivals has went forth, Billy Graham's, and Jack Schuller's, and Oral Roberts. Oh, just hundreds of them have combed every little crack and corner… What did I tell you from this pulpit? Last year [1956] America made her fatal mistake. I said, "Fatal mistake," sure did… They're trying to go right over and hook up with the Arabs. Don't you know, God's Word said, "Ever who curses Israel, will be cursed?"

Questions And Answers, May 27, 1962: "You remember about four years ago, in Chicago one day, the Spirit of the Lord came upon me and I said, "This is it! And the revival is over, and America has turned down her opportunity." It's on tape. "And there won't be no more. Her last opportunity, she's turned down." …And so just watch what's happened since then, see, the revival has stopped

An addendum to this tale occurred in the mid-90s:

[Towards the end of 1995, Bob Jones rang up Paul Keith Davis and asked: "I keep hearing January 16. Do you know what that means?" Paul Keith realised that the next January 16th would be the 40-year anniversary of Branham's prophetic word that brought the great Healing Revival to a close. Rick Joyner decided to host an invitation-only gathering for a number of the prophetic ministers on that date. They gathered in a cabin at Moravian Falls, and Paul Keith prepared to begin.

"No, we can't start yet. There's two more men due here," Bob Jones protested.

"No Bob, this is everyone we invited," he was told, but he was adamant. "God said there were two more." So, they waited, fellowshipped, had lunch, and then decided they had to make a start. Paul Keith started to tell the story, when a car pulled up outside. There was a knock at the door, and two men were there.

"Excuse us. I believe the Lord wants us here."

"Them's the ones," Bob Jones said."

Paul Keith Davis began again, "On January 16, 1956, William Branham prophesied the end of the Healing Revival in Chicago…"

"I was there," interrupted the elder of the new arrivals, a man called Ray Kirschke. They all looked at him in shock. "I always wanted to hear Branham preach," he explained, "and that was the only chance I got."

Ray was the last disciple of the great healing evangelist John G. Lake. Lake had spent his last 18 months mentoring Ray. "The day before Branham spoke that word, we were going through hospital wards cleaning them out," he told the group. "The day after, nothing." **The general anointing for divine healing shut off like a tap and the Voice of Healing Revival dwindled away.**]

To give some insight into how unrighteous some of the evangelists had become (remember the Lord told Paul Cain 'You're in a Rat Race), I share the following stories Paul related:

* In the last Voice of Healing meeting he attended before he stepped away in response to the call of the Lord, Paul was horrified to see two evangelists actually engaging in a fist fight out the back of the auditorium over who would receive the offering money.

* Paul at one stage shared an office with another prominent evangelist. A wealthy lady (the heiress to the Woolworths fortune) had built a "Prophet's room" in her house, where she would invite Paul to come and pray. While he was there the elderly lady said she felt much better.

One day she asked Paul to come quickly from Phoenix, as she wasn't feeling well. He told her, I'll be there as quickly as I can, but I'm in Phoenix, Arizona. He drove two days straight, and when he arrived, was asked:

"Why did you take so long?"

"Sister, I left immediately. I told you I was in Phoenix. It took me two days to drive this far," Paul replied, surprised.

"Why didn't you come in the plane I bought for you?" she queried.

"Sister, you never bought me a plane."

"Yes, I did. I sent a cheque for $25,000 to your office months ago, with a note for you to buy a plane to get around."

The other evangelist had taken the cheque and bought himself a plane!

For some years, Paul warned the other man "I keep seeing you in a plane crash…" He wasn't teasing—the Lord was having him warn the men. The other man sold the plane, and confessed to Paul before he died that he'd taken the money for himself.

*   William Branham also had a significant sum of money stolen from his ministry by another pastor. When he was driving nearby that man's town, he suggested to his assistant that they stop off and see the men, and preach for him. The assistant exploded—"You **know** what he did to you?"

"Yes," Branham replied, "but I still have to love him. God will deal with the rest."

Not all of the men were corrupted by the competitive spirit that crept amongst them.

Paul Cain mentioned in 1990 that John Wimber was receiving a lot of phone calls at the time warning him away from any association with Cain, because of his history with the Voice of Healing Revival and the Latter Rain movement (an offshoot movement that was inspired by the Revival, but had a distinct emphasis on the 5-fold ministries). "You can't afford to have this," they were telling Wimber.

Paul responded, "So what? Because those things started right. The only difference between what happened then and what happens now is that was then…. This is now. We're gonna do it right this time. We're gonna see the Lord come on the scene."

"If only 10 per cent of what happened in the Healing Movement, and what happened in the Latter Rain, and what happened in the Charismatic Movement…if only 10% was truly of God, that 10% of power was greater than 1000% of all the deadness and all the church activity put together. It was real!"

It is interesting to note that few of the Voice of Healing ministers continued seeing miracles into the 1960s. Of the well-known ministries, only A. A. Allen and William Branham saw significant healings continue (Paul Cain was in hiddenness for 25 years).

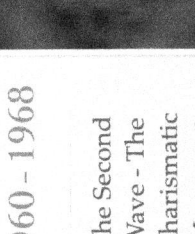

1960 – 1968

The Second Wave - The Charismatic Movement

- Few of the survivors of the VOH Revival continued in power during the 60s - exceptions being Branham and A.A. Allen
- Oral Roberts settled down and started his university. Others went overseas.
- Mainstream Denominational churches began to experience the outbreaks of spiritual gifts, first recorded at St Mark's Episcopal Church of Van Nuys, California, where Dennis Bennett was the priest (Apr 3, 1960). Larry Christensen (Lutheran) soon after. Michael Harper (UK) in 1962.
- Most had no choice but to adopt the Theological explanations of the first-wave classic pentecostals and move back to a more theologically sound position.
- Many Charismatic churches were forced to leave their denominations and become independent after they experienced the outpouring of the Spirit. The Catholic Churches began to experience this from the late 60s

11

The Second Wave—The Charismatic Movement

After the Branham prophecy of 1956, the Voice of Healing Revival, and its spin-off, the Latter Rain Revival, both declined rapidly. In just a few short years, nearly all the travelling evangelists had left the field. Some were exposed in sin—immorality, financial issues (it should be noted the IRS had made a specific target of the Healing Revivalists in the mid-50s), and few were untarnished by the glory-hunting self-promotion that had crept amongst them.

William Branham continued to challenge the fanaticism that had emerged amongst Christians, and the sectarianism and self-interest that still prevented true unity in the Body of Christ. As he touched on issues that certain groups were determined to hold on to, he began facing more and more opposition. His large-scale Healing Campaigns became less frequent, though no less powerful and effective, and he began to spend more time in Jeffersonville. He even lost some from his own team—Brother

THE SECOND WAVE—THE CHARISMATIC MOVEMENT

Bosworth died in 1958, others walked away. He himself remained faithful and followed the continuing instruction from the Lord.

Oral Roberts began to focus on building the University the Lord had told him to establish, though he kept doing evangelistic and healing campaigns, and branched out into television. A. A. Allen set up a Bible School and community in Miracle Valley, Jack Coe died, and Paul Cain retreated into seclusion. Others, like T.L. Osborn went into the mission field. Of the huge group of ministers that had held healing revivals in the 50s, those who continued moving in power within the USA into the 60s were only those like Allen and Branham whose personal anointing enabled them to do so—the general anointing for healing shut off.

But the Holy Spirit had used this time to initiate change in the hearts of many denominational ministers, who now began to seek the Lord for a greater knowledge of His ways. This led to what was later termed the Second Wave of the Holy Spirit in the 1900s, the Charismatic Renewal.

In the mid, 1950s, Jack Coe believed he was seeing what he called the "second call", as people from traditional denominations began to pour into his healing services. Traditionally, the main supporters of the Voice of Healing Revival were the Pentecostals—generally poor people from the working classes. It was generally recognised that the education, especially theologically, of the Pentecostals was lacking, compared to the well-financed Methodists, Presbyterians, Lutherans and Episcopalians (American Anglicans), most of whom demanded that their ministers had completed theological training. But as the Revival continued into the 1950s, more and more people from the "chosen frozen" (as many Pentecostals viewed them) were beginning to attend meetings and witness the manifestation of the gifts of the Holy Spirit.

Donald Gee, editor of *Pentecostal Evangel*, wrote: "There is this increasing new gale of the outpoured Spirit that is penetrating the old denominations with such intensity that we can hardly keep abreast of all the news of all that is happening," (*Pentecost*, no.64, 1964). Gordon Lindsay also recognised the change: "Pentecost is being taken into the so-called liberal churches," (*The Voice of Healing*, Nov 1961).

Possibly the biggest impetus for the social and spiritual change was the relatively-new organisation, the Full Gospel Business Men's Fellowship International, founded by Demos Shakarian in 1951 to reach businessmen with the gospel. This organisation grew out of the early years of the Revival (when it was still pure) and was mentored by Oral Roberts. The potential impact of Christian businessmen free of denominational politics and restraint was obvious to Roberts, who, though he himself managed to keep the support of the Pentecostal denominations, was keenly aware of the problems some of his peers were facing.

The FGBMFI grew astoundingly quickly—a group of Charismatic businessmen witnessing and encouraging other businessmen for Jesus. By the mid-60s, they had over 300 chapters with about 100,000 members. At least part of the impetus was the feeling amongst Pentecostal laymen that they were excluded from decision-making, and the Pentecostal groups nervously watched this new challenger to their perceived authority. The FGBMFI offered a much-needed financial base to many of the Revivalists, and a way to bypass the jealous attempts of church officials to control them.

The FGBMFI began to reach new audiences far removed from the dusty tents and auditoriums of the early revival—and touched a broader and more sophisticated strata of society, who, it should be pointed out, were generally educated to a higher level than the masses. Oral Roberts quickly caught onto this new direction of the Holy Spirit. His efforts to build a Charismatic Christian University faced opposition even within his own team, many of whom came from traditional Pentecostal backgrounds. "… Their religious and educational background was based on the traditional belief that the power of the Holy Spirit and higher education don't mix …" he commented in an interview. Roberts then stunned many when he joined the Methodist Church, which to many seemed to be turning his back on his Pentecostal Holiness heritage.

One of the biggest stumbling-blocks to members of the traditional denominations was the traditional Pentecostal theology of the Gifts of the Spirit. The "First Wavers" had little theological basis for their beliefs, and a recognised over-emphasis on experience, which unsettled many from traditional backgrounds. The traditional Pentecostals taught that there was a "second Baptism" of the Holy Spirit "with the evidence of speaking in tongues." They believed that the power gifts of 1 Corinthians 12 were a permanent blessing for a believer, and one shouldn't expect to operate in ALL of the nine gifts. Many Pentecostal ministers lacked the extensive Bible training of those in the older denominations, who couldn't even be ordained without years of study.

To the developed theology of the traditional churches, this seemed to be gross error—the Bible states clearly "…one Lord, one faith, one baptism…" (Ephesians 4:5). Many ministers were greatly offended by excitable Pentecostals who told them they didn't have the Holy Spirit if they didn't speak in tongues, or some taught they weren't even saved. Many knew the "still, small voice" of the Spirit in their hearts, and were assured of their salvation, and they continued to reject the incomplete theology of the "untrained" Pentecostals.

Nevertheless, there were a growing number who recognised the reality of what God had done during the Voice of Healing Revival, and set their hearts to seek Him for a fuller understanding of the Holy Spirit. They then began to experience the operation of the gifts within their denominational churches, though they had to "work backwards" from the Pentecostal theology to a more balanced middle-ground. Gradually the Holy Spirit began to influence others within the traditional groups, though many were put in a position where they had to leave their denomination and go independent.

A. A. Allen had been advocating this for years, pointing out the rigid control structures of many, even Pentecostal, denominational groups. He had personal experience of the attempts to "get a slice of the pie", and the unrighteous acts that had been done to attempt to discredit him and his ministry. As the old guard of the Revivalists moved on, into pastoring, missionary work, and so on, new ministers from the highly educated denominational backgrounds were experiencing the power of the Holy Spirit, and the Lord began to do something new amongst them, about which most Pentecostals were largely ignorant.

Father Dennis Bennett was an Episcopal (American Anglican) Priest in Van Nuys, California. A colleague came to him with a problem: a young couple who were previously intermittent attendees who were now in church every Sunday, and during the week for events, and looked HAPPY! They said they had been baptised in the Spirit and had spoken in tongues. It was the tongues that caused the problem—Bennett felt it was some kind of "off-beat emotionalism", despite the fact that they tithed, were willing to help with anything, and as the pastor said, seemed to glow.

Bennett was unable to forget the tale, and eventually met the couple. They said they had been "baptised in the Spirit, just like in the Bible," which, as a minister he felt was a "low blow"—he was supposed to be the expert on what was in the Bible. As they left afterwards, his wife commented, "I don't know what those people have, but I want it."

Bennett began to search the Scriptures, noting all the references to the Holy Spirit, and the experience of speaking in tongues. Over time, with continued conversations with the couple, he became convinced that what they had was scripturally valid, and that he wanted it. His friends encouraged him to ask for it, and they began to pray quietly together. After a while he noticed he was praying in words and syllables he didn't know. As he persisted, he felt the presence of God envelop him in a way he hadn't felt in years, filling him with joy and peace.

Bennett shared his experience with his church on April 3rd, 1960, and was soon shown the door, as a group rose up protesting against the very idea of speaking in tongues. A Bishop from Seattle asked him to take over the struggling St Luke's church, and to "bring the fire". Over time, St Luke's was transformed, and other ministers began to experience the "baptism in the spirit".

Lutheran Seminary Student Larry Christenson became intrigued with the subject of Divine Healing when he read Agnes Sanford's book *The Healing Light*. He claims to have read "omnivorously"—20-30 books on the subject. His intellect became convinced that Jesus Christ really was "the same yesterday, today and forever" (Hebrews 13:8), though he claimed his inner man came along much more slowly. "The Old Adam has quite a hold there, and knowledge alone isn't enough to drive him out!" he wrote in a 1962 article in Pentecostal Evangel.

His interest led him to investigate the other manifestations of the Spirit, particularly the reports of speaking in tongues. "Again my intellect became thoroughly convinced that this was real and true and absolutely grounded in Scripture." Christenson asked for wisdom, and was eventually invited to a nearby Pentecostal Revival where he was willing to receive prayer, and eventually found himself praying in tongues.

Larry Christenson became a major leader in the Charismatic renewal, and his San Pedro Lutheran church became well-known by those seeking more understanding of the Holy Spirit. He was always careful to direct them back to the place where the Lord had planted them to be a witness. Although many orthodox theologians criticised the Charismatics as being too reliant on shallow emotionalism, Larry Christenson's sharp intellect and quite confidence challenged their preconceptions.

Michael Harper was a Church of England Curate under the well-known theologian John Stott. One weekend, where he was speaking at a retreat, while reading through Ephesians he felt waves of wisdom and knowledge pouring over him. In following weeks, he noticed prayers being answered in a new way, worship became revitalised in his life, he began praying in tongues, had a deeper awareness of Christ in his life and a new ability to help people.

The issue of tongues led to friction with John Stott and other conservative Evangelicals, and Harper eventually left the curacy to found the Fountain Trust. He wrote numerous books explaining the Charismatic experience, and the flow of history from the Pentecostal tradition, and was considered one of the leaders of the Charismatic Renewal in Britain.

The major theological contentions of the Second Wave were over the issue of tongues, and the concept of a "second baptism". The general position of the Charismatic leaders was that tongues was NOT necessary for salvation (as some Pentecostals claimed), nor was it the required evidence of being "filled with the Spirit". It was a valuable tool that had led them each to a deeper experience of Jesus working in them and through them.

As previously stated, most Charismatic theologians were engaged in defending the Biblical validity of their experience, working backwards from a traditional Pentecostal theology to a more balanced middle-ground. It was not for another two decades that a leader would emerge who worked in the other direction, and had a theology developed from the gospels themselves.

The issue of a second experience remained divisive, although Scripture records exactly that in the book of Acts (those baptised by Apollos). Whether this was an issue of incorrect terminology or understanding, or a demonic deception is still hotly debated in orthodox circles. To deny experience completely as a valid influence on one's spiritual walk is ridiculous—certainly in scripture there are numerous occasions where this is reported, though it MUST ALWAYS be consistent with "the whole counsel of Scripture".

Few Charismatic leaders or lay-people were able to remain within their home denominations, and they all faced loud criticism and rejection. Many churches where wide-spread experience of the "baptism of the spirit" (there is simply no point in avoiding the easily-understood terminology, regardless of one's theological position) found that they needed to leave the denominations and became independent, which drew further accusations of being "out of authority."

What is undeniable is that the Second Wave of the Holy Spirit made the exercise of the 1 Corinthians "gifts" more accepted and well-known within the traditional denominational boundaries.

1965

Dec 24, 1965

The Death of William Branham

- Dec 18, 1965, Branham and family driving on two cars back to Jeffersonville
- Branham had publicly rebuked his followers, some of whom were calling him "Elijah". He told Paul Cain the Lord would take him home soon.
- Head-on accident. Media had no signs of life. Branham was thrown through the windscreen, left arm mangled in the driver's door and left leg wrapped around the steering column.
- Prays for Meda and she returns. He died six days later.
- Billy Paul begged him to "say the word", but he turned away.
- Did he get it wrong at the end?
- Heavenly position.

12

The Death of William Branham

Meanwhile, William Branham continued to minister, and see remarkable results. Many were shocked when he died in 1965 as a result of an automobile accident, feeling he was "taken before his time." There are a number of conflicting stories being circulated about what exactly happened, and what I have pieced together here is the result of testimonies of those who were present, and those who knew Branham in his final years.

One of his biggest concerns in the mid-60s was the fact that some of his "followers" were elevating him in a way in which he was not comfortable. Branham's detractors have publicly stated for years that he started to claim he was the "End-time Elijah". There were even those who were baptising in the name of William Branham, and who still await his second-coming. Certainly, there was gross error among the most extreme of his followers, which continued after his death, though examination of the many recordings of his sermons and the testimonies of those who knew him best refute these derogatory claims.

In the message from 1961, in Jeffersonville, called "Bruised Servant", Branham said the following:

"If there's anything that has been in my heart to do, was to hear those Words of our Lord Jesus at the end of this journey, to say, "It was well done, My good and faithful servant." And many times I have said I'd like to have been standing there when He said, "Come unto Me"; but I did desire to hear it say, "Well done." That I did not hear the voice in the original say, "Come unto Me," back in the times of the writing of the Bible; but I do desire to hear it say, "Well done."

And if anything I always wanted to be, and desires of my heart to be, was a true servant to Jesus Christ, my Lord and Saviour. I want my testimony to be clean, clear cut, that I stood, in all my mistakes I yet loved Him with all my heart. And I do that this morning with all my heart.

And because of that, it forces me to say I am leaving the ministry *[of the travelling evangelist]*, is because that there's something arose up amongst the people that's caused me to do it; that is, that I have been taken from my bracket of a minister or a brother and being called Jesus Christ, and so call... And that would brand me as an antichrist. **And I'll meet God as a quitter before I would meet Him as an antichrist to take away from Him.**

I--I heard of it a--a few years ago and I thought it was a joke. And I met a couple brethren (which I don't see neither one of them in the meeting this morning), two or three of them one time in a fishing trip, and they approached me by the subject of saying, 'Brother Branham, aren't you the anointed Messiah, the Christ?'

And I put my arms around the neck of both brethren, or all of them, and I said, "Brethren, as much as I have tried to be a true servant of Christ, I would not that you would say such a thing as that. And if it would ever be said of me, then I will leave the field with a clear conscience, and you who do that will be responsible for every soul that I would've saved during that time (See?), for taking me from the field." And I thought that ended it."

Paul Cain spoke many times of his personal relationship with the much older Branham, and the bond they had because they were so similarly gifted. Paul felt that he had finally found a friend who understood him—he had always felt isolated because of his gift. Others were jealous of the attention Branham gave Paul, and the fact that Branham would often ask Paul to continue his meetings when he himself couldn't continue. He spoke of the accuracy of Branham's prophetic gift—many others also testified that they never knew Branham to "miss it"—every detail was accurate. Paul was present at many Branham meetings over the years and they ministered together many times (off the platform, usually in the tents outside). Branham said on many occasions that the healing of Paul's mother Anner at the time of his birth was the greatest miracle he'd ever heard.

Paul told in a video interview with Mike Bickle in 1990 of his last conversation with William Branham, some months before the tragic accident. He said they had arranged to have some time together in February, 1964, when they were both in Bakersfield, California.

"He came to my motel room early the next morning, …sat down across from me, … And began to tell me what I'd dreamed the night before and what that dream meant. And also, he told me what I'm doing right now (in 1990) and that I'd see behind the Iron Curtain.

"As far as I'm concerned William Branham was the most humble, and the most powerful of all the healing evangelists put together…he manifested a truly Christlike Spirit. The last two years of his life there is controversy about who said what—whether it's William Branham talking or whether it's someone else writing his name on it. I don't have permission to get into that.

"There were meetings where he would call out every person along a row—any row he would pick out. I would have to say the William Branham I knew had more of the Spirit of Christ than anyone I ever knew. Though I didn't have anything to do with him from Feb 1964 till December 1965 when he had the fatal car wreck.

In that final meeting, Branham told Paul of his concern at his followers' behaviour. "Brother Paulie, the Lord's gonna take me home soon. They're saying I'm Elijah, and I can't make them stop. The Lord won't share His Glory..."

There are audio recordings where Branham rebukes his followers publicly, accusing them of making him an antichrist by their extreme claims. There is certainly NO evidence to support the accusations that he believed such things himself, or ever claimed them. He was aware of the Elijah nature of his ministry (best explained in *The Elijah Task*, by John and Paula Sandford), but never believed that he was anything more than a messenger who heard the Lord clearly.

Branham told a similar thing to young Buford Dowell, whom God had supernaturally taught to play the organ. He ended up playing for several of the ministries of the day, and was stunned when Branham offered to take him to lunch during this period. Overwhelmed by the ministry he had observed, he said "Brother Branham, if you let me promote your meetings, I'll make you the greatest prophet ever..." Branham smiled quietly and responded, "Oh no, son, that's not what it's about. My time is almost done..."

On the 18th of December, 1965, Branham and his family were driving back to Jeffersonville from Tucson, a distance of 1,750 miles, in two cars. William Branham and Meda were in his Ford station wagon with his daughter Sarah, and his son Billy Paul was with his own family driving in front. Near Friona, Texas, Sarah said Branham and Meda were discussing an issue, and William turned to look at her as he made his point, and a car hit them head on. Billy Paul saw the crash in his mirror, and turned around.

Branham was thrown forward through the windscreen, with his left arm trapped in the mangled door, and his left leg wrapped around the steering column. Meda had no pulse in the front seat. Billy Paul had no idea how to extract his father, and begged him to "speak the word and you'll come out of there", but Branham turned his head away. He reached across and felt for Meda with his right hand, asking "Lord don't let Mommy die", and she immediately moved and moaned.

On Christmas Eve, 1965, William Branham passed into Glory.

I, personally, have always felt uncomfortable at the incongruity of the event. Branham raised his wife back to life but dies three days later himself? God raises his wife but not him? Please consider the following, which is my personal belief, based on what the Lord has put on my heart.

Branham grew up in an old-school Baptist setting, and he honestly believed he would pay the price for his followers' errors. He did not seem to note the passage where God says he won't punish people for the mistakes of others. He trusted what he had been taught and it seems never asked the Lord for clarity about it. He spoke this out on several occasions, and it gave the enemy a "foothold" to take him out, as it became a curse, he'd spoken over himself (the understanding of spoken-word curses didn't emerge in the wider body of Christ for many years afterwards). We all need to be very careful what we speak over ourselves. I believe Branham was "taken-out" before his time, and if he had lived, he would have been able to halt or even mollify the error his followers have fallen into and the damage they have done to the Body of Christ by their error.

As one person said, he left behind one of the worst messes in Christendom!

Nevertheless, his followers preserved so much original material that we can listen to his sermons in his own voice, and judge for ourselves the truth of the claims about him. God can, and will, sort out the rest. I have faith that, whatever the error and deception some groups may have fallen into, if they hold fast to Jesus, He will correct them in His time. Our job is to love them.

One final note: In the 90s, a well-known leader had a prophetic experience in heaven, where he saw William Branham sitting in a high place of honour in heaven among the great cloud of witnesses. Jesus wouldn't allow him to speak to Branham, "I just wanted you to know the place of honour he has with me."

1970

June 11, 1970   *San Francisco, California*

The Death of A.A. Allen

- The Assemblies of God wanted Allen to hold meetings in churches, not the Tents and large auditoriums - money!
- Fall 1955, in Knoxville, Tennessee, Allen stopped for a drink of milk at a cafe on the way to a meeting. He commented to Bro. Rogers "that milk tasted funny". He felt dizzy after a few block and pulled over. The press were waiting for him, with several denominational pastors and the police.
- According to Gerald King and Bernie Schwartz, "We were in the Jack Tar Hotel in S.F. in the late afternoon, and Bro. Allen said, Boys, I feel tired, I believe I'll rest a bit, before we go to dinner." Bernie said, "I went to my room, and about 8 p.m. began to be concerned, because I hadn't heard from Allen." "I phoned his room, got no reply, so went up and knocked on the door, and still got no reply." "I then proceeded to get the manager, and he opened the door, and we found Bro. Allen slumped over in an easy chair, dead."
- Medical Examiner: "…apparent heart attack" NOT alcoholism.
- In 2006, a former AOG pastor publicly repented of being involved in spiking Allen's drink

13

The Death of A.A. Allen

Few will dispute the broad details of A. A. Allen's ministry, though there are always sceptics who will sow doubt over ANY claim to Divine Healing. As the general anointing for healing was removed in 56-57, Allen seemed to be hitting his stride. His personal breakthrough with the Lord enabled him to continue in Miracle ministry until 1970.

In 1958, a wealthy admirer (Urbane Leiendecker) approached Allen and offered him 1,280 acres (5.2 km2) of land in Arizona, which became the headquarters for his ministry, and was name Miracle Valley. Allen established a Bible College and Christian community. The same year he purchased Jack Coe's former tent, which seated around 22,000 people, and continued regular tent revivals. He was active on radio and television, and his Miracle Magazine grew to over 450,000 subscribers.

Allen had resigned from the Assemblies of God soon after the drink-spiking incident of 1956 in Tennessee. Allen set up his own, independent Miracle Revival Fellowship, and was loudly vocal about the problems within the denominations of the day. He claimed Sunday School teaching classes had replaced the altar of repentance from sin in many churches, whose ministers were not willing to seek the Lord for miracle power themselves.

"Revivals are almost a thing of the past. Many pastors, and even evangelists, declare they will never try another one. They say it doesn't work. They are holding "Sunday School Conventions," "Teacher Training Courses," and social gatherings. With few exceptions the churches today are leaning more and more toward dependence upon organisational strength, and natural ability, and denominational "methods." They no longer expect to get their increase through the old-fashioned revival altar bench, or through the miracle working power of God, but rather through the Sunday School" (http://voiceofhealing.info/04_other%20ministries/allen.html).

At his peak, Allen was ministering on 58 radio stations each day, and 43 television stations. By 1970, Miracle Valley had swelled to 2400 acres. Allen himself had knee surgery, and was about to have his other knee operated on. He was found dead in his hotel room in the Jack Tar Hotel in San Francisco, California on June 11, 1970 at the age of 59. His death certificate states "Heart attack" as the cause, though a coroner's report a few days later claimed "acute alcoholism and fatty infiltration of the liver." Reports that his hotel room was littered with pill bottles and alcohol bottles emerged later, but were not part of the early newspaper reports, and may have been fabrications designed to discredit his ministry. None of the early police reports mention evidence of alcohol consumption in the room.

One particular Pentecostal denomination had always maintained that Allen was a drunkard since the incident in 1956. Soon after his death, a story emerged from a Miracle Valley student that a cheque for $10,000 and letter asking for forgiveness was sent to Miracle Valley by the Coroner, who apparently claimed to have been paid to lie about his cause of death. This unsubstantiated story may not be true. The report can be found on several websites, with the "testimony" of the person who opened the letter. Miracle

Valley archives also have photographs of several early newspaper clippings of Allen's death.

Well-known Southern Baptist prophetic minister Bobby Conner tells of an experience he had after repeating the initial story of Allen's death as a drunkard, where the Lord appeared to him that night and accused him of lying about "my servant Allen."

It is up to you to decide which reports you will accept, and to prayerfully seek the Lord for the truth you believe. All of those close to Allen refute the accusations, and various testimonies are online. There are still people alive today who were healed in Allen's meetings, and some of the miracles God did through Allen were remarkable.

One in particular is the story of Gene Mullenax, who had had his right lung and three ribs removed by surgeons, and an open wound with a drainage hole in his back. In May, 1958, he passed by what he thought was a circus tent in Little Rock, and went inside. He kept going back, and eventually obtained a prayer card and stood in line. He was totally healed, and later x-rays confirmed the "missing" organs had been restored.

Personally, I see a pattern of the Holy Spirit's work. None of these men, however gifted and anointed, were sinless, and ANY sin can give the devil a "foothold" from which to attack us. We should be very cautious about judging any ministry by what we see—Jesus was pretty clear it's by FRUIT. I have heard so many stories of wonderful men of God who have made horrific mis-judgements of people, others slandered, others fell into gross sin (and later repented and were restored). It's not the incident that defines their ministry from heaven's perspective, but the repentance and overcoming by the Blood Jesus shed on our behalf. King David committed most of the worst sins listed, but he truly repented. We need to be faithful in our walk to "take up our cross" and follow Jesus, every day, ourselves.

As regards Brother Allen and the accusations against him, whatever conclusion you come to—don't throw out the baby with the bathwater… God did incredible miracles through him for an extended period, and he inspired many others to believe God for themselves and reach out to the lost.

Late 60s to Late 70s

The Jesus People

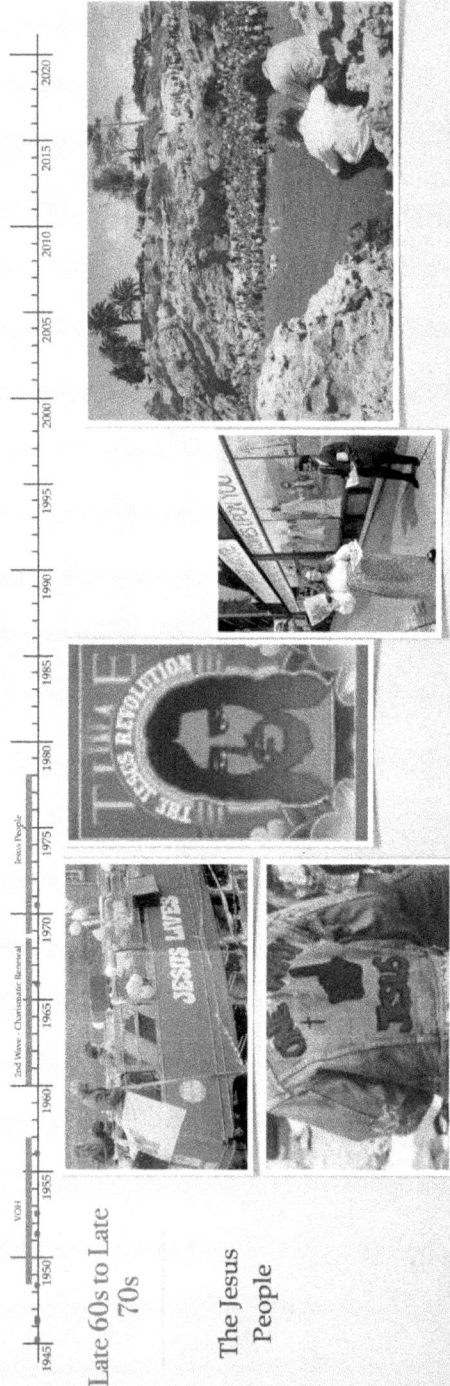

- A ground-swell movement linked to the hippie counter-culture of the late 60s, it saw the birth of Contemporary Christian Music, and thousands of people making commitments and being baptised.
- Various individuals experienced a revelation of Jesus despite their drug trips, and lives changed
- Halfway Houses, Christian coffee shops, beach meetings and street evangelism
- Birthed Calvary Chapel - Chuck Smith's teaching and Lonnie Frisbee's Power Evangelism - influenced the Vineyard
- Names such as Keith Green, Arthur Blessit, Barry Maguire, Larry Norman, Dave Hunt, Hal Lindsay and David Wilkerson

14

The Jesus People

The counter-culture revolution of the 1960's birthed an extraordinary move of the Holy Spirit that became known as the Jesus People. While the church was working through the challenges of the fallout from the Voice of Healing and Latter Rain Revivals, the sin many evangelists had fallen into, and continuing controversy surrounding William Branham, A. A. Allen and the fledgling Charismatic Movement, the world was struggling to cope with the ever-present threat of Nuclear War, the Kennedy Assassination, and the unpopular Vietnam War.

The involvement in Vietnam had spawned massive protests in the US, and introduced Eastern mysticism, culture, food and drugs into the American mainstream. At the same time a revolution in the world of music was underway, led by bands such as the Beatles, with a new sound and less orchestral instruments. The rebellious tone of the youth was summed up by the slogan: "Make Love, not War!" and groups of hippies flocked to San Francisco in 1967 for the "Summer of Love", where sex, drugs and Rock 'n

Roll dominated their approach to life. Their long hair and jeans were symbolic of their rejection of the traditional forms of society—no suits and ties. However, the Summer of Love was not all peace and joy: overcrowding, crime, sexually transmitted diseases and bad drug trips were rife, as penniless young people would "crash" wherever they could, often in the streets. The leading hippie newspaper, The Oracle, advised those making the trip to San Francisco to forget the "flowers in their hair" and bring "a sleeping bag, warm clothes and money."

A few years before, a drug-using sailmaker named Ted Wise was saved after a bad drug trip. With his wife Elizabeth and a number of hippie friends they began attending the local Baptist Church. Their unconventional ways, long hair and relaxed dress caused friction amongst the members, who took time to accept these hippies into their midst. When 75-100,000 young people migrated into San Francisco in 1967, Ted and others began to move among the homeless, hungry and sick on the streets, urging them to follow Jesus and give up drugs and promiscuous sex. By their dress and appearance they had an acceptance among the youth that their well-dressed minister did not, and the churches began to see the need to reach out to the lost on their doorstep.

The message of the Jesus People was a repudiation of the institutional churches and their weak and meaningless "Churchianity." Instead, they stressed the need for a personal relationship with Jesus, who, in their telling, was not far from being a hippie himself. This led to a revolution of evangelism outside the church buildings, and a focus on studying the Bible, praying and singing together, and believing God would directly intervene in the lives of those who sought Him.

The support of the churches enabled the establishment of a diverse number of Christian coffee-houses, where the hippies could get a hot drink, donated doughnut, sing simple gospel choruses and hear about how others' lives had been changed by Jesus. Christian communes appeared to challenge the sexual freedom of the hippies with true community living. By 1971, the movement was featured on the cover of Time magazine, and photos of thousands of Jesus People being baptised at the beach were circulated.

The revolution in Christian music spawned by guitar-led choruses in coffee houses rapidly exploded into mainstream churches, especially those whose youth had been influenced by the Jesus People. Christian artists such as Keith Green, Larry Norman and Barry McGuire laid the foundation for what is today known as Contemporary Christian Music.

Many of these new converts to Jesus found their way into mainstream denominations, though large numbers were attracted by the lively independent Charismatic churches. Street Evangelism and Youth outreach efforts spread quickly onto University Campuses, where Campus Crusade for Christ and others preached to students. Many of the Jesus people were keen to return to a "first-century" Christianity, and were keen to adopt the Gifts of the Holy Spirit they read about in the Bible.

One of the better-known groups to emerge from this period was the Calvary Chapel churches, initially founded by the Bible teaching of Chuck Smith (who oddly enough had been Paul Cain's manager in the 50s) and the casual faith of Lonnie Frisbee. Frisbee had been saved in a coffee house in 1967, and "radiated love" as he enthusiastically preached Jesus to the street people. He loved the presence of the Holy Spirit and expected God to work as he was faithful to go out. Numerous miracles and overt evidence of the Holy Spirit's presence accompanied Frisbee's ministry, though his secret personal life was in shambles. He came from an abusive background and struggled with homosexuality until he died of AIDS in the 90s. Nevertheless, the Calvary Chapel group was instrumental in influencing the leaders of the Holy Spirit's next major move during the 80s.

I remember growing up as a young boy during this time in Australia, where as an Anglican minister's son I had no idea of the broader work the Holy Spirit was doing. In the strict orthodox evangelicalism of Sydney Anglicans, the gifts of the Holy Spirit were opposed as demonic deception, yet I saw many people saved after a simple gospel message was preached. I thought that was normal.

My father was the leader of a Scripture Union Beachmission team at Gerroa, south of Sydney. Children's Special Service Missions (CSSM), or Scripture Union Family Missions (SUFM) as they later became, are a continuing evangelistic work that are widespread in Australian Caravan and holiday parks in the weeks after Christmas. I loved the 10 days we spent living in tents and caravans and ministering to the children in the park, running morning sessions with choruses from Bible verses, Bible talks, games and craft, then a morning beach service (on a giant stage made of sandbags and decorated with a Bible verse in fake flowers), and the evening family activity, where we saw many saved every year. The older teen-twenties team members were enthusiastic evangelists who paid their own way to go, and introduced us to Christian rock, movies, the bookstall and guitars, electric pianos, and of course, the accordion, which is unbeatable for open-air singing. Scripture Union is an organisation dedicated to promoting Bible Study, and daily Bible reading is encouraged, and SU produces age-appropriate study notes to assist new believers.

This period was also memorable for the spread of miraculous missionary books, detailing the outreach endeavours of heroes such as Brother Andrew (*God's Smuggler*), David Wilkerson (*The Cross and the Switchblade*), Jackie Pullinger (*Chasing the Dragon*) and Elisabeth Elliott (*Through Gates of Splendour*). Christian comics using characters from Archie, or retelling *The Hiding Place*, or the story of Tom Landry and the Dallas Cowboys became available, and taped messages of Bible teachers from all over the world began to be widely circulated.

All of these influences were used to set the stage for the next Wave of the Holy Spirit. In the meantime, God was still working and moving amongst the traditional denominations, and using other remarkably gifted individuals to achieve His purposes.

A final note about Lonnie Frisbee and his battle with homosexuality. Although popular culture insists that homosexual behaviour is "natural" for some people, the "nature versus nurture" debate has been settled in the literature for many years, though few Psychologists and Psychiatrists are willing to torpedo their careers to speak publicly on this issue. Homosexuality is a demonic spirit, and most commonly enters through childhood sexual abuse. Over the years I have seen several people totally set free by deliverance ministry at the Healing Rooms in Adelaide, though they then need to walk in freedom themselves. Those who have not been set free from the driving compulsion of the demonic spirit will struggle for years, or simply give in to the lies being popularly told.

The Bible is absolutely clear that homosexuals (along with those who make their peace with a host of other sins) "have no inheritance in the Kingdom of Heaven". Dealing with this issue is serious, and the church will not be true to her calling until we start honestly setting people free. We need to keep in mind that all these people are victims first, but Jesus died to "set the captives free." Buying into the lie that "God made them that way" only leaves them desolate and hopeless.

The tragedy of Lonnie Frisbee, and others who battled against this sin, is that there was no-one around who could set them free.

1975

August 8, 1975

Alabama

Bob Jones Dies - Billion-Soul Harvest Prophesied

- When only seven years old and walking on a dirt road in Arkansas; the Arch Angel Gabriel appeared to Bob Jones on a white horse and blew a double silver trumpet in his face. He then threw an old bull skin mantle at Bob's feet. Although terrified at the time he ran from God. Many years later (early 70s) he returned to pick up that old mantle which is that of a Seer Prophet.
- Aug 6, 1975 - Open vision driving back from the lake bringing warnings against abortion and homosexuality infiltrating society
- Aug 7, 1975 - Demon threatens to kill him if he won't stop warning about those two issues
- Aug 8, 1975 - Satan kills him, meets Jesus in 'the Tunnel'
- "Have you learned to love?"
- Jesus prophesies the "Billion-Soul Harvest" after 2000
- Get the church leaders ready

15

The First Death of Seer Bob Jones

At nine years of age, Arkansas cotton-picker's son Bob Jones was walking down a dusty road in mid-summer, when a large Angel on a huge white war-horse carrying a double silver trumpet came to rest in the middle of the road, about 50-100 feet way. When the angel came close Bob knew (by revelation) who he was and that the trumpet was silver. He had heard that "when Gabriel blows his horn time will be no more" and "everybody's gonna get burned up". The Angel blew the trumpet and Bob was paralysed with fear. The angel just looked at Bob, and disappeared. He stood frozen for some time before he was able to move. It was three days before he felt that he wasn't going to die, though he avoided that place for years.

When he was 13, Bob had been working picking cotton. He was walking along another road when he heard his full name (Bobby Joe Jones) being called from the cane field. He knew it was the Lord, and again related it to death, but didn't understand it was death to the old man. He stood for a while waiting for the lightning to strike, then He ran in terror and hid under the bed covers.

When he was 15, he was struggling at school. A faceless man (he later came to understand it was the Holy Spirit) came to him and he was taken by the hand out of his body to the Throne Room. He saw the elders worshipping around the throne, though had little understanding of what he as seeing till years later. He saw things there that so frightened him that it took three months for his nervous system to settle down. He experienced the Fear of the Lord—"everything within you shakes and quakes and burns". The Lord showed him a seat he would sit in one day, and again he related it to death. He saw the glory and power of the Lord and started seeking anything that would make him forget those things. He had no understanding of this calling but knew that it was real, and VERY different from the God that he knew from the Baptist Church. This "wasn't the God that you could stand before and have sin in your life in any way". He was also a God of judgement. He felt the sin inside of him burning in his bones ("I hurt!").

The Throne looked like golden crystal light, but the light "went through you. It would go through you and it would show what was in you, ... I wasn't that much interested in knowing what was in me, and to see it to that detail I sure wasn't interested in it. And to have to look at Him, now that really frightened me. And if I hadn't had that guide with me, to stand before me and that light, I don't think I'd have got out of there alive."

He understood that the 'guide' was the Angel of the Lord—the Lord Jesus Christ (Bob always maintained the two were the same). He understood later that the Lord had prepared a 'seat' for him in his purposes. At the time he only thought the Lord was calling him to death and to give up sin, "and I didn't want to do either one of them."

Bob immediately became an excellent student and started studying and reading to stay out of sin (except the Bible, because of the terrifying things in there), and though his grades improved, he would shake and burn every time he remembered the experiences. He didn't want anything to do with that power and ran from it, trying to find peace in sin. He joined the Marines at age 21, drank heavily, gambled and fought. He noticed that others would follow him in sinful pursuits, and those he loved would suffer consequences, though he personally didn't. He "got more and more miserable", trying and failing to drown his sorrows in alcohol and bar fights.

On one occasion a man pulled a gun on him behind a screen door. Bob went through the door to get him. The man tried to shoot him in the face but the gun wouldn't go off and Bob beat him badly. A friend picked up the gun, pointed it at the ceiling and pulled the trigger and it went off immediately.

Another time he was drunk with a bunch of Marines in California. They ran off the edge of the Santa Monica Palisades. Everyone else got hurt except Bob—all that happened was the seat of his pants got torn out. He began to see that there was a purpose he was running from, and a hand that was keeping him from getting killed. But still he looked for peace in sin.

After the Marine Corps he decided to try and get rich, though every scheme failed on the verge of breakthrough, leaving him broke. At one time he was going to buy commercial property (12 acres) in the centre of town. He only needed $5000 to make the sale, which would have set him up for life financially, and was set to borrow the money when it all fell apart.

In his late 30's his nerves went, and couldn't even get drunk anymore. His shaking would never let him rest—"the damned can't rest". He lived days with no sleep, but his mind was clear. He went to the psychiatrist and was put on heavy dosages of drugs, which made him sleep but didn't help the shaking. He ended up at the Veterans Hospital in Topeka, Kansas. He ran away several times, but they took him back.

A Christian doctor who had been praying for one more man to save before his heart gave out took him off the drugs, and he ended up walking the halls of the hospital every night. The other doctors thought he would be there for life. The Christian doctor got him to mop the floors to stop him shaking. So, every time he started shaking (midnight till 6am) he would mop the floors.

A man who was praying for him sent him a book called God's Psychiatry, about the 23rd Psalm. Bob realised that he was terrified on the inside—terrorised of going to hell. He began to cry out "Lord, Help me. Be my shepherd," and would repeat the 23rd psalm over and over. About 3am one night, after he had been mopping since about 10pm, he was tired and knelt by his bed. While he was repeating the 23rd psalm over and over, a demon came and spoke to him.

"Everybody has mis-treated you all your life. No wonder you're like you are. You deserve a break. You deserve to get even with them. They got you in the Veteran's Hospital in the Crazy Ward, and you truly are crazy. There's about. 12 people who are the reasons why you're here. Why don't you run away tonight and go back to town and get your gun and go kill them people. Then come back and sign back in. You'll be here the rest of your life anyway."

Bob cried out to Jesus for help, and heard the Lord's voice: "I can't help you Bob until you forgive them. You'll kill them or forgive them." He started forgiving people through his life as the Lord reminded him of names and incidents. The next thing he knew, the demon was shaking him awake—he'd finally slept for the first time in days, though he felt like he'd only slept one minute. Bob said he would have given anything he had for just one more minute—"you have no idea how blessed it is to sleep with a clear conscience."

The demon said: "Poor old Bob. You're just a born loser. You was born the son of an ignorant cotton farmer in Arkansas, and you're just dumb. You're just a loser and you always will be." Bob cried again to Jesus for help. Again, he heard the audible voice say: "One of your biggest sins is self-pity. You blame everyone else for your problems but the real problem is your selfishness."

He went to his knees and repented. "I'll never let anyone give me sympathy as long as I live," and I won't give it to others. He maintained that sympathy is 'agreeing with their problems... Instead of dealing with them." He woke up in the morning and realised he had slept!

He was walking down the hall and started to whistle. The first person he met was the doctor, who called him back and asked what had happened. Bob replied "What do you think?" The doctor put him in charge of the padded cells as a test, and then discharged him. He told him to find a simple job for a few months to get himself back on track.

Bob said the mental wards are full of born-again Christians who won't forgive those who've hurt them. Unforgiveness and self-pity have made the Christians mentally ill!

Bob began to read the Bible night and day for 4 years. He joined a Baptist Church where many were spirit-filled and responded to salvation calls every week, until the Lord finally gave him assurance of his salvation. He had a hatred for the demons who were oppressing Christians and began to minister in deliverance. He had authority because he himself had been delivered. He began to have visions and words of knowledge during the praise and worship, which he would share with the body. They knew his background and knew the God was using Bob. He said: "I never experienced persecution or rejection in the Baptist Church…. It was the spirit-filled body that always clobbered me." He had specific words such as: "Patty Hearst will be taken captive in 30 days", which would occur as he had predicted. It would always begin when people started to lift their hands ("which made me uncomfortable") and praying in tongues ("which really bugged me") and when they entered into praise. Bob didn't understand what was happening and would plead the Blood of Jesus over himself over and over. This became a regular occurrence, and the brethren recognised that God was using Bob in an extraordinary way.

In 1973, he began to pray against the legalisation of abortion. He tried to rally the churches but couldn't overcome the apathy. The Lord began to show Bob this was Satan's strategy to kill the deliverers throughout history, and that God's deliverers were being released at that time. The Lord showed him the aborted babies growing up in heaven, saved and free from the trials of earth. The Lord said: "They didn't get my main deliverers—they just killed off their own…"

In 1974, a week after he was baptised, he was down at the Lake with some of the spirit-filled brethren, who wanted to lay hands on him to receive the Baptism of the Holy Spirit. Bob wasn't keen, but didn't want to disappoint these people he trusted, so he agreed, thinking he had "only a few minutes he'd have to put up with this junk." They began pleading the Blood of Jesus over him, just like he himself did, and he felt something warm running down over his body. His mind went into the prophetic realm, and heard a voice say "Look!" He saw a technicolour landscape almost at sunset, and heard a voice say: "Surely it will that where no man can go into the labour field. Pray that the Lord raises up labourers now, for the Harvest was ready." When he came out of the vision, he found he had been speaking and singing in tongues. He asked the Lord not to allow him to go through the exuberance and depression he had observed in many others—he wanted the "even walk'. After about 3 months he prayed; "Lord, I think I got robbed. Everybody else is talking about their experience when they get baptised in the Holy Spirit. I wouldn't mind having just a measure of that joy." For about 3 months his feet didn't touch the ground. From the time he was filled with the Holy Spirit he experienced around 5-10 visions and dreams EVERY NIGHT. [In 1984, Bob came to Mike Bickle, his pastor, asking if they could see anything wrong in him, any sin or quenching the Spirit, because he hadn't seen any visions and dreams in two nights. "God's shut the whole thing down", he complained.]

On August 6, 1975 he had been down at the Lake fishing with his wife Viola. On his way back in his truck, the Holy Spirit came over him as a ball of light, and he began to prophesy. The first thing he prophesied about was Abortion. He saw visions of the different ways that men would advance abortion, and it was making him sick. He saw babies being cut apart with knives, burned with acidic salts, and eventually a pill that would cause the foetus to be expelled from the womb. The Lord told him: "As you destroy the first-born, as you destroy the fruit of the womb, you will be destroyed." [Since that time there has been a judgement on the Western world, where their youth are destroyed through the drug wars.]

The second issue was homosexuality and immorality. Some churches were beginning to justify homosexuality, and it was becoming popular to have a homosexual in their midst, and some were starting to claim it to be normal. Bob was prophesying that if you oppose this unrighteousness, "those who want free will get free," but if you accept it, you damn them to Hell for eternity (1 Cor 6:9-10). He prophesied homosexual diseases and venereal diseases that couldn't be cured, and that in the end times it would be popular to be faithful due to the incidence of these diseases [NB: This has been taught in high school sex ed. classes since the mid-90s, though few have listened]. Bob prophesied that 5,000,000 people would die from "a homosexual disease that couldn't be cured" (AIDS) before the year 2000, and it would double after that. He warned that homosexuals would be demonstrating publicly in the streets and even elected to government, which was unthinkable in the society of the 70s. The Lord told Bob "Mark the 30, when the generation I've raised up that he didn't abort will appear. Satan did not get my Deliverers." So, 30 years from that day (Roe v Wade—Jan 22 1973), which was 2003, then the Lord's inspired priests would begin to come forth and challenge this evil.

Bob got home and began to call pastors around the area and tell them what the Lord had shown him. The words were too confronting for the churches, and they didn't like it, and told Bob to be quiet.

The next morning, on August 7th, 1975, a demon looking like a skeleton in a dark robe appeared to him and told him if he kept speaking on the two issues of abortion and homosexuality he had "authority to kill" Bob. The demon said: "If you knock that off, we'll back off and you can do all the signs and wonders you want to. You can heal people and prophesy day and night, if you leave these two subjects alone. We'll get you a couple of spiritual wives too."

Bob told him to get lost—"I know who you are. I don't work for you no more. You can't touch me. It was too hard getting here to back up." He went and picked up the telephone (while the demon was still there) and dialled up someone else and shared the word. "You got to show him who's boss." The demon left.

The next day, August 8th, 1975, some of the sisters in the church called and asked Bob to share again what the Lord had shown him. Soon after he went out to pull a stump with his son, and was overcome with cramps and pain throughout his body. He said it felt like his lower body was turning to stone. Things got worse, and the doctors didn't know what was wrong, so he went home—he wanted to die in his own bed. The pain was really bad, and got worse with each pain pill. Blood began to shoot out of his mouth and nose with each heartbeat, and he wrapped a wet towel around his face and lay on the bed. He lay in agony for some time, then all of a sudden, the pain was gone.

Bob found himself in a dark tunnel with the most beautiful person he'd ever seen standing at the mouth, surrounded by living light. He knew it was Jesus, like a form of light within light. He wondered how the devil had been able to kill him. He then worried if he had "messed his garment" and was afraid to look. The faceless man (the Holy Spirit) was next to him, and said "Bob, it's okay to look." He looked down and saw he was dressed in a spotless white robe, and exclaimed: "thanks you Lord, you brought me out of such deep sin and you kept me clean." He felt that for the first time in his life he "had it made" and that he was "coming home".

The faceless man led him along the tunnel. He could see along the left of the tunnel a long line of people on a moving walkway, wrapped in whatever they had worshipped on earth, whereas Bob was wrapped in light. Some were wrapped in dollar bills, some in "Sod" or earth—they'd worshipped their yard! Others worshipped their own intellect—they had huge heads and no body. This walkway would carry these people along till they saw Jesus at the entrance to heaven. They would have a witness of the truth, and then it would go down deep into the ground to Hell.

A much smaller line was waiting for the Lord, about 98 times smaller than the other. People were accompanied by angels as they waited for their turn. Bob asked the Holy Spirit, "What's going on here?" He was told that the angels were those assigned to help them in ministry.

When they stepped up to Jesus, He would ask them a question, give them a kiss, and then accept them into heaven. Of all the questions one would think the Lord would ask a believer at the gates of heaven, the only question was: "Have you learned to love?" Bob said it was impossible to lie. One big black lady with many angels (the Holy Spirit told Bob she was an evangelist) answered: "Oh yes Lord, I've learned to love." Jesus gave her a kiss and it was like his heart opened up like two big doors, and she went through into heaven. Another 12-year-old girl had been crippled her whole life, but had interceded for everyone who would walk past her window.

A third lady was wrinkled up with arthritis, and had been crippled for years. When the Lord asked her The Question, she replied: "Only you Lord. I got widowed and bitter very young. I stayed in the church my whole life, I loved You, but I bit (criticised) the saints." Jesus told her: "You kept trusting in me for salvation, so you're saved by Grace, by the skin of your teeth; but you don't have much reward." He kissed her and she entered heaven.

Bob was next, and said: "I was just about ready to pucker up." He Jesus put his hand up and said: "No Bob. Satan killed you before your time. I want you to go back."

Bob answered, "No Lord, I don't want to go back. I'm not doing any good back there."

Jesus answered, "You're a liar. You spoke what I told you to, and what I speak will always be profitable. Some of the things you spoke will be 20, 30 to fifty years before they get ahold of it."

"But Lord, it's so painful back there, all that rejection—it hurts."

"Yes you always were sort of a coward—not one to face those coming up at you. But I called you out of the Baptist Church 'cause you had a great love for souls. If you want to come on in, I'll let you in, but I want you to look at this line one more time," pointing towards those destined for Hell.

Bob was now in front of their faces and could see the utter devastation and loss of all hope as the realisation of their poor choices hit home. Jesus said "I want to bring many to me in the last days."

Bob looked back at Him and said: "Lord I'd go back for just one…."

Jesus told him: "I don't want you to go back for just one, I'm going to save much more than that. I want you to go back for one billion." He then prophesied: "In the year 2000, when there's six billion people on the face of the earth (the global population in 1975 was about 3 billion), I'm going to begin a work. When it's completed, over a billion souls will be swept in to the Kingdom in three great waves. I'm sending you back to prepare the leaders of the church."

Bob went back to his room thinking he would be healed, and there were two large angels there, praying for his body on the bed. Behind them was a spirit of death that was being blocked from his body by the angels. The demon vanished when Bob looked at him. Bob overheard the Resurrection Angels talking to each other saying: "At this time praise will raise up like a light, and it will go all over the world." Bob said this light will be like atomic light that will drive darkness out of people. It will start in small places and travel at the speed of light over the whole earth and raise up the Tabernacle of David, setting whole cities free from darkness. Praise will release prophecy—revelation of how to pray. Praise is an enema for the soul.

Bob went back into his body to great pain, though the bleeding had stopped. It was now about 3pm. Bob's senses were still extremely sensitive, and he heard in the spirit a phone ring—somebody calling an intercessor saying: "Bob Jones needs prayer." As more and more people began to pray for him the more the pain receded. Bob said it got noticeably worse during the Saturday afternoon baseball game!

On Sunday morning the church gathered, and the pastor called them to pray for Bob 'before we do anything else." Bob was instantly healed and made it to the end of the service.

Please note: the two issues that the devil wanted to kill Bob over were not bible reading, evangelism, healing the sick, or attending church, they were abortion and homosexuality.

1976

Feb 20, 1976 *Tulsa, Oklahoma*

The Death of Kathryn Kuhlman

- She intentionally distanced herself from the practices of many VOH evangelists
- Rarely prayed for individuals - focused on creating an atmosphere of worship and faith where the Holy Spirit was welcomed and healing just happened
- "Just praising God— not asking for a single thing but just praising Him— always brings the power. It's pleasing to the Lord. ... You do not manipulate the Holy Spirit."
- Diagnosed with a heart problem in 1955. She maintained a very busy schedule and overworked herself, particularly into the 70s, where she was the only major healing ministry still operating in the US.
- She died following open-heart surgery in 1976.

16

The Death of Kathryn Kuhlman

Kathryn Kuhlman had continued her own healing ministry since 1946. She intentionally distanced herself from the Voice of Healing Revival, being concerned about the showmanship she saw and the habit of some of blaming the sick if they weren't healed. She hated some of the practices she had witnessed, such as invalids being "steered out" of the prayer line to a tent out the back as the evangelist approached. She favoured a model of creating an atmosphere of worship and faith where the Holy Spirit would move amongst the people.

Some see this as direct criticism of Branham and others. Remember there were a lot of evangelists holding healing revivals in the 50s. Branham was sent with a particular gift and mission. A. A. Allen certainly didn't shy away from the hard cases. There are **many** testimonies of people being healed in the meetings apart from the prayer-line, and, as we have mentioned, many of those involved did fall into error or sin at some level.

Kuhlman was an established evangelist before her healing ministry broke out. She went through her own period of sin, being the "other woman" in the break-up of a marriage. It took some time before she "surrendered fully to the Holy Spirit" around 1946, and her marriage fell apart. It was after this that her ministry really entered the realm of the supernatural.

Kathryn became widely known during the Charismatic movement of the 60s, as her presence-focused approach meshed neatly with the more balanced theology of the Charismatic period. She rarely prayed for individuals, and often asked people not to approach the stage until they had already been healed. "When the power of the Spirit is there, miracles happen. … I discovered that certain things brought the presence of the Holy Spirit… You do not manipulate the Holy Spirit. The Holy Spirit is a person. He is not an 'it.' He is God. He is to be reverenced, to be worshiped. He is not to be presumed upon by anyone" (Kathryn Kuhlman: The Woman Who Believes in Miracles).

In the 60s, she began a television show, called *I Believe in Miracles,* which aired nationally, and had a 30-minute national radio show where her preaching a ministry would be broadcast. She had been diagnosed with a heart condition in 1955, but maintained a very busy schedule, holding meetings that went for 5-6 hours. The financial demands of her media ministry were growing, but she refused to cut back her workload, feeling that there were souls that needed saving.

In 1975, her heart trouble flared again, and she died on Feb 20th, 1976, after open-heart surgery from which she did not recover.

An amazing testimony of her death is recorded on YouTube by the young nurse on duty at the time. The young Presbyterian believer came on duty about 11pm on the 19th, for her first shift as nurse-in-charge. Kathryn had cardiac arrest on the day shift, was on a respirator with kidney failure, and was incredibly frail—totally unresponsive.

The nurse could tell there was still fluid in her lungs, but was concerned because the respirator was doing all the work keeping her alive. She looked up at the monitor just as Kathryn went from normal rhythm to flat line, which doesn't naturally occur. Thinking that a lead had fallen off, she went in to record the feed. At that moment the entire hospital had a power failure.

After 15 seconds the emergency generator should have kicked in, and she found the leads were all connected. As she listened for a heartbeat, the lights flashed on and immediately off. She called the supervisor and reported Kathryn had passed away, and the super was in the other wing across the road.

While the nurse was confirming there were no signs of life, a powerful smell of roses and warmth flooded the room, and the nurses had to step outside the room to breathe. The supervisor arrived, and the power returned, and the super said: "Oh this is where the smell is coming from. I could smell it on 3-East (the other side of the 4-lane road)."

The young nurse pointed into Kathryn's room and said: "That is where the smell is coming from." The super replied, "Well You guys aren't allowed to have roses in here."

The super went into the room and examined the body, and asked what was the time of death. The young nurse had forgotten to look, and picked 1:13am as the time.

When the day shift came on in the morning, they asked "Where's Kathryn Kuhlman?" and they were so excited to hear that she had died. They rushed to check the notes, and showed they had written down her prediction of the date and time of her death.

Kathryn had also told them the only flower she wanted at her funeral was roses. The young nurse had not yet told them of the strange smell. She slumped in a chair, overwhelmed. The next October, she gave her life to Jesus at a home group meeting.

With the passing of Kathryn Kuhlman, the era of the "big name" healing evangelists had passed. Some continued the ministry of their mentors, like R.W. Shambach, Paul Cunningham and Benny Hinn, though few would argue they moved in the raw power of the Branham meetings or those of A. A. Allen. For most of the mainstream of Christianity, Benny Hinn was the only name we were familiar with, and usually in a negative context. It was not for several more years that we would encounter the reality that *"I, the Lord do not change"* (Malachi 3:6) and *"Jesus Christ is the same yesterday and today and forever"* (Hebrews 13:8).

1977

Bob Jones' Sands of Time Vision

- Draft notices for the Army of God (2nd Order). To be sent out when the US post reaches 20c (1981).
- Children born since 1981 are the Army of God. Those born since 1973 are the deliverers.
- "I'm going to glorify myself in the last days more than anything they've ever seen. These are the Children of Promise (Isaacs)." A.K.A. the Generation of the Righteous (GOTR).
- "They will walk with God and carry his power to the world."

17

The Sands of Time Vision

Bob Jones' unusual Seer ministry continued in the Baptist church. One night the Lord came to Bob and took him to a beach on the ocean (he was living in Kansas, Missouri at the time). Bob found himself on a beach that stretched backwards through the Ages. He saw Jesus striding along the beach as time progressed with the saints trying desperately to walk in his footsteps. Many couldn't for very long, and were jumping from footstep to footstep (as children do).

Every so often the Lord would stop and point to a place in the sand, and instruct someone to dig. Bob saw the Apostle Paul, who dug with great excitement, saying: "It's going to happen in my time!" After furious scrabbling in the sand, he pulled out a shoebox. "It's us, It's our generation." Though when he ripped of the lid the box was empty, and he was crestfallen.

Bob saw other men throughout the ages have the same experience, Jesus would walk up to them, point to a place in the sand, and command them to dig. With great excitement they would obey, only to have their hopes dashed. Bob saw around 100 awesome men and women of God through the Church age all of whom were disappointed.

Jesus walked up to Bob and said "It's your turn to put your hands in the Sands of Time, dig there." Bob wondered what was the point as the boxes were empty. Jesus said: "Do it!" Bob put his hands into the sand and pulled out a box, though with little expectation, unlike what he had observed in all the others.

He pulled the lid off the box, and found it was full of letters, or certificates. The one on top said: "Greetings. You are inducted into the Army of God." There was no stamp, and Bob mentioned this to the Lord.

"These are My draft notices for My End-Time army," he was told. "When it costs 20 cents to mail a letter I'm going to start sending them." (At the time the US post was 11 cents, and Bob said they thought it would never go up. On October 13, 1982, the US post put stamps up to 20 cents.)

The Lord continued: "These are who I will pour My Spirit out upon. These will be some of the greatest Evangelists you have ever seen, and there will be no place they won't go. They will tread on all that Satan saw and have no fear for their own life. Death will have no sway over them."

"Those born since '73 will be My inspired priests, my leadership (the Deliverers), but this will be My Army."

So, Satan rose up in 1973 using abortion against the Deliverers—they will be the leaders who will build a church without walls.

In a later story from around this time Bob warned the youth leaders of another church that they were angering the Lord by their promiscuous behaviour, and needed to repent. He called them out with specific details of who and when. When the young sinners began to die one after another in freak accidents Bob was accused of putting them under a curse, and told to leave. Prophets who warn of consequences of sin are never popular….

1977-1982

May, 1977   Yorba Linda, California

John Wimber's progress to the Vineyard

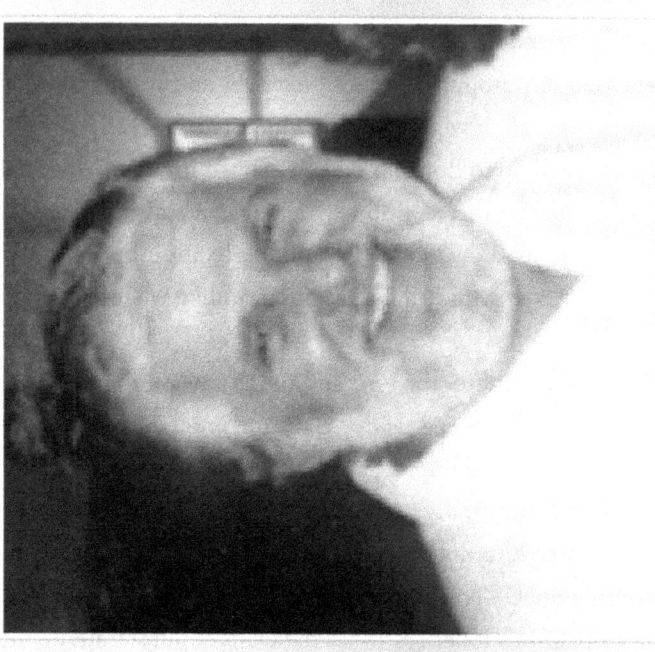

- Wimber was a founding member and keyboard/Sax player for the Righteous Brothers
- 1963 saved in a Quaker Bible Study Group
- 1974 Wimber offered position by C. Peter Wagner as Founding Director of the Department of Church Growth at the Fuller Institute of Evangelism and Church Growth.
- 1976 - small home group seeking more of God
- May 1977 - due to Calvary Chapel's experience of the Holy Spirit as part of the Jesus Movement, founds Yorba Linda CC.
- 1978 - after 10 months teaching on the healing ministry of Jesus, experience first healing
- Became associated with the Vineyard Churches led by Ken Gullikson who were within the CC movement
- John Wimber's Yorba Linda Calvary Chapel grew from 400 in May, 1980 to over 1700 in three months, baptizing 700 people in their swimming pool.
- 1982 - As the Lord began to train them in deliverance, caused problems with CC. Mutual decision to separate, and Wimber took over leadership of the Vineyard.

18

John Wimber's Progress to the Vineyard

John Wimber was a successful professional musician, who could play a variety of instruments. [His testimony is on YouTube, and is very funny]. He said he was a "typical pagan, from a pagan background." He was a founding member of "The Righteous Brothers", who he managed for a time, but his personal life was in shambles. At age 29 he described himself as a self-proclaimed chain-smoking, beer-guzzling, drug abuser, who had gone through a marriage crisis. In his pain after separation, he started looking for help, but the only people he knew to speak to were musicians and drug addicts. One man suggested that driving into the desert to watch the sun come up was a good way to "groove" a religious experience, so John tried it. One day as he was driving, he was reflecting on the shambles of his life, and began to weep. Feeling weird and embarrassed, he pulled over, and walked around "cussing and kicking the cactus." At one point he looked up at the heavens and said "Oh God, if you're there, Help me." Thinking he was no insane "talking to the sky", he went back to the hotel to change before going to the hospital. As he walked into the hotel the concierge told him there was a message from his wife. When he rang, she said "I've decided to give it one more try." In shock, he fell back against the wall, and thought "Wow, I'm in touch with the Supernatural," realising that God had answered his prayer. On the way back to California, he prayed his second prayer, "Attababy God," and started to ask God about other issues in his life. Carol had been raised Catholic, and explained that "talking to God is called prayer." She told him God had a book out—the Bible, so John bought a Bible and began reading it. He was shocked to find out that "God was Jewish." He would take the book to work with him and read it at the bar during intermission. He started to read it but found it very hard (he opened it at Ezekiel). They began to read it daily, and would use children's books to get some understanding.

He said the first time he met a Christian was when friends of his came to see him in Las Vegas, inebriated after having drunk gin on the way to keep warm. The next day they were embarrassed, as they were brand-new Christians, and had wanted to preach Christ to John and Carol. A few weeks later, Dick told John he'd become a Christian, and John replied "What's that? Isn't everyone in America a Christian?" He was told about the need to be born again spiritually, which John did NOT understand. Over the next weeks and months he came by and shared regularly with the couple, explaining the basics of what it meant to follow Jesus.

John said the weirdest things was that they invited them to go to church in Yorba Linda. John wasn't impressed by the building or the sign out the front, and suddenly realised he was the only one smoking. He couldn't find an ash tray and finally put it out on the ground, where "some guy with a flower looked at it." His recounting of the first church service as a totally un-churched perspective is hilarious. After a few weeks he asked one of the deacons "when are we going to do the stuff?" What Stuff?" the man responded. "The stuff Jesus did in the Bible—healing the sick…." He was told "Oh we don't do that anymore—we just sing about it."

They agreed to go to Bible Study, where a welder named Gunner started to explain things and answer John's questions, with his friend interpreting. John went home and read the Bible all night—excited that he was finally understanding. After many weeks the couple were saved—Carol first, and John was quite suspicious, but he found himself on the floor sobbing. John determined in his heart that "if Christ was worth coming to at all, He was worth coming all the way with," and he would do "the foolish thing in the eyes of the world." He continued: "I didn't know it would be the foolish thing in the eyes of the church too."

Over the next few years John was constantly witnessing to his friends and filling the little church, but there was tension between the unchurched newcomers and the newly saved, who weren't "cleaned" first. The growth continued and John was appointed to the staff and ordained. One day he had just "set straight" a young man who had come to him with various problems he was having in his life. The Lord spoke to his heart and asked him "John, would you go to this church if you weren't paid to?" He had a moment of revelation, and realised there was something wrong.

God began to show him that he'd become caught up in the institution and lost touch with the people. He started to sob as God began to show him where he'd gone wrong, and he realised he'd begotten something that was not of God. Three weeks later he was gone, and took a role at the Fuller Evangelistic Association, developing the Department of Church Growth.

As Wimber travelled, he discovered that most of the church in America was not really active in doing the things the Bible taught. He himself was operating in the gifts of the Spirit without realising that was what was happening, in order to earn a living and he became very "bankrupt inside". Again he began to cry out to God, and he opened the Bible to read for himself. It opened to Psalm 61, and he saw all the things that he was doing. After falling asleep, the Lord spoke to him: "John, I've seen your ministry. Now I'm going to show you mine."

The Lord began to restore him, and he began to be exposed to the operation of spiritual gifts. At one conference, a friend brought a lady who said she had "a word for God for you." The sceptical Wimber eventually agreed to meet the lady, who sat down and started sobbing. After nearly half an hour Wimber exploded, "I'm busy. You said you had a word from God for me. What is it?" She looked up with tear-stained face, and said, "That's it!"

John realised God was weeping over **him**, and he was undone. When he had composed himself ("I shook it off") she approached him again, and again. He eventually accepted that God was trying to get his attention, and the Lord spoke to him 19 times over the next two-and-a-half months: "Go Home. Start a church. God's going to show you His ministry." At least two-thirds of what he was shown were things Wimber himself didn't believe God was still doing: dreams, visions, prophecy, tongues and interpretation.

He and a small group of believers started a church, and connected with the Calvary Chapel movement. They had a wonderful experience of the presence of God, and people were being saved each week as they gave themselves to worship. After some months the Lord told him to teach on the Gospel of Luke, and he had to cover the Healing Ministry of Jesus. He said the trouble was, that when you're teaching such a topic, the people don't know that you don't believe it, and they wanted to start praying for the sick. God told him to start praying for the sick, but "nobody got well. In fact, some of us got sick praying for the sick." For eight months, nobody got healed, but the Lord kept telling him to keep going. Over half the congregation left, and he himself was angry with God. One day he slammed the Bible shut, and said "I'm not gonna do it." the Lord spoke very clearly: "Either do it, or get out. Do not preach your experience, preach My word."

In those days they would take people behind the stage curtain to minister, and one Elder had had enough of the failures. He stormed out and said "I'm not going behind that damn curtain ever again." On the way home from church the Lord dropped a Scripture reference into his mind. He got home and looked it up: "the Lord dwelleth behind the curtain" was the gist of the passage.

John said they didn't realise that the Presence and the Power were the same. They would pray weak prayers: "If it be your will…" John said he'd "named it, claimed it, commanded it…" with no result. God said: "Why don't you pray the way we did?" so he went home and studied the prayers of Jesus—"you know they're really short!"

After eight months of failure, he fell on the floor and complained "God it's not fair. You're not doing what you said you'd do." The next morning he received a call from a new family in the church "I've got a new job. I have to go to work. Can you come over and heal my wife so she can look after the kids?" All the way over, Wimber was complaining "It's still not right. It's a mess."

When he arrived at the house he was led into the bedroom. "This woman was **sick**. No woman would let you see her like that." He mumbled a faithless prayer, and then turned to the husband to start explaining how sometimes people don't always get well when you pray for them. He noticed the man looking over his shoulder and grinning, and turned around to see the wife out of bed with her housecoat on, making the bed.

"What happened to you?" he asked in surprise.

"I'm well. You healed me," she answered. "would you like to stay for some coffee?"

John walked out on the front lawn and yelled "All right. We got one."

As he was driving home, he had a vision, where he saw, superimposed over the landscape as far as he could see, a honeycomb dripping honey.

People are weeping and grabbing the drips and sharing it with their friends. Others are really irritated, trying to get out of the honey. He pulled over and asked "God, what is it?"

"John. That's My mercy. For some people it's a blessing, and for others it's not. John, don't ever beg Me for healing again. Look at it. There's plenty for everyone. The problem isn't on My end. The problem is down there where you are."

From 1978 the church grew rapidly, especially after Lonnie Frisbee ministered there in May 1980, on Mother's Day. God told Wimber to "let that young man preach tonight." Frisbee finished preaching and asked the young people to come to the front. "Come, Holy Spirit," he cried, and bedlam ensued. People started falling on the floor and speaking in tongues. One kid fell right next to the microphone, and was talking with tongues into the microphone. When it finally stopped Wimber copped a lot of criticism, and was so anxious he couldn't sleep. He looked through the bible for "Holy Spirit come," followed by speaking in tongues. "Oh God, you gotta do something for me," he prayed. He was reminded of similar occurrences in the ministries of Wesley, Whitefield and others. Feeling a little better, he said "God is this really you."

Just then the phone rang—Tom Stipe from Denver. "It's the Lord. That's exactly what happened to us in the early days of the Jesus People revival." Over the next three months the church grew from 400 to 1700 people. Youth were witnessing to their friends in parking lots and praying for them, and they would fall as well. They baptised 700 new converts, and Wimber began to discover that everyone he spoke to felt that it was "wonderful", and they had grown closer to God as a result of the experience. It was hard for him to argue with results.

Over time God began to train them in deliverance, which caused a theological difference with Calvary Chapel. John tells of his first encounter with a demon in his book *Power Evangelism,* when he was asked to pray for an 18-year-old girl thrashing around so violently that the pickup truck she was sitting in was shaking on its wheels. When John arrived, a rasping voice spoke out of the girl "You can't have her. She's mine. And you don't know what you're doing." John began to pray, and kept at it, through 10 hours of terrifying manifestations (smells, blasphemy, supernatural strength, eyes rolling back), calling on the forces of heaven to set the girl free, and eventually overcame.

The erroneous idea that saved people cannot "have a demon" is still common today, and one of the main reasons why "*God's people are destroyed through lack of knowledge*" (Hosea 4:6). Few churches and pastors are willing to deal with demonic oppression in their flocks, because it's messy, scary and divisive. Yet, it is a major part of our six-fold Mission Statement in Matthew 10:8. The leadership of Calvary Chapel were very troubled at what was happening in Yorba Linda, and suggested they find another home. They joined the small association of Vineyard Churches led by Ken Gullickson, and in 1982, Ken asked John to assume the leadership of the Vineyard.

1978

June 18, 1978 *Boise, Idaho*

Angels Visit Roland Buck

- Repeated visitations by Angels, including Gabriel and Michael to Pastor Roland Buck
- Messages that God CARES
- If only ONE member of your household is living for God, each individual is highly favoured
- A host of Angels is assigned to work to bring these highly favoured people to God
- They have orders to hasten people to a point of choice
- If the person chooses unwisely, they begin again!

19

Angels visit Roland Buck

William Branham mentioned on several occasions that a "change" would occur in 1977. In numerous sermons, he **predicted** (NOT prophesied) that certain events would occur by that time. Many have accused him of being false when the events didn't occur when he had thought they would, but a careful search through his transcribed sermons reveals he was very clear to state that it was his personal extrapolation, not revelation from God.

However, something amazing DID begin in 1977. Firstly, the year itself is the 70th Jubilee Year from the establishment of Jubilees in Leviticus. Secondly, it was the 25th year (Silver Jubilee) of the Reign of Queen Elizabeth II of England—a godly ruler like her predecessor Queen Victoria.

Finally, and of most interest to our discussion, the next year, 1978, angels began to repeatedly visit a humble pastor in Boise, Idaho—Roland Buck, with a message that God Cares!

On the night of June 18, 1978, at about 3 in the morning, Pastor Buck was awakened by someone grasping his arms and sitting him up in his bed.

I the dim light he could make out the shape of a huge being. He could sense the supernatural presence of God in the room, and the angel told him not to be afraid, that he was sent from God because the prayers of God's people for their loved ones had been answered.

"Pastor, I have a message for you from the Father. A message that He will help you bring to the whole world."

God was mobilising angels to bring people to a place of decision for Him. If they chose wrong, they would start again. The Lord would not violate their free will, but He would work to give them every opportunity to choose Him.

The angel said: *"I am here right now leading a great band of angels in order to clear the way, to scatter the enemies, to move away the roadblocks, and to let people know that the heart of God is toward them."* The two-hour encounter covered a lot of scriptural references, and an instruction to share the message, which God would bless.

Although understandably reluctant to risk his reputation with such a message, Pastor Buck told his family and a few trusted friends. After three weeks, he still hadn't shared the message, and the angel appeared again, reinforcing the urgency of the message. *"The Father knows how you feel, and He will be with you, and help you to obey Him."* He had asked the angel his name, and was told *"I am mentioned in Luke 1:13-19,"* where Gabriel speaks with Zacharias.

In the first week after the sermon had been taped, he received six calls from people whose lives had been turned to God as a result, and had the privilege of leading several to the Lord himself.

Over the next two years, Pastor Buck had twenty-six more visits from angels, described in the books *Angels on Assignment*, and *The Man Who Talked with Angels*. He gained many insights into Scripture and the workings of Spiritual Warfare, prayer and the Holy Spirit, through extended conversations with various angels, including Gabriel and Michael—both mentioned in Scripture. Much of what he shared is extra-scriptural, but it certainly does not contradict scripture. It is encouraging, informative, but NOT for establishment of doctrine. It is worth mentioning that the great Evangelist, Dr Billy Graham, wrote his book "Angels—God's Secret Agents", not long before these encounters.

1982-1988

Nov 1982

Mike Bickle and KCF

- Sep 1982 - While spending a night in prayer in a hotel room in Cairo, Egypt, Mike heard powerfully the voice of the Lord say, "I will change the understanding and expression of Christianity in one generation."
- Nov 1982 - Mike moves to Kansas City to lead Kansas City Fellowship. Bob Jones is already in KC waiting for the young people known for "prayer and intercession"
- Mar 7, 1983 - Mike meets Bob Jones (wearing winter coat as a sign for double winter) - "Worship and 14/7 prayer", "Pray for Israel", "Harry S Truman property in Grandview", "unplugged TV sets in China", "You won't believe me now…", "First of spring when the snow melts you'll believe me" (21 March, 1983)
- May 7, 1983 - After receiving specific direction from the Lord (and a comet), Mike called churches in Kansas City to a 21-day solemn assembly of prayer and fasting. During that time, the Lord gave a prophetic word to do "24/7 prayer in the spirit of the tabernacle of David." This birthed 16 years of prayer meetings held three times per day at the church Mike was pastoring.
- 1984 - Bob Jones prophesied "Noel is coming" (Noel Alexander), "Civil War in the Church", Mike's Heavenly visitation (August 1984), meeting Paul Cain (highest mantle prophet…), John Paul Jackson's arrival and the "group of kindergarteners on the West Coast" (Jan 1984) - cross pollination with Compassion and Worship
- April 1987 - Mike finally meets Paul Cain. Paul confirms their meeting place is the vision he saw of Joel's Army. Now In Training….
- Oct 1987 - Bob tells Mike John Wimber will call him in three months
- Jan 1988 - Wimber invites Mike to speak to his staff

20

Mike Bickle and Kansas City Fellowship

In 1971, while still a student, Mike Bickle was saved, and it immediately had a profound effect on his life. At the time in America, it was common for brawls to erupt between the greasers (generally working-class origin, jeans and leather jacket, slicked-hair rebels) and the jocks (generally wealthier origin who were athletes), and Mike, who was committed to several athletic programmes, was seen as a leader among the jocks. When an incident arose, Mike refused to fight the greasers, even after being punched in the face, saying, "Jesus says I have to love you." He developed a great passion for the Bible, and a life-long habit of praying the Bible back to the Lord. At age 20 he was invited to leave University and lead a small group of Christians in St Louis, Missouri.

Some years later a man named Augustine Alcala was driving past the church, when the Lord gave him a prophetic word for the pastor. He asked a friend in the town to make contact with Mike, for he had an urgent "word from the Lord" for him. Mike politely declined, not believing such things still occurred. Augustine decided he would have to visit the church himself.

It happened to be a morning when Mike arrived late and sat in the sound booth at the back, while another leader took the service. Augustine eventually stood up and introduced himself "God uses me to speak prophetically," and began to call out accurate words for members of the congregation. Mike was initially suspicious but began to realise the accuracy of the words. Suddenly Augustine called out "the young man at the back of the room" and pointed directly at Mike, not realising he was actually the pastor. He prophesied that God was calling "that young man" into something completely new.

At the end of the service, he asked Mike out for lunch, still unaware of who he was. When he learned the truth, he told Mike that the audible voice of God had spoken to him, and that he was to move to Kansas City. Mike had no framework to accept or deal with prophecies and audible voices, but the Lord confirmed to him over the next months that He was leading him to Kansas City. So, eight people who felt they had received the call sold up and moved.

Their hunt for a suitable building took a while, as with only eight members they didn't seem to have the ability to meet the rent on a 400-seat building. Eventually, they found a place but needed to come up with $21,000 by Wednesday of that week. The next day two different people donated $20,000 between them, and Mike received a gift of $1000.

In September 1982, Mike went on a ministry trip to India, and then to Egypt. While praying in a hotel room in Cairo, he heard the audible voice of God saying "I am going to change the understanding and expression of Christianity in the whole earth in one generation." He was overcome by the fear of the Lord, weeping and trembling, and said "Yes Lord, Yes." The Lord answered "many have said Yes but they've not yet done it." The Lord highlighted 4 values that would accompany this work, which, in the fullness of time, became International House of Prayer (IHOP-KC):

- Night and Day Intercession (I)
- Holiness of Heart—Loving God and Loving People (H)
- Commitment to the poor—embracing a simple lifestyle so they could give more to the needy (O)
- Unwavering faith strengthened through the prophetic (P)

On his return, Mike again ran into Augustine, who encouraged him with several more words, and warned him of a false prophet who would be there from the beginning: "If you are patient and will discern him you will save the church great heartache." Augustine gave Mike four specific points that the Lord would initiate in Kansas City.

For eighteen months the little group had gathered every night to pray for several hours, and once they began public meetings, they began to meet three times a day. In January on 1983 an excited Christian brother told Mike about a local Prophet Bob Jones: "He's been talking for years about a group of young people the Lord was bringing who'd be led by a 27-year-old man (Mike's age). They'd be talking about Intercession and Revival (his current sermon topic)" Augustine's warnings came back to Mike and he declined to meet Bob. A month or so later another member came up and mentioned Bob, saying he was a prophet, and Mike reasoned that he'd better sort this out sooner rather than later.

On 7th March 1983, when the winter cold had long disappeared, Bob walked into Mike's office wearing a full winter coat. Mike stood up to shake hands, but Bob was busy looking around, holding up his hands, and muttering: "Yep…Yep… Them's the ones. This is what I seen." Mike offered to take his coat, but Bob said: "No, the snows are coming again on the first of spring (21 March in the US). Bob asked Mike about all the things he'd seen: are you a singer? musician? Do you pray for Israel? Do you have a connection to Asia? To which Mike said "no." Bob told Mike you will, "you're going to have 24-hour prayer with the spirit of the Tabernacle of David," … "You're going to pray for Israel," … "I see you over in Grandview on the corner of Grandview and Blueridge, next to Harry S. Truman", and "people all over Asia are going to be watching you on unplugged TV sets in their hands." Mike couldn't relate to ANY of it, and after two hours, was convinced he had found his "false prophet". Bob told him "on the first of spring when the snow melts, we'll be sitting around the table in fellowship, and I'll tell you the secret of your heart and you'll accept me as a prophet of the Lord." On his way out the door, Bob stopped, and turned back. "The Lord said you don't believe me now, but I have to tell you these four things you already know…" and repeated the same four points Augustine had given Mike.

A few weeks later Mike's friend Art Katz, a messianic Jew, had flown into Kansas City in a private plane. The weather closed in and they couldn't fly out, so Art visited Mike's new fellowship. At the end of the service Mike saw art in intense conversation with Bob Jones, and thought, "Great! Art will sort him out." After Bob had finished, Art came over to Mike: "That man is a true prophet. He just told me the secrets of my heart. I have to have more time with him." At Art's persistence Mike rang Bob later in the afternoon to ask if they could come over. "I've been waiting for him all day," Bob answered.

So a small group sat around the table at Bob's house talking till late in the night. At one point, Bob spoke a phrase to Mike that was his biggest secret—the promise he had made to his father to look after his paralysed brother Pat: "He ain't heavy, he's my brother." Mike looked at Bob and said, in shock, "You are a prophet of the Lord."

"Quick, what day is it today?"

"21st March," Mike answered, confused.

"And what's happening out the window?" Bob persisted.

"The snow's melting," Mike told him, not following.

"It's the first of spring, the snow's melting. We're sitting around the table in fellowship and you've just accepted me as a prophet of the Lord."

Bob had been saying for some weeks that God was going to send a comet "unknown to scientists" as a sign God was moving in Kansas City. God began speaking to Mike in April from Daniel—Chapter 9 where Gabriel speaks and Chapter 10 about a 21-day-fast, which he felt should begin early in May with 500 people. He rang Bob Jones to see if he had any insight on "a very scary word" he'd received. Bob said "Yeah I already know about it." When he arrived, Bob told Mike he had seen the angel Gabriel, who told him: "Give the young man Daniel 9 and he will understand."

Mike called the "solemn assembly" to the derision of many local churches, yet over 700 people crowded the church for the first night. The next day the newspapers announced a comet unpredicted by scientists. They prayed from 6am to midnight for three weeks, and on the final night Bob Jones stood up and said a three-month drought was coming on the city because the churches had rejected the call to fast. There was no rain at all till August 23, when it poured.

Bob Jones walked in an amazing level of prophetic revelation, but was still just a sinner, saved by grace. He regularly received 5-10 visions and dreams every night, and often if someone had a dream or experience from the Lord Bob had "seen it" himself and could interpret. If he "only" heard the audible voice of God twice in a month—that was a "slow" month!

A year after all this, they began looking for a larger building, which could seat around 5,000 people. Two Christian businessmen wanted to sell a Sports complex on Grandview Road that wasn't doing so well, and so they moved to the exact spot Bob Jones had told Mike about—right next to the family property of Harry S. Truman! Some years later the Lord gave them the Truman property as well.

One day two denominational pastors were driving past the church, and on the spur of the moment decided to drop in on Mike. After chatting for a while, they commented they'd really like to meet Bob Jones. Mike said "Oh, really? Then let's go over there now." The pair were surprised, and asked whether they should ring ahead. "Oh no," Mike said. "He already knows you're coming."

"How can that be?" they protested. "We didn't know we were coming."

"Trust me, he always knows," Mike told them, then picked up the phone, "Just listen."

"Hello Bob, … Yep, …Yep, …See you then."

The two pastors looked on in astonishment, and asked, "So what happened?"

Mike said: "Hello Bob, …Denominationals? … Yep, … Two of 'em? …. Yep, … Come on over…"

In various ways over the years having Bob Jones in his church was a major blessing for Mike. Bob often knew ahead of time by revelation when important figures would show up, like John Paul Jackson or Noel Alexander, whom the Lord had told him about in 1976. In 1984, Bob had an experience where the Lord told him: "I'm going to give you a friend who's a prophet like yourself, but I never want you to get this confused. For every dream and vision I give you I give him twelve. This man is the highest mantle prophet on the face of the earth at this time." Some time later they met Paul Cain, after several divine encounters with people preparing the way.

Another time Bob walked into Mike's office and announced "The Lord's been tellin' me of a group of kindergarteners on the West Coast that we're going to meet up with. We're going to help them some, and they're gonna help us, and the Kingdom will be advanced as a result. Their name in the Spirit is 'Worship and Compassion'." He'd been saying for years that the Kansas City Fellowship was known as 'Intercession and Prophecy'.

Mike was keen to go look for them at once. "Oh no," Bob said, "We're not ready yet."

"But you said they were kindergarteners," Mike responded.

"Yeah, we're still in nappies," the seer told him. Perspective!

Over the years many gifted prophetic ministries became part of the Fellowship, and they began to be called the Kansas City Prophets. Naturally this drew criticism, particularly from Cessationist pastors who refuse to accept that God still chooses to speak through vessels he anoints. Jim Goll, Larry Randolph, John Paul Jackson, Dave Parker and Mike Sullivant were all gifted ministers and part of the team.

Mike Bickle was asked once what was the benefit of the prophetic. He replied: "Without prophets, your losses will be very great." There were undeniably messes that needed to be cleaned up, and people pastored through the issues, but Mike had become firmly convinced that the benefits outweighed the drawbacks, though public criticism increased.

John Paul Jackson had been called from the womb—his mother had been told by an angel she would be pregnant for 11 months, because he would have an 11th-hour ministry. From a young age he would "see" things before they happened, and his parents encouraged him to go into ministry. He preferred to work in the corporate world, but the Lord supernaturally worked to change his heart. Many wonderful prophetic words were spoken over John Paul during his time at Kansas City. Paul Cain particularly had a revelation of God's plan for John Paul, which sadly never came to pass.

Prophecy is an invitation, or a call, to walk into a particular place with the Lord. Definitely NOT a set-in-concrete prediction of the future, as many believe. The Bible says "Many are called, but few are chosen" (Matt 22:14). The part in-between is called training. There are always conditions on a word from God, whether or not they are spoken at the time: faith, obedience, humility and so on. Even salvation, can be rejected—Jesus will "never leave you or forsake you" (Joshua 1:5, Hebrews 13:5), BUT YOU can turn your back on Him!

Mike and his team learned a lot about how to manage the prophetic and prophetic people—often through their mistakes (as we all do). Several books on the topic were written and are worth reading. Put simply, the church needs to learn to separate the Revelation (what the prophetic person actually experiences) from the Interpretation (what that means) and then work out the Application (what we should do in response). Few prophetic people are accurate in interpreting their own revelations—God made the church a community for a reason.

In April, 1987, Mike was scheduled to be a keynote speaker at a conference on the prophetic. Paul Cain was attending, and it was suggested to Mike that Paul should be invited to say a few words. To the shock of the Kansas City team, Paul then publicly confirmed many of the words the Lord had given them over several years. A few weeks later on 10-12 May, Paul visited them in Kansas City.

For several decades Paul had been seeing a particular recurring vision. He had been afraid to go looking for the building, concerned that the people there might not have the right Spirit for what God wanted to do. He said he would be taken to the "crossroads of life", and see a large building with a sign out the front reading "Joel's Army. Now in Training!" He recognised the Grandview Worship Centre as the building he had seen so many times.

Joel's Army was a revelation that came out of the Latter Rain Movement, which drew accusations of elitism against those involved. It was the unstoppable, end-time army of God, described in Joel Chapter two, which would, in great discipline, carry the Lord's message to the whole earth—an army of deliverance, not destruction. Paul immediately saw a connection between the work the Holy Spirit was initiating through the team at Kansas City and God's eternal purposes. Paul described this Army in a number of ways: 'The Nameless, Faceless Generation' (from his recurring Stadium vision), and the 'Generation of the Righteous' (Psalm 14:5). The KCF team were greatly encouraged that their faithful obedience in daily corporate prayer, intercession and fasting was meaningful, and part of God's plan.

We should NEVER assume that ANY such group is the only such group. God has done similar things in unknown groups around the world, whose stories will be told in heaven. The spiritual pride that accompanies such prophetic words is always an issue to be overcome, and we need to learn to walk in humility. Mike used to say that God gave them the grace to pray three times per day, and maintain it for years. Without that grace, like so many programs in so many churches, it would eventually fail.

The stage was set for the next big move in the Holy Spirit's plan—the "cross-pollination" with the West Coast "kindergarteners", which shook the world at the time—literally!

Doug Addison made the following comment about the operation of the prophetic at Kansas City in those days:

"Now, the Kansas City prophets—Bob Jones, John Paul Jackson, James Goll, Paul Cain—those were some of the names of the prophets that were part of the Kansas City movement. Now some people, you know, can Google it and find some bad stories, but I tell you what. The Lord used those people. He used those people to rebirth the prophetic movement like we've never seen before. They actually bore the weight of it. They bore the stripes for what we do today.…"

One of the interesting issues that emerged at the time was the discussion and understanding of the Ephesians 4 Office Ministries.

> *And He gave some as apostles, and some as prophets, and some as evangelists, and some as pastors and teachers, for the equipping of the saints for the work of service, to the building up of the body of Christ; until we all attain to the unity of the faith, and of the knowledge of the Son of God, to a mature man, to the measure of the stature which belongs to the fullness of Christ.* (Ep 4:11-13)

The five Office ministries appear again in 1 Corinthians:

> *And in the church God has appointed first of all apostles, second prophets, third teachers, then workers of miracles, also those having gifts of healing, those able to help others, those with gifts of administration, and those speaking in different kinds of tongues.* (1Co 12:28)

Note that the order is the same, except in Corinthians the pastors and evangelists have been substituted with gifts of helps and administration, miracles and healings. Could these be the Biblical qualifications for pastors and evangelists?

It has been claimed that the Offices disappeared from the church in order of authority, as time passed. Apostles vanished first, then prophets, and so on, though there have always been some who were fulfilling these roles. Whether they met the standards of the end-time Offices is a matter for debate.

The Offices have been being restored in reverse order since the Reformation. We saw the restoration of widespread pastoral and teaching ministries first, which took a few hundred years, based on Luther's understanding that Salvation is "by grace through faith" (Ephesians 2:8) rather than legalistic church attendance. Evangelism underwent a huge boost after the Moravian 100-year prayer meeting, which in turn sparked the Wesleyan revival and the 1st Great Awakening, which in turn led to the Missionary Age of the church in the 19th and 2oth centuries. One could argue the Evangelistic Office has been fully restored in men such as Billy Graham and Reinhard Bonnke. Since William Branham, we have seen a progressive restoration of the Prophetic, which was catapulted into international awareness in the Third Wave of the late 80s, and has been clawing its way towards maturity. I believe we are going to see the full restoration of the Apostolic Office in the future, though many who claim the title at the moment are premature. They might be functioning in an apostolic calling, but very few are actually Commissioned in the Office.

Mike Bickle said years ago, "We believe that End-Time Apostles must actually 'see the Lord'," which Paul indicated was a marker (1 Corinthians 9:1). I suppose we'll find out. Again, there is a difference between the Calling and the Commissioning—the part in between is called training and maturing.

1982 – 1993

The Third Wave - The Vineyard Movement

- May 1980 - Lonnie Frisbee asks "Come, Holy Spirit" and the then Calvary Chapel experiences the Spirit's power, and explosive growth occurs
- Conference ministry began which soon exploded worldwide. Kids saved off street part of the ministry teams
- Power Evangelism, Power Healing, Holiness Unto the Lord
- 1987 - Jack Deere leaves Dallas Theological Seminary and joins Vineyard, First Australian Conference in Canberra (Nov 1987)
- 1988 - Lean on Holiness - dealing with sin, meeting the Prophets, Earthquake prophecy, son Saved
- 1989 - Platform for the Prophetic, The Ranch, Melbourne Conference
- After the 1990 conference in England, where Paul Cain prophesied Revival, Wimber copped increasing criticism about the prophetic, and 'backed away'. This prompted a fall-out with Associate Pastor Jack Deere (1992), and eventually Metro Vineyard Fellowship, Kansas City (formerly KCF).
- In 1995, he gave the Toronto Blessing leaders an ultimatum, resulting in their separation from the Vineyard
- Went to be with the Lord on November 17, 1997, after a hallway fall had led to a massage brain hemorrhage
- "Jack and the Beanstalk" prophecy - did he fulfil it all???

21

The Third Wave—The Vineyard Movement

After the explosive growth after Mother's Day, 1980, John Wimber began to receive invitations to share his experiences. C. Peter Wagner at Fuller Seminary encouraged him to put together the 'experimental' course MC510—Signs, Wonders and Church Growth, which they began teaching in 1981.

They were soon invited to teach at a conference in England, and took a group of their young converts along as the ministry team. Wimber believed that "everybody gets to play", and that it was vitally important to involve all believers in the power ministries the church was supposed to be exhibiting to the world. He tells a story of that trip, where they were invited to attend an Anglican service in St Paul's Cathedral, where the Lord taught him a lesson. He said the service was "dead and dry", and he couldn't wait to be out of there. At the end the reaction of the young people surprised him. These young recent converts, who had been saved off the streets and had no church background at all, went hunting for a bookshop to buy copies of the

Prayer Book. "Man, can those guys pray," one commented. They wanted to learn the prayers to use themselves at home. It is a timely reminder of the faithful prayer that went into the crafting of the Anglican order of service—designed for uneducated people. The idea was that by weekly repetition of the prayers in church they would be learning the fundamentals of the faith—the creed, communion, repentance and forgiveness for sins.

Wimber's experience teaching at Fuller meant that the Vineyard conferences were accompanied by well-presented notes, outlining the teaching and Bible references. Power Evangelism conferences were held in a number of countries over the next few years, teaching the churches to pray for the sick, and introducing them to the simple worship songs the Lord had been releasing into their network. Wimber himself continued to grow in experience of the supernatural, as the Lord taught them a different way of introducing the Holy Spirit's gifts to the mainstream.

Wimber's greatest advantage was that he developed his practises of ministry from the Bible, by paying attention to what Jesus himself did. Unlike the ministers of the Charismatic Movement, who tended to work backwards from the Pentecostal experience to a better theology, Wimber's Bible basis made his teaching far more acceptable to orthodox evangelicals. The Vineyard did not emphasise tongues as the "only valid evidence" of the baptism of the Spirit, and taught that a believer could operate in all of the nine "manifestations of the spirit" listed in 1 Corinthians 12.

A careful reading of the passage will bring out verse 7: "*To each one the* **manifestation** *of the spirit is given for the common good.*" A manifestation is a short-term event, not a long-term blessing or gift. This challenges the traditional Pentecostal teaching that some would receive certain permanent "gifts", but not others. Wimber learned a manifestation can be for a certain time, and all believers should expect to operate in ALL of the gifts at different times. This was a major reason why the Vineyard taught believers to operate in teams when praying for someone—one might get the word of knowledge for that person, another wisdom, another the healing gift. But the next person ministered to could see a different mix of the team operating in the gifts, as the Holy Spirit manifested in each case.

The Vineyard began to host conferences all over the world. Power Evangelism was followed by Power Healing, Holiness Unto the Lord, Worship, Doin' the Stuff, Prophecy and others. Believers would travel across national boundaries and oceans to receive instruction on the "Third Wave" teachings, and many mainstream denominational churches began to experience Renewal. The term "Third Wave" originated from the Fuller Seminary, where proponents saw the First Wave as being the Pentecostal outpouring beginning with Azusa Street, the Second Wave as the Charismatic Renewal, where there was greater influence on those from mainstream denominations, and the Third Wave where the Holy Spirit was moving with more prominence within those traditional churches.

My own experience with this "Wave" began back in 1978, when I went over to my Father's study in the back of the Hall at Northbridge in Sydney. Twelve years old, I wanted to know why we didn't see the healings and miracles we read about in the Bible in church. I remember Dad explaining about Pentecostals who claimed they did see them, and some of the errors he had experienced (he was told by a Pentecostal pastor he wasn't saved because he didn't speak in tongues). He said "I know I have the Holy Spirit. He speaks to me through the Bible and in my prayer." I remember asking him "So what do you think?"

"I'm waiting to see," he answered. I walked out of his study to head back to the rectory, and the thought struck my heart: "Of Course God's still doing such things." I **knew**! I found out years later that by 1983 Dad was so disillusioned at the lack of success reaching the affluent people of the lower North Shore he was seriously considering leaving the ministry. All of his experience at Beachmission, and the many evangelism courses run by Sydney diocese—nothing worked. We had no idea that the Jesus People era was over—that wasn't understood by Sydney Anglicans. Unbeknownst to everyone, the rector's warden, Ray Spencer, had been sneaking off to Charismatic Prayer Conferences with Intercessors for Australia, and he offered to pay for my parents to go along. They were so crushed they thought "we might as well." In my mum's words: "They had their socks blown off." They witnessed tongues, healings, demonic manifestations and so on, and were impressed by the godly character of the people they met and the gentle movement of the Holy Spirit in their own lives. They returned, determined to "look into it some more."

We began attending the weekly Healing Ministry in St Andrew's Cathedral in town—a very low-key service led by Canon Jim Glennon, where each week we would be involved praying for those who wanted it, believing that God would "do something". From the folk there, we learned about John Wimber, and the conferences others had attended in New Zealand. By 1985, I was at Uni, and Mum and Dad were keen to go to a Wimber Conference. Michael Green was visiting Sydney at the time, and spoke openly of his experience in Renewal, and a Renewal Conference that his church, St Aldgate's in Oxford was hosting in July. They expressed interest in the Conference, but their priority was to hear John Wimber, at his next Conference in New Zealand, although they were having difficulty getting there.

"Oh, don't go to New Zealand," he told them. "John and I are both speaking at Acts '86 in Birmingham, two weeks after we have our Renewal Week in Oxford. Come to England and you'll be our guests." Later in '86, Bishop David Pytches, former missionary bishop of Chile, now pastoring at St Andrew's Chorleywood, came through Sydney. That was where we first saw people falling spontaneously "under the power" when the Holy

Spirit was invited to come. Dad was soon asked to take the leadership of ARMA—Anglican Renewal Ministries of Australia in Sydney, and we began to grow in different areas, as the Lord exposed us to demonic manifestations (thanks Jackie Pullinger), inner healing, and so on.

Wimber himself didn't come to Australia until 1987 in Canberra (and I couldn't go). Dad went and came back with all the tapes, but John returned to California to a year of great trouble. Jack Deere, former professor of Old Testament at Dallas theological Seminary, had been pushed out of his academic position and joined the Vineyard team, and had known of Paul Cain from his time in Texas. During 1988 John was receiving messages from Paul, Bob Jones and others, about various leaders in the Vineyard movement who were in sin. Detailed words, including office numbers, views from the window, and who was doing what with whom unleashed a mess that John spent most of the year dealing with, as the Lord began to "clean up" the gross unrighteousness that had crept in.

Brent Rue, pastor of the Lancaster Vineyard, told of a time in the middle of the year when all the Vineyard pastors had gathered with the intention of becoming a formal denomination. John had the documents in front of him, ready to sign, when Jack Deere burst through the door.

"I've just got off the phone with Paul Cain," he said, "and he says this is not of the Lord, and I believe him. If anyone disagrees, let him stand up and let the Lord judge between us." Brent was convinced someone was going to die—it was that intense.

John simply tore up the documents, "Well, that's that." Though he had not yet met Paul Cain, he had heard stories from both Mike Bickle (with whom they'd recently connected) and Jack Deere, and he had observed the accuracy of the prophetic words that unmasked the sin in the camp.

Not long after, the Lord spoke to Paul Cain, and told him to go and see John with a word from the Lord. Jack Deere walked into John's office and said, "Paul Cain is on the phone. He wants to come and see you. He says he has a word from the Lord for you."

John handed Jack a list of dates, "This is when we're gonna be around. Tell him to pick when he wants to come."

"Yeah, about that," Jack began. "He said to tell you there'll be an earthquake in our area on the day he arrives as a sign that his coming is from the Lord, and the word of the Lord to us is Jeremiah 33:8. There's something else significant about the verse, but he doesn't know what it is, but he'll know when he gets here."

John said later that picking a time of year for an earthquake in California is not hard. Picking a date when the date hasn't been picked "separates the men prophets from the boys."

Jack had asked Paul, "Is that the Big One everyone keeps talking about for California?" referring to the prophecy William Branham had spoken.

"No," Paul told him, "but after I leave there will be a major earthquake somewhere else in the world. Because what the Lord initiates when I come to the Vineyard will end up shaking the whole world." John wasn't really sure how to take that—he had no frame of reference for what was about to happen.

The final weekend of November, 1988, Paul Cain arrived to visit Kansas City fellowship, to meet with the leadership. He had told Mike that he had a "staff infection" and the Lord wanted to make the leadership "as white as snow", and as a sign there would be unseasonal snow on the ground. Mike made sure he personally had dealt with things before the time arrived, but many others were very worried. The morning Paul arrived the snow was there. Two days later, Paul was due to arrive in California.

At 3:38am (Jeremiah 33:8), there was an earthquake of 5 on the Richter Scale under to Rose Bowl in Pasadena. John Wimber woke up, saw the news reports, and dialled Mike Bickle in Kansas City.

"Who is this guy who can predict earthquakes? Did the snow thing happen?" he asked.

"Oh yes," Mike laughed, "and the team got cleaned up."

John was getting worried. "You got snow. I got an earthquake. Am I gonna die? What should I do to get ready? Is it too late for prayer and fasting—he's going to be here in an hour?"

"It's never too late for prayer," Mike said.

Jeremiah 33:8 says: *"I will cleanse them from all the sin they have committed against me and will forgive all their sins of rebellion against me."*

Paul didn't want to tell John he didn't yet know the word the Lord had—he hadn't yet been told. After John had dropped him off at his hotel room, he had a nap, and woke up to see the clock reading 5:55. Since 5 is the number of grace, Paul understood the Lord's word to the Vineyard, which was "Grace, Grace, Grace" and they had a wonderful time of healing after a difficult year.

Brent Rue said a rumour was going around amongst the leaders that you couldn't get within ten feet of Paul Cain or he could read your mind. When they all went out to a Chinese restaurant, Brent and other made sure their table was at least 10 feet away from where Paul and his assistant sat with John, Jack and their wives.

"He must have been laughing himself silly," Brent said. "We found out later he can pick you up across the country if he needs to." Mike Bickle told a similar story about Paul's ability to discern over a distance, which I told earlier.

The day Paul left Anaheim was December 7, 1988. A major earthquake hit Armenia, causing many deaths and a lot of damage. Please note, God did not **send** the earthquake—he merely used the event for His own purposes.

Paul then began to travel and speak at various Vineyard conferences throughout 1989, as the Lord began his re-emergence into public ministry. He was in Melbourne, Australia later that year, where my Dad got to go again without me. It was through the Vineyard, after all these confirmations, that the rest of the world was shaken by the prophetic, and we began to hear the amazing stories of how God was using these men.

A lot of criticism began to be levelled at John Wimber because of this association. Many people had preconceptions and assumptions about the prophetic that were unfair, unrealistic, and unbiblical. Much New Testament prophecy operates on a different level to that of the Old Testament. Under the new covenant, we are adopted sons and daughters of the King, and our heavenly Father treats us differently to the "servants" of the Old covenant.

When Wimber came to Sydney in 1990, with John White, Jack Deere and Paul Cain, the orthodox evangelicals were there in force, and caused many problems. I remember Paul Cain ministering in power, calling out faces from the crowd with accurate prophetic words that we were able to confirm afterwards. A local church magazine, *The Briefing*, opposed to just about everything that was happening, published an appalling issue misrepresenting much of what happened, twisting words and making many slurs against the team. Unfortunately, it is still being circulated today. Wimber's comment was, "Well, we've met the Pharisees."

In 1990, the Kansas City Fellowship held a Leadership Conference, with 8,000 in attendance, including a team from Wimber's Anaheim Vineyard. As well as Mike Bickle and Paul Cain, the speakers included Mahesh Chavda, Francis Frangipane and Rick Joyner, who had a special prophetic gifting, and would develop a worldwide ministry. My Mum and Dad were also there, and reported that there was a great move of God throughout the meetings, and Paul Cain ministered prophetically in much greater power than we had seen in Sydney.

Kansas City Fellowship joined the Vineyard that year as Metro Vineyard Fellowship Kansas City, to benefit from the broader oversight. A fierce public accusation by a local pastor had been widely circulated making serious accusations about the Kansas City Prophets, and Jack Deere had led an investigation into the allegations. Some minor issues were unearthed for which Mike publicly repented. His attitude was that if there was any rebuke from the Lord contained in the mess of wild accusations, he wanted to be diligent to repent. The vast majority of the barbs were baseless. As it turned out, the pastor behind the accusations had some major issues in his own life which came out some years afterwards.

When Wimber and his team returned to Sydney in 1991, Paul Cain did no prophetic ministry in his first session. I spoke with Jack Deere about it, and he said, "I've told Paul if he doesn't start calling people out on Friday night, I'm not going to let him off the stage. People need to see the truth."

On the final night, Paul simply turned and walked off. "The Lord won't let me," he told Jack. "They rejected Him last year, and they don't get another chance."

Also in 1991 was the infamous conference in England, where Paul Cain prophesied that revival was coming to England. When nothing had happened after some months, a lot of public criticism was directed at John, and accusation he was harbouring a "false prophet". Eventually, Wimber "backed off" on the prophetic, which prompted a massive falling-out with Jack Deere, and Wimber began to distance himself from Paul Cain.

Harsh words were spoken, and Wimber told Jack he was fired as his assistant. He repented the next day and asked him to stay, but Jack felt it was time to move on. He couldn't un-see the things he had witnessed, and felt the Vineyard was moving out of the Call of the Lord.

In 1994, the Toronto Blessing, arising from the Toronto Airport Vineyard, broke out around the world, and had a huge impact in Britain, fulfilling all the things Paul Cain had prophesied years before. But the damage had been done. Again, in response to concerns over the strange manifestations of the Holy Spirit that were being reported at the Toronto Airport Vineyard, Wimber became involved. It was felt that the ministry occurring was not what the Vineyard had taught and modelled around the world, with many strange manifestations occurring. This put the Toronto team on the spot. They realised God was at work in the midst of these manifestations, but with so many visitors coming, they needed to restrict ministry to their own, known and trained ministry team.

Wimber, however, was not satisfied, and early in 1996, the Vineyard leadership voted to sever ties with the Toronto Airport Church. Later that same year, Kansas City left the Vineyard, Mike Bickle sent a 14-page directive to the Vineyard leadership saying he had been "confronted by the Lord," ... "in a sudden, yet dramatic, way concerning an issue of compromise grounded in the fear of man," referring to the Toronto decision. Believing they were now on different paths; they resigned their membership of the Vineyard association.

Wimber's personal health declined. He had heart issues, sinus cancer, which he beat, a stroke, and triple bypass surgery. He passed away in November, 1997, after a brain haemorrhage following a fall.

My personal belief is that John Wimber "lost the plot" when he backed away from his support for the prophetic ministers. I felt at the time his reaction to the criticism of Paul Cain's 1991 word was premature, and the action to cut loose Toronto was ridiculous. Jack Deere had taught many times at the Vineyard that throughout history the leaders of the previous move of God tended to be the persecutors of the next. While John never persecuted the Toronto leaders, his public withdrawal of oversight was seen by many as a backwards step.

THE THIRD WAVE—THE VINEYARD MOVEMENT

Years before, Bob Jones had given John a prophetic word, the well-known "Jack and the Beanstalk" prophecy, Jack being a common nickname for John. He said that John was called by God to do three main things:

1. To recover David's Harp of worship from the enemy
2. To restore the "golden eggs" of healing to the church
3. To mobilise the church to lay the axe to the roots of the enemy's kingdom.

The Vineyard was certainly instrumental in promoting worship and healing within the mainstream churches, but I do not believe John ever "walked into" the final call, when he separated himself from the Prophetic.

I do not intend this as a judging criticism—I have never had to face the decisions and vitriolic attacks that John Wimber did. He was a wonderful, caring man of God, and I really miss his gentle teaching and self-depreciating humour, and I personally owe him so much for the things he brought that affected my life. But I feel we need to learn from the mistakes our leaders make as much as from their victories.

It is also worth saying that few ministers know their divine calling, fewer still have had mature prophetic ministers to help them on any part of their walk, and of the one or two I know who were called to a specific purpose, I believe only ONE actually saw it all the way through—Jesus Himself. The rest of us will find out when we stand before Him.

Pray it through. Ultimately, you are responsible for your own walk.

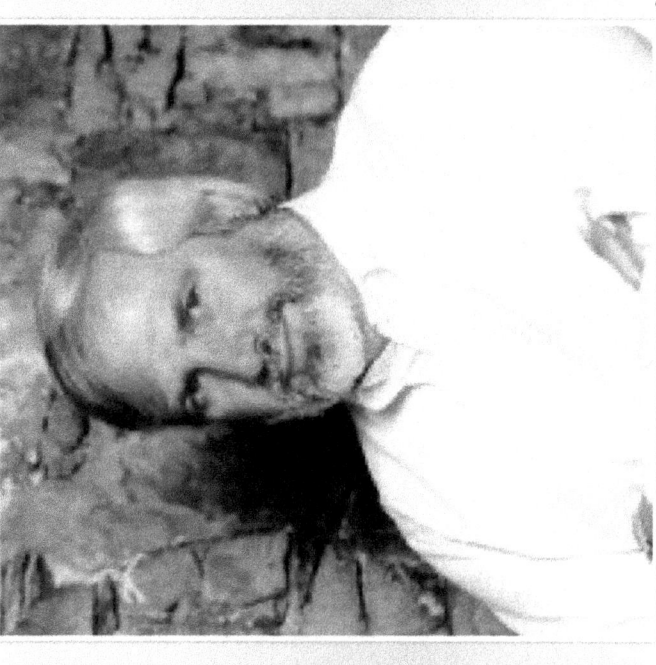

1987

September, 1987 *Charlotte, North Carolina*

Rick Joyner's Vision of the Harvest

- Rick was grieved by the distress he had witnessed in the Church after the Televangelist controversies of 1987.
- He went into his study and was "caught up" in a tow-and-a-half day Prophetic Experience where he was shown a detailed panorama of things to come.
- He went from "deep discouragement" about the Church to having great faith that she would become all that God called her to be.
- *A Vision of the Harvest* opened doors, and Rick was quickly connected with Leonard Ravenhill, then Mike Bickle and Bob Jones, Jack Deere, John Wimber and Paul Cain.

22

Rick Joyner's Vision of the Harvest

After leaving the Navy in 1970, Rick Joyner was determined to enjoy whatever the world had to offer. His childhood memories of church were of "intolerable boredom", and though he read extensively on philosophy, history and religion, he never seriously studied Christianity.

He says the day he was saved he was introduced to personal prophecy. He went to a home group, where he experienced beautiful worship and witnessed tongues. A man prayed for him, detailing events he had experienced over the previous days. He was led through a prayer of repentance, and then delivered, "something very dark left me."

The change in his life was dramatic, and he began witnessing and seeing results. He also began having vivid dreams and visions, and was fortunate in being connected with people who could help him grow and mature, without dismissing the experiences as demonic. He became captivated by the Bible, and by the fellowship of the Charismatic house churches he was linked with.

He tried to be a pastor for a while, but felt he failed miserably. He said he had a lot of knowledge "but no experience and less wisdom." Returning to a flying career, he began to see success, but the Lord was calling him in another direction. After forming Morningstar to self-publish his first book, *There Were Two Trees in the Garden*, he felt the Lord calling him back to ministry. He asked the Lord to free him from the pride and entanglements that were preventing him from following his Call—in thirty days his business crashed.

At the end of 1987, Rick was very discouraged at the state of the Church, and concerned about supporting his family. At the time the church was reeling from the public embarrassment of the televangelist controversies. He went into his study to do paperwork, and was "caught up" into a two-and-a-half-day prophetic experience, where he was shown the end-time church becoming everything God had called her to be. He wrote a brief summary called A Vision of The Harvest, which immediately began drawing attention, and led to Rick meeting Mike Bickle. He had heard of the prophetic ministry coming out of Kansas City, and been intrigued by the reports, and the encouragement he witnessed in the church as a result.

Rick met Bob Jones at a Conference in Greensboro, North Carolina, where Mike was speaking with Jack Deere. Bob ministered to Rick and explained many of the events of Rick's life that had caused him so much confusion. He wrote, in A Prophetic History, "Almost every person Bob met would be left on their knees and crying because of the love of God that touched them through him," (p. 73).

Jack Deere invited Rick to his home in Dallas, and introduced him to both John Wimber and Paul Cain. Rick had been so isolated from much of what had been happening in the wider church he had not heard of the Vineyard, but John had heard of Rick, and called Jack's house, asking if the Lord had shown him anything for John. He began to say "no", when the Lord told him, "Tell him that a scandal is about to be released in the Vineyard." The next day, details began to emerge about a key Vineyard leader in adulterous relationships.

Rick's meeting with Paul Cain was even more dramatic, as Jack Deere wouldn't tell him anything in advance. The day they were to meet, Paul Cain had a heart attack and was rushed to hospital. As they prayed for Paul, Rick had a vision of the spirit of death coming for Paul but it couldn't touch him. Bob Jones rang the next day—he had had the same vision.

The connections with the Kansas City team, the Vineyard and Paul Cain both encouraged Rick and opened even more doors for him. He began releasing The Morningstar Prophetic Bulletin, to share words the Lord was giving to the broader church community, and was invited to speak at a major Conference in Kansas City, where he met Francis Frangipane. Morningstar itself began to grow and develop, and the Lord led them step-by-step as they investigated property and established a church. Rick's full-length book of the 1987 vision, called The Harvest, has been reprinted multiple times and sold millions of copies. Most of the things he was shown have happened already in the years since 1989, and only a few are still outstanding.

Rick believes that the vision he was given, and the exciting re-introduction of the prophetic ministry to the wider church, was used by the Holy Spirit to encourage many, and help bring a harvest into the Kingdom of God.

What impresses me most is that the Holy Spirit was weaving together so many different strands, from so many different backgrounds, into a web of purpose. He established a base through these events from which God would launch His next work, and many, many people were saved. Some estimates are that since the publishing of The Harvest and the introduction of the prophetic by the Vineyard in 1989, more people have come to Christ than in the whole of the rest of Church History put together. But we STILL haven't seen the Billion-Soul Harvest Bob Jones was told about in 1975.

1989

Jan 1989 *Los Angeles, California*

Paul Cain's Re-Emergence

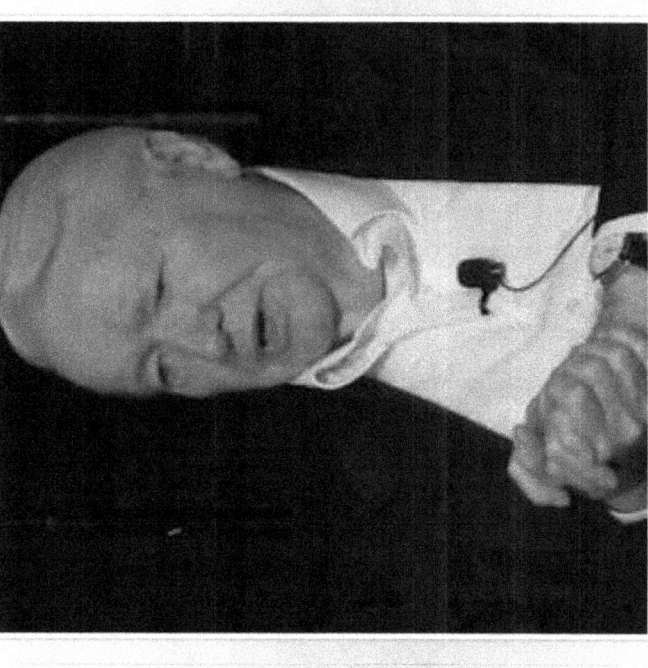

- Paul had 'stepped away' since 1957, only ministering a few times a year. "I still can't trust you," the Lord said
- In the early 80s, God told him to go and visit Evangelical leaders – "I will lead you to the one who will provide a platform for your re-emergence into ministry"
- Benny Hinn, Oral Roberts, Yonggi-Cho, and Jimmy Swaggert - he saw what would happen to Jimmy but God wouldn't let him speak (Bob Jones did too).
- After his encounter with the Vineyard and the Earthquake Prophecy on 1988, God spoke to him in a plane above LA and said: "John Wimber is the man. Go and spend time with the Vineyard."
- Then followed the two years of amazing ministry and appalling opposition. In Sydney 1990, Wimber commented: "We have met the Pharisees…"
- Wimber backed away after the English Revival failed to happen immediately - when it did in 1994 (Toronto Blessing) most people failed to make the connection

23

Paul Cain's Re-Emergence

In 1957, as we have seen, the Lord called Paul Cain to leave the life of a travelling evangelist, and spend his time waiting on the Lord for the "new breed of leaders" God had promised. Paul thought it would only be a few years, and went from over 300 engagements a year to one or two. He lived with his mother in Texas, waiting on the Lord up to 10 hours a day and studying the Bible.

Every time he would be allowed to minister, the power of the Lord would operate as it always had, and he would think "This is it." But the Lord would always say, "Not yet. I still can't trust you," and send him back to Texas. In all, he spent 25 years waiting on the Lord. God had told him he was a "sovereign vessel", and that he was never to take a job to support himself, and the Lord supernaturally supplied his living needs for the whole time. In the early '80s, the Lord told Paul it was time for his re-emergence into ministry, and he was to go and visit major leaders in the Church. God would lead him to the man who would provide him a platform for his end-time ministry.

Paul visited a number of the big names of the day: Oral Roberts, Paul Yonggi Cho, and Jimmy Swaggart. Many would comment that it was great to see him "making a comeback", not understanding the process of preparation and humility God had been nurturing in Paul. He saw what was happening with Jimmy Swaggart (who was later publicly exposed as being involved with a prostitute, to the great humiliation of the wider church), but the Lord "wouldn't let (Paul) say anything." Just think about that!

One amazing story that Paul shared publicly was, according to Paul's last assistant Dan Reise, the first meeting he did after his re-emergence. Dan first met Paul at the second meeting, a small house meeting with about 17 people.

This earlier meeting, Paul said he was in San Francisco, in an auditorium of about 5000 people, with a large overflow of several hundred off to the right of the stage. He saw the "amber light of God", as he described it, hover over a number of women throughout the crowd, and the Lord told him "Ask those women to stand." He pointed at one after another, as the light moved around the room, until a number of women all over the auditorium were on their feet. He said he had no idea why, until the Lord said, "Tell those women they all have the same thing in common," so he did. He said, "It felt so good to say that," though he had no idea what the thing was. Then the Lord said, "Tell them they all have unsaved husbands."

The room buzzed as the response of the ladies was obvious to all. Paul then said "The Lord wants you to know that your husbands are going to be saved soon." He then pointed to one lady near the front, and called her by name.

"Your name is Mary-Ellen. Mary-Ellen, your husband is going to be saved not many days hence ... No scratch that, he said 'Right away!'" Then, without missing a beat, he swung around and pointed to a young theological college student in the overflow auditorium to his right.

"Steve! Shame on you. The Lord has a little divine sarcasm for you. As I said that to Mary-Ellen your mother, about your father, you said in your heart, 'No Lord. Stop that man. He can't be a prophet or he'd know that my father is a hard man, and an unemotional man, and he's resisting the gospel. You've got to stop him Lord or my mother's faith will be destroyed'. Just for that, Alex will be saved within 24 hours. And you told the Lord he was a self-made man and an unemotional man. Your father is going to come into the Kingdom of God shaking and quaking under the conviction of the Holy Spirit."

After the meeting Mary-Ellen went home, where her husband had just flown home from Washington D.C. and she told him what had occurred. As she was speaking, the Holy Spirit fell on him and he began to weep. They had houseguests, and he entertained them by sobbing, weeping and shaking. He couldn't stop, and wept all night and throughout the next day. He was the first at the front the next night to give his heart to the Lord, and his eyes were swollen shut from weeping non-stop.

My favourite part? That was the prophetic sign to all the other women that their husbands would also be saved!

Another time in Kansas City, Paul was beginning to call people out with words from the Lord, when suddenly, as Mike Bickle said, it went to a whole new level. The manifest presence of God suddenly entered the room, and Paul began calling people out in great detail for about a minute and a half. He pointed at a woman and called her name, "Mary." "Yes", she squawked. "You and (Phil) have been praying for (Bob). He's going to be saved right away." She fell to the floor under the anointing. Paul went on like a machine gun, about seven people around the room. After that, it seemed to lift, and Paul said, "Well, it's kind of hard to get going again after that. Brother Mike, you'd better close the meeting."

Mike said it was hard to move—it was like the whole room was stunned by the power of God. He got up and mumbled, "you're dismissed," but only a few people quietly began gathering their things. "It was like the holiness of God had entered the room. It was hard to breathe." Suddenly, the doors at the back crashed open, and firemen in full kit "with axes" burst into the room, yelling "where's the fire?" Mike said, "It was so rude. Couldn't they see something holy had just happened?"

After a few minutes the fire chief came back to Mike and said, "Well we can't find a fire, but something happened here. About 10 minutes ago a power surge went through this building that blew every alarm circuit down at the station."

"Oh, I'm sorry," Paul said. "That happens sometimes. It's been so long I forgot."

Mike told a story when he first met Paul. They went out to a Cafe after a meeting. Sitting at a table, the waitress had just brought their food, and Paul complained of being tired. "Can we move to that booth in the corner?" he asked. "I'm so tired." Mike didn't understand, but called the waitress. "Do you mind if we move to that booth in the corner?"

"Not at all," she replied. "Any particular reason?"

"He's *tired*," Mike told her, as if that explained everything. The waitress helped them resettle. Paul sank back into the corner, and sighed in relief, "Oh that's so much better."

"What on earth do you mean?" Mike asked, privately wondering if Paul had 'lost it'.

"Well Mike," Paul began. "When I'm tired, I can't shut down. That waitress has kidney problems, and every time she walks past, I feel like my kidneys are on fire. That man over there is a homosexual, and that couple have marriage problems… And he went around all the people in the cafe."

PAUL CAIN'S RE-EMERGENCE

"Great. Let's go pray for her," Mike said with enthusiasm, starting to get up.

"No. Please don't," Paul said rather forcefully, "I'm too tired." Mike clearly didn't understand.

"Surely if the Lord is showing you this stuff we need to pray for them?"

"Well Mike, some time ago the Lord visited me, and He called me His friend," Paul said, with tears in his eyes. "and from time to time, He tells me things *because* I'm His friend, so I know He's on the job. If I went and prayed for that lady now, she would be healed, and then a crowd would gather, and I'd be picking up every detail in 100 yards. I'm just too tired."

In the years since I've learned that the Lord **often** shows us things just so we know, or so we can intercede. I remember someone saying, "Prophets are known on earth by what they say publicly. They're known in heaven by what they **don't**." We need to learn to ask the Lord what to do in each case, not just assume it's a divine appointment to minister. One of the problems we have seen in Adelaide is the lack of discernment in deliverance ministry. Some witches are going along to Charismatic churches to get delivered, knowing full well they'll get "seven times" more powerful when the spirits come back, as they had no intention of repenting. Always ASK the Lord!

After the events of 1988, and the earthquake prophecy at the Vineyard, Paul was still looking for the man God had sent him to find. He never expected it would be John Wimber, as John's background was so totally different from the stature of the men he was expecting—well-known Pentecostal leaders with large, established ministries.

In January 1989, he was in a plane over Los Angeles, and the Lord spoke to him, "John Wimber is that man. Go back to the Vineyard. He will provide a platform for your emergence into your end-time ministry."

And we know what happened next.

1983 - 1997

The Prophetic History of the Toronto Blessing

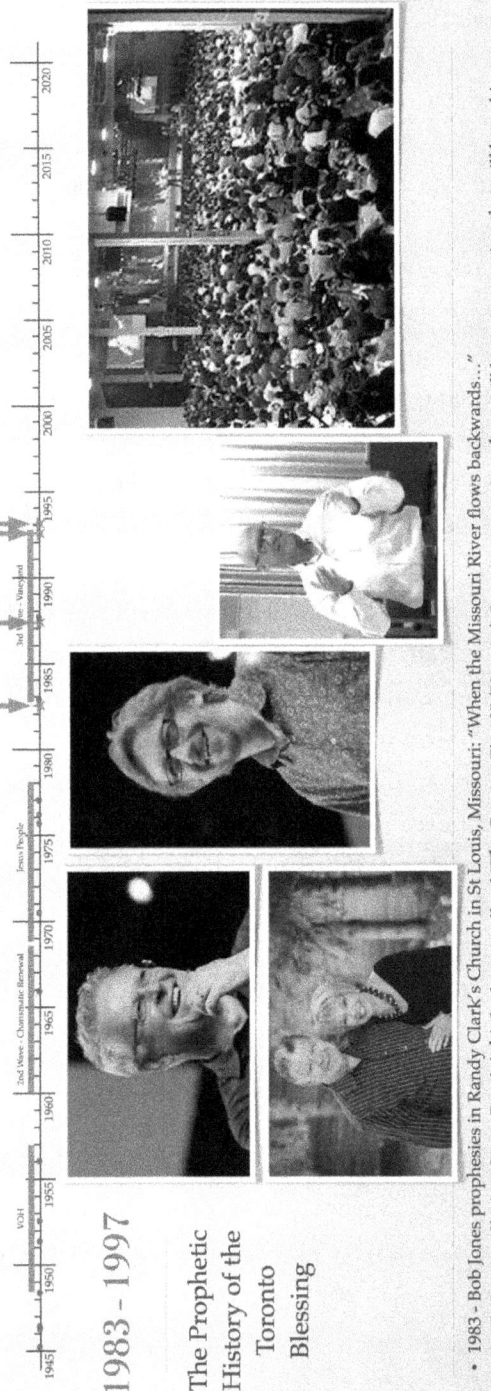

- 1983 - Bob Jones prophesies in Randy Clark's Church in St Louis, Missouri: "When the Missouri River flows backwards…"
- 1987 - Jesus walks into Larry Randolph's bedroom, tells of "The Coming Flood" (Harvest). In seven years time there will be an outpouring that will be so big you'll think that's it - it's the precursor…
- Early 90s, Larry has a dream where he sees a laser beam coming from Argentina Revival to Missouri, then to Toronto, and exploring worldwide
- John and Carol Arnott go to South America and are prayed for by Claudio Friedzon: "Receive it…"
- 1993 - Huge rainstorms across middle US cause Missouri River to flow backwards. John and Carol Arnott go to South America and are prayed for by Claudio Friedzon: "Receive it…"
- 1993, Rodney Howard-Browne, who had brought the Laughing Revival from South Africa to the US in 1987, was ministering in Kenneth Hagin's Rhema Bible Institute in Oklahoma. Feeling dry, Randy Clark attends. John and Carol Arnott go to South America and are prayed for by Claudio Friedzon: "Receive it…"
- Randy Clark shares with his church and things start happening. Later that year he shares with Vineyard pastors, and is invited to Toronto in Jan 1994
- The one week of meeting went even night for 6 weeks as crowds flocked to experience what God was doing. Baptist minister Guy Chevreau likens the manifestations to those recorded by Jonathan Edward in the First Great Awakening (Mid 1700s)

24

The Prophetic History of the Toronto Blessing

The early 90s was a very confusing time, as the Vineyard began to distance itself from the prophetic. We watched in shock as attack after attack was levelled at Wimber, Kansas City, and it seemed that everything was falling apart. My parents went over to the States each year, and came back with armloads of tapes from conferences, which kept me going in my own "Desert experience." They were in the Kansas City Leadership Conference where the Million-Dollar offering Bob Jones had prophesied years before was taken up, to get Bibles and worship cassettes into Russia after the collapse of the Iron Curtain. Terry Law had been sharing of the opportunities the Lord had opened up, and that it cost them $1 to get a Russian Bible into the hands of a person. Among the 5000 or so pastors and their wives, the donations and pledges were over a million dollars. Mum told of ladies putting their $15,000 engagement rings into the bucket, wanting to give to the Lord's work (*who* walks around with $15,000 on their finger???).

For all the confusion that many were experiencing, the Lord had already been setting up for his next move. In a time where many pastors were saying they were feeling "dry" and "burned out", God was preparing to release "rivers of blessing" that would impact the Western Church.

In 1983, Bob Jones had been ministering in a small church in St Louis, Missouri, pastored by Randy Clark. He gave them a word that seemed to make no sense: "When the Missouri River flows backwards, revival will break out in your church." The Missouri is a major river that runs into the even bigger Mississippi—it's like saying that the Darling River will run backwards towards Queensland. No-one knew what that meant.

In 1987, one of the Kansas City prophetic ministers, Pentecostal-raised Larry Randolph, had an experience where Jesus walked into his bedroom in the middle of the night. The Lord preached to him, and he sounded slightly Pentecostal. Larry awakened around 11pm to the sound and smell of rain. He jumped up, and ran to the window, but there was nothing, so he went back to sleep. This happened twice more, and he remembered the story of Samuel, and said, "Speak Lord. Your servant is listening."

At once the Lord was standing at the foot of his bed, and He began to speak out of Luke 17:26, "as it was in the Days of Noah…" The Lord said "Your generation is poised for one of the greatest outpourings of the Holy Spirit in recorded history. On your generation the ends of the earth are going to come. As it was in Noah's day, it's going to be duplicated in your day." He was told of a spiritual Flood of revival that would inundate the globe, and it would start in seven year's time (i.e. 1994). People would think it was the last days outpouring, but it would be the precursor to "a Flood like you have no context at all."

The Lord began to tell him that 1994 would herald the first drizzle. Then around the end of the '90s they would go through the eye of the storm. And then the backdraft of this spiritual hurricane would hit with a "velocity like you've never experienced before." When the Lord finished, He left with the statement, "The Glory of the Lord will cover the earth as the waters cover the sea."

Jesus told Larry that he would go through times where he would doubt, and the church would doubt, but he must remain faithful. Around this time he also had a dream of a laser beam coming from Argentina, touching down in Missouri, going up to Toronto, and then exploding with branches travelling all over the world.

In 1993, Larry Randolph began to prophesy over a radio show that a deluge of water was coming, and that year would be the wettest year they'd ever seen with Floods throughout the mid-west United States. Within 40 days they had mudslides in California, torrential rains in Europe, and huge floods across the mid-west. So much water was flowing into the Mississippi River that the Missouri River flowed backwards.

At that time, Randy Clark, pastor of Vineyard Christian Fellowship in St Louis, Missouri, was feeling dry. After years of ministry, he was desperately seeking more fruit in his Church and power in his ministry. He heard about unusual manifestations of laughter occurring in Rodney Howard-Browne's meetings, and decided to go to one nearby in Kenneth Hagin's "Word of Faith" Rhema Bible Church in Tulsa, Oklahoma. He said at one time, "It had to be God. It was held in the only church group I'd ever spoken against publicly from the pulpit." The Lord told him he had a denominational spirit. "How badly do you want to be touched afresh?"

Randy went and received prayer, but still had doubts about the experience. In previous experiences, he had shaken under the power of God, and therefore was thinking that this would happen again. At a later meeting, he told the Lord he would continue fasting until he'd been filled. He went in the prayer line 5 times, eventually noticing God was healing him, despite the lack of shaking. The final time, the Lord floored him, and his life changed forever.

He had no intention of telling his church what had happened, but God overruled him, "I'm God." He shared his testimony, and the believers rushed forward for prayer at the end. He started to lay hands on them and they started going down, some laughing, some crying, all testifying to a powerful experience of the Holy Spirit. One young man said "I don't want prayer. I don't believe it is real," but was stuck to the spot and couldn't move. Randy prayed for him and he was healed of a deep emotional wound. This kept happening every week.

John and Carol Arnott, pastors of the Toronto Airport Vineyard, had spent most of 1993 seeking a fresh anointing from the Lord. They spent time every morning seeking Him and praying. They had been powerfully impacted by Kathryn Kuhlman, John Wimber and Benny Hinn. They also went to a meeting with Rodney Howard-Browne, but John wasn't overly impressed—he wanted to see more healing and salvation rather than people falling around laughing.

In November 1993, they went to Argentina themselves, and were ministered to by Claudio Friedzon, which lifted their faith. John had heard Randy Clark sharing the testimony of what God was doing in his church at a Vineyard Leaders meeting in Palm Springs, and invited for a series of four meetings starting on Jan 20, 1994.

At the end of 1993, on December 15th, Larry Randolph was invited to go and speak at the Arnott's church in Toronto. The Holy Spirit fell with strange laughter and Larry went away angry, thinking that the people had gone mad. A few weeks later Randy Clark visited, and the Toronto Blessing broke out. "The Lord fell powerfully," and the meetings continued indefinitely.

1994 - 2000

The Toronto Blessing Outpouring

- In a year the movement had spread globally, as many 'dry' Christians sought to experience "more" of God
- First such outpouring spread via the Internet
- Criticism due to the unusual manifestations that were common
- Personal experience, Father's Day 1994, Friday Fire - only good fruit
- Directly responsible for the spiritual hunger that followed - Pensacola, Heidi Baker, Todd Bentley, Lakeland Revival
- Recent estimates are more salvations as a direct result of Toronto than the whole of the rest of Church History put together - mostly in the Third World, as the Evangelical Western Church opposed it and the Pentecostals largely ignored it
- By Oct 1995, it was clear that the 'wave' was receding - Next Wave Visions

25

The Toronto Blessing

It sounds ridiculous to say, but there are many faithful Christians attending church every week who have never heard of the Toronto Blessing, and are totally ignorant of the amazing work the Holy Spirit has done around the world as a direct result. The Internet Pharisees continue to loudly denounce the movement, using emotive accusations such as "heretical", "false", "New Age", "subjective" and "experience-based." Their criticisms ignore the wealth of church history, which is littered with similar manifestations throughout, though not often so many happening all at once. Quakers, Methodists, Moravians… Even Baptists and more recently Pentecostals have all had odd manifestations of the Holy Spirit at some point. The Great Awakening experienced by Jonathan Edwards and his compatriots in the 1750s was accompanied by many of the unusual manifestations that were later observed in Toronto, as were some of the meetings of John Wesley, though few had studied the history to any great extent.

The main argument against the outpouring is that the specific manifestations are not mentioned in scripture, and are therefore invalid. They fail to recognise that most of what we do in church is not mentioned in scripture. What human flesh does at moments when it is impacted powerfully by the Holy Spirit is not clearly spelled out, yet even in the Bible there are several mentions of people falling, crying out, speaking in tongues, or having visions, dreams and trances. Modern authors attempting to write these off as "New Age" are pushing a Cessationist barrow, and need to be pointed back to the Bible itself. If there is a false—it stands to reason there is also a real.

Jesus is quite clear that fruit is the only way to judge. The testimonies of changed lives that arose from the Toronto outpouring of 1994-1995 are numerous. One of the most unusual features of this outpouring was that it was transferable. Initially, John Arnott and Randy Clark held meetings every night for 6 weeks. After that, they realised they needed some time off, because God didn't seem to be stopping. As the news spread, people began to travel from all over to the tiny Vineyard Church. If a leader or elder of a congregation attended, and was impacted, they had authority to release it in their home church.

The outbreak quickly spread to England, and found a home in Holy Trinity Brompton. Huge crowds began to attend the services, resulting in long lines of people standing outside who hadn't been able to get in. They eventually had to sell tickets to services, just so that people didn't drive for hours, only to find out there was no room. The Revival that Paul Cain had prophesied in 1991 had arrived, and began to impact the English churches.

As with ANY move of God, it involved humans, so there was undeniably flesh involved (God seems to be OK with that). However, critics tend to accuse everything that occurred as being false and fleshly, and refuse to credit anything as being anointed by the Lord. The weirdness of the manifestations that some were experiencing was commented on by all. One man lay on the floor, blowing raspberries like a small child. When asked, he said the Lord was treating him like a father with a small baby, blowing raspberries on his tummy. It was deeply significant to him as an individual, not so much to the casual observer. Another man was crowing like a rooster—"it's the dawn of a new day," he cried when asked.

Church Historian Guy Chevreau became involved early on, and taught about the similarities of the manifestations that were occurring in 1994 with what had happened during the Great Awakening. Jonathan Edwards had read out his notes in the sermon *"Sinners in the Hands of an Angry God,"* and a great movement of repentance had swept the nation. What is not so widely known is that there were many reports of people falling under the presence of God, or laughing, weeping and so on. Edwards' own wife kept a diary for a few weeks—she would "fall out" at the mere mention of the name of Jesus. After grace one Sunday lunch she was found face-first in the mashed potatoes. Another time Edwards was ministering to some people in the parlour, and mentioned the name of Jesus. There was a loud thump on the wooden floor in the hall outside—his wife had been walking past at that moment and was slain in the Spirit in the hallway. She wrote in her diary about being overwhelmed by the joy of the Lord in the early hours of the morning so that she could barely keep from crying out loud.

The common testimony of ministers who attended Toronto was they were feeling dry and barren, desperate for God to inject new life into their lives and congregations. After visiting Toronto, they were renewed and encouraged, and they saw God impacting individuals again.

Many books have been written on the Toronto Blessing and its flow-on effects. My personal involvement happened on Mother's Day 1994, when my parents visited the Airport Church (once again, I was left behind…). They were told they were the first Australian pastors to visit (no idea if that is accurate) and were called up the front for prayer to release the Blessing in Australia. They had planned to go on to England after Canada, and visit

Holy Trinity Brompton and several friends, so they didn't arrive back in Sydney until October.

By the time they got back, several other ministers from Sydney had made their own visits. Greg Beech from Randwick Baptist and Brian Houston from Hillsong among them. They all arrived back in Sydney within a 7-day period.

I remember Dad coming to our Home Group meeting to share what he had experienced. He told strange stories of the unusual manifestations, and the ministry team playing like little kids in the presence of God. I asked him what happened to him when he got prayed for, and he said, "Not much. I just fold over in the middle. I can't stand straight."

A week or so later we went to visit the Seeker Service at Hillsong, held AFTER the regular night meeting (which I felt was wrong at the time. I believed that giving place to whatever the Lord was doing was more important than the regular program). Brian was talking about his own experience and asked the Holy Spirit to come and do what He wanted. As we waited, wondering what to expect, I felt the Holy Spirit descend through the room. I was in the row behind Dad, and suddenly noticed him fold over like he'd been punched in the middle. Not much else seemed to be happening, and I felt the anointing on my hands, so I said to Rob Holmes next to me, "Let's get him."

We both began to pray quietly for Dad from behind, "More Lord. Just bless him." He suddenly jerked like he'd been hit with a shock and folded onto the floor between the seats. I looked at Rob, and nodded towards Mum, waiting with her eyes closed. She went down soon after, so we kept going along the row. Brian was wandering around reporting on different things the Lord was doing around the room. "There's an Anglican Minister on the floor down here," he told the audience.

At a Kevin Prosch Concert at Brookvale Christian City Church Dad shared about Toronto, and a number of people wanted to know more, so a Wednesday morning meeting was arranged a Northbridge for pastors and lay people. It was a relatively small group, but the Holy Spirit moved powerfully, and one lady had to be helped out because she was 'drunk in the Spirit', or overwhelmed by the presence of God. Dad felt that he needed to host a regular meeting for those who wanted to know more, called Friday Fire. The initial one was set for a Friday night, December 8th, 1994. I was in the habit of getting up early for a quiet time before I had to go teach, and that morning the Lord spoke to me from Ezekiel 37—the Valley of Dry Bones. He put on my heart that what we were seeing was the beginning of the prophetic sequence—the "rattling sound" of the bones coming together. There was certainly a lot of "noise" associated with the Toronto move, and the pastors were all commenting on how dry they had been feeling. The "tendons" were the relationships the Lord was forming between ministers from different parts of the body. I knew the "flesh" represented the maturing of what was happening, and understood that would take time.

I asked Dad and shared it that night at the meeting. In our tiny congregation of about 45 adults, if you were on the music team, you were on the ministry team. There were several prophetic words spoken through the evening, and I ended up collating them all into a summary sheet that we gave away each time. After Dad finished sharing, we invited people up the front for prayer. When numbers quickly overflowed the church building, we had to move to our church Hall, which comfortably seated around 200.

People kept coming, and we ended up with a full house. After Dad had finished sharing, he invited people to come to the front for prayer. We went around praying in the Vineyard fashion we were familiar with, and God began to touch people. Every person was different. Some would laugh, some would cry, some would shake, or fall. I found that I would be led to pray certain things over people that were prophetic—secrets of their hearts stuff. Several asked me "how did you know?" I really didn't—it just felt right to say that at the time.

We saw people's lives being put back together as we prayed for hundreds of people we'd never met till early the next morning. Dad had announced another meeting for January 20th in the New Year.

In January, 1995, we had about 450 people present—some were standing around the edges till after midnight waiting for prayer. We had managed to find some pieces of carpet to cover the wooden floorboards of the 'ministry area' at the front. Late in the evening I had a bit of a break from ministry as the crowd was thinning. There was a white-haired man with glasses sitting with folded arms in the second row, watching closely everything that was happening, but he hadn't come up himself. The Hall floor was littered with people who were just resting in the presence of the Father, "letting God be God."

"You should get some prayer," I encouraged him, but he glared at me, and I thought I may have offended him. Around 1:30am I was talking with Dad at the front and he appeared at my shoulder.

"I think I do need some prayer," he said, "but I can't get too much. I have to drive back to Maitland tonight (about 3 hours North of Sydney).

"No worries," I said. "Let's just see what God wants to do." He closed his eyes and I just asked the Lord to come and do what He wanted. The man crashed to the carpet, face-first. His glasses fell off, and he began to sob. He spent the next half hour praying out loud—"They keep saying things about me, Lord, but You know I'm not like that," and banging his fists on the floor. His wife came up, and said, "Oh this is good. He really needed this." He went on for about half an hour and I went to others waiting for prayer (this is around 2am!).

I went past him banging and complaining and the Lord 'nudged me.' "Lord give him peace," I asked, touching him lightly on the back. It was like an electric sock hit him. He convulsed off the floor, flipped over onto his back, crashed back down, and sighed in relief. The Lord spent the next half hour putting him back together.

We finally helped him to his car around 2:30am! A few weeks later this man came back with a busload of youth from his church in the Hunter Valley. He was full of excitement, and shared about the amazing things the Lord had done in his home town when he went back. He was the youth pastor and had been sorely wounded by people opposing him and speaking against him. After the January meeting, he went back and shared with the young people what God had done in him, and they all wanted prayer. They were so impacted they were praying for their friends in the McDonald's carpark, and they were getting saved. The youth group exploded, and many lives were changed.

A few weeks later, Dad asked a Baptist pastor to share, who had just come back from Toronto himself. He had opposed the movement, but gone to safeguard a number from his church who were keen to go, and while he was there God blasted him. As he was starting to speak, a Holy Ghost bomb hit the front few rows. A big guy called Pete who was there every fortnight cried out in surprise and hit the floor, taking out chairs all around. Pretty much the front quadrant all hit the ground, laughing crying and so on. The Baptist pastor leaned on the lectern, and said:

"You know. A few weeks ago, this would have really bothered me. I felt that the most important thing about meeting together was the preaching of the word, and nothing should disrupt that. I've come to learn that what God is doing one-on-one with these people is far more significant than anything I have to say. My lot do this to me each week now. So, I'll just talk to those of you who are still conscious, and we'll leave these ones to God."

In the meantime, the Friday Fire Prophecies sheets were passed around across the country, unbeknown to us. So many people were saying they were thirsty for more of God, but the vocal critics were increasing, and loudly denouncing everything as deception. Suddenly, two new ad campaigns hit the TV screens: Sprite Lemonade—"Style is Nothing. Thirst is Everything. Obey Your Thirst!" and Nike "Just Do It!"

At the time, Australia was experiencing the worst drought in years, and it was dominating every news report. By April 1995, we had noticed a trickle of country folk driving long hours to Sydney for the meetings, just to see what God was doing. During the Royal Easter Show, many more were there for the Show. I had been feeling all week we should call them up to the front and pray for the drought. Rob Holmes showed up with a Word about Spring Rains, and Dad said "Let's do that."

A 6 am the next morning the phone went off. My groggy father listened to an overly excited farmer from Jerilderie (7 hours south west), who had gotten back to the hotel at 1:15 am and decided to check on the kids on the farm. "You won't believe what happened to us…," she began, when she was rudely interrupted. "Mum! Shut up and listen. It's raining, right now."

That night un-forecast rain fell right across New South Wales and broke the drought. Now, we knew we weren't the only ones praying, but we definitely **were** a little spooked. It's not often that we had seen prayers answered so dramatically, so quickly.

I have heard numerous accusations and criticisms made about the Toronto Blessing over the years, some truly weird, some valid. I can testify that I only ever saw good fruit. I witnessed lives changed by the love of the Father.

By October 1995, I was noticing that the power was waning. The raw power just wasn't as present as it had been a year before. I began to pray about this, asking the Lord in the context of Ezekiel 37, "You said it would continue, Lord. You said it would mature."

Over a two-week period, as I waited on the Lord, I had a series of visions (the only ones I've ever had). I first saw a picture of a huge roller of a wave out in the middle of the Pacific Ocean. I knew it was a Tidal Wave, and it was heading for Sydney. I began to "look", as the prophets said in the Bible, reflecting and praying about what I had seen. Was it a real wave, or spiritual?

A few nights later I had another picture: A man and a woman wearing brown robes like monks, which I understood as representing "doing ministry". They were on the beach, looking down at their feet, which were barely damp.

"What's going on?" they were asking. "We thought this would last. We thought it would get deeper (ie. more mature), but the tide's going out."

Again, I had several days of reflection and waiting, before I saw the third instalment. I saw the same picture, but this time as I looked it zoomed backwards, until the figures were tiny, still looking down at their feet. Poised above them, hanging, was an enormous Tidal Wave, ready to drop. It was bigger than a skyscraper compared to the figures on the beach, and was drawing up into itself all the water they were looking for, but they couldn't see it because they were looking down.

The final image a few days later saw the Wave drop. It fell vertically, and cut the beach from under the 'ministers'. They went from barely damp soles-of-the-feet to struggling to stay afloat instantly. The Lord spoke clearly into my heart: "Suddenly the Lord God whom you are seeking will come into His temple. The Next Wave will be as far beyond Toronto as Toronto was beyond anything you'd seen till then."

I believe we've been "fleshing out" the work of the Spirit in our lives and hearts ever since.

The Toronto Blessing continued to spread out over the next few years. It branched into new churches, where an outbreak would occur for several months, and then it would move on. It reached Adelaide in 1996, and the Lord moved us down there a year later. In the Toronto Airport Christian Fellowship, waves of new outpouring would continue, and birth new moves of God around the world.

Back in 1990, at the Sydney Wimber Conference, one of the teaching emphases all week was "God offends the mind to reveal the heart." Though not explicitly mentioned in Scripture in that way most of the Ways of God are NOT specifically stated in Scripture, it nevertheless can be clearly seen in the way God deals with people throughout the Bible narrative. He always expects us to trust and obey—even when the instruction seems weird. I believe many were offended by the Toronto Blessing, and rejected it because to their minds, the exotic manifestations were not "decently and in order." A Biblical principle is that you must receive a prophet AS a prophet to receive the prophet's reward (Matt: 10:41). Rightly discerning both the presence of the Holy Spirit and what He is doing is vital to know how to respond. We don't want to be like the city of Jerusalem, where Jesus *wept over it, saying, "If you had known in this day, even you, the things which make for peace! But now they have been hidden from your eyes. For the days will come upon you when your enemies will throw up a barricade against you, and surround you and hem you in on every side, and they will level you to the ground and your children within you, and they will not leave in you one stone upon another, because you did not recognise the time of your visitation"* (Luke 19:44).

As the Lord had shown Larry Randolph in 1987, the Toronto Blessing was just the precursor. It gave rise to the Brownsville Revival, The Mozambique Revival, and the Lakeland Healing Revival, which was broadcast around the world. More people have been saved as a direct result of the Toronto outpouring than in the whole of the rest of church history put together, though nearly all of these salvations have been in the third world, as the Western Church rejected the move of God—they again didn't recognise the time of their visitation, just like in the Voice of Healing Revival.

The relationships that formed between ministers across denominational boundaries (Ezekiel 37's 'tendons') are still present, and in many cases far stronger than those within the traditional groups. Many ministers still hunger for more of God than they are experiencing, and are well aware of the internal work that has taken place in their hearts in the decades since 1994.

The Critics and Internet Pharisees continue to denounce the movement. I would answer with this verse:

> *"Which of you, if his son asks for bread, will give him a stone? Or if he asks for a fish, will give him a snake? If you, then, though you are evil, know how to give good gifts to your children, how much more will your Father in heaven give good gifts to those who ask him!"* (Mt 7:9-11)

If people are genuinely asking their heavenly Father for more of himself, do you really think He would allow such gross deception?

1995

Early 1995 *Charlotte, North Carolina*

Rick Joyner begins having the Final Quest revelations

- The condensed version of *The Hordes of Hell are Marching* was published in *The MorningStar Prophetic Journal*.
- As Rick began to seek the Lord about the battle he had seen, the revelations continued, and grew in intensity.
- He would go to his cabin and sit in his armchair to spend time with the Lord, and thy would pick up where it had left off.
- There are now 5 books in the series.
- This is the book EVERY Christian should read.
- I believe we are living the first section NOW!

26

The Final Quest Visions

Around the mid 90s, Rick Joyner began having a series of ongoing dramatic prophetic experiences. Mike Bickle had made a habit of always asking Bob Jones, "Was it a dream? Was it a vision?" Bob would reply, "No it weren't no dream. I was THERE."

"I was there" had become a catchphrase to describe an experience so realistic that the subject couldn't tell whether or not they were in the spirit or actually translated. Rick would go up to his cabin to spend a day with the Lord, sit down in his armchair, and find himself back where it left off the week before.

He had initially shared the first part of the vision as "The Hordes of Hell Are Marching" in the Morningstar Prophetic Journal, and as he began asking the Lord about what he had seen, the revelations continued. He put the first section together as the book, *The Final Quest*, which I personally think is the book every Christian should read. I used to read it with my Yr. 9 Bible Class at the Christian school. The revelation highlights Biblical truths in an amazing way, and reveals the Lord's heart about a number of issues.

In the experience, Rick found himself moving through a progression of events. Beginning with the 'Hordes of Hell,' he was involved:

1. Battling the Demonic Army with the Army of God, then
2. Climbing the Mountain of the Lord to the top, where
3. He met with Jesus in his garden.
4. He returned to the Battle empowered and encouraged others to climb higher.
5. He was taken to a treasure room and given greater understanding of the triumphs of Jesus over the world in different areas.
6. Finally, he was taken to the Hall of the Judgement Seat of Christ, where Jesus' throne is made up of a large number of smaller thrones—those who have overcome the world to a degree where they will "rule and reign with Him". Most of those thrones are still empty! As he walked towards the throne, a number of people from the great cloud of witnesses stepped out to speak to him. What they told him is amazing. God's values are WAY different to ours.

Rick copped a lot of criticism for writing the vision in the way he did—he was told he would have offended fewer people if he'd claimed it was an analogy, or dream, like *Pilgrim's Progress*. He felt that God is a God of truth, and that he wanted the vision to be as raw as possible, with as little of himself as he possibly could manage.

Judge for yourself. Just read it!

There were initially three books: *The Final Quest*, *The Call*, and *The Torch and the Sword*, and then the visions stopped for nine years. In the early 2000s, they started again, and the second trilogy has two books so far: "*The Path*", and "*The Valley*".

Rick also kept publishing various revelations in the *Morningstar Prophetic Journal*. Two in particular are very relevant to events today: "Civil War in the Church" and "War and Glory". In 'Civil War' the Lord likened the situation in the Church at the time to the American Civil War. The people were being kept in bondage, and needed to be set free. I believe this is a warning to all leaders in ministry. The people belong to the Lord, not to our particular group. 'War and Glory' also mentioned the 'Civil War' being fought between parts of the Body, to the extent that millions of unsaved couldn't come and get help and salvation because of the War. The Lord sent a huge wave that washed the whole place clean, and then began to build His house from the people who were faithfully His in each group or movement.

You should find both on the Internet. Read and pray about them.

Since about 2005 we having been living through "The Hordes of Hell Are Marching." The violence of the attacks on the church, individual Christians and Christian marriages has been incredible. Every Christian I know says they have been through the worst trials they've ever experienced since around 2005.

But as I'm trying to show in this book. God has a plan. Stay firm to the end.

1995

June 18, 1995
Brownsville
Pensacola
Revival

- Characterised by widespread repentance and call to holiness
- Broke out Father's Day, 1995
- Various Prophetic heralds over the years, John Kilpatrick spent two years calling the church to pray for Revival
- Evangelist Steve Hill visited on Father's Day and a 'mighty wind' swept through the building, bringing widespread repentance
- By 1998, estimates of over 2.5 million people had visited the church. Nearly 200,000 people surrendered to Jesus
- Ended in 2000 when Steve Hill left to pursue other works.

27

The Brownsville Pensacola Revival

On Father's Day, 1995, missionary evangelist Steve Hill shared his testimony of being impacted by the Toronto Blessing at the Brownsville Assembly of God in Pensacola, Florida. Steve had been greatly influenced by Carlos Annacondia, who sparked the Argentine Revival of the 1980s, during his time in South America. He hungered for more of God, and visited Holy Trinity Brompton in England to investigate the Toronto Blessing. He was powerfully impacted, after being prayed for by Vicar Sandy Millar, and was keen to share his experience of the Lord.

In 1993, Pastor John Kilpatrick had called the Brownsville assembly to earnestly pray for Revival, and made this his focus for the next two years. He made corporate prayer for major issues a feature of every Sunday evening service. The power and presence of God at these intercessory meetings was so strong that attendance began to increase. The Assembly experienced a new appreciation for sharing Communion, and made it a meaningful part of their worship every week. The same year, Dr. David

Yonggi Cho, pastor of the world's largest church in Korea, was preaching in Seattle, Washington. He was asking the Lord if He would ever send revival to America. In a vision, he was told to get a map of America, and point his finger at the map. His finger was drawn to Pensacola, Florida, and the Lord told him revival would come to Pensacola "and it will spread like a fire until all of America has been consumed by it."

Shortly before the Father's Day outbreak, a pair of brothers from South Africa led a series of worship meetings, which many felt set the stage for what was about to break loose. The anointed worship led many into a powerful sense of the Lord's presence, and many people began to wonder what was going on in the spiritual realm.

When he finished sharing, Steve Hill asked people to come forward for prayer. Pastors later told of a "mighty wind" that swept through the auditorium.

"Over 1000 people came forward to pray that morning, and Kilpatrick stood on the platform praying with Hill and another man when he suddenly heard a sound like a "rushing mighty wind" sweep over his right shoulder. As Kilpatrick looked over his shoulder, he said his ankles slipped, his knees bowed out, and a sudden "river of the glory of God" moved between his legs. "It felt like a telephone pole," he said. "An endless telephone pole was coming through my legs and it was coming in the church." With some help from another man on the platform, Kilpatrick stepped back and listened to the sound of the "rushing mighty wind" and what he described as the "river of the glory of God" as it swept into the church. He suddenly jumped to the pulpit and screamed, "My God, church, get in! This is it! This is what we've been praying for! Get in!" (Costella 1997).

Daniel Norris explained, "The moment Pastor Kilpatrick spoke those words, the heavens above the church opened, and the Spirit of God filled the room. Whole groups of people began to be swept right off their feet.

From his vantage point on the stage, he saw people falling everywhere. John Kilpatrick had never seen nor personally experienced anything like it. Even he found it difficult to hold himself up as the weight of God's glory began to increase around him. He started to descend the steps once again, but instead collapsed hard to the floor. His head bounced on the marble floor of the stage. He would lay there for nearly four hours under the glory of God," (https://www.openheaven.com/2017/04/08/never-knew-steve-hill-brownsville-revival/).

John Kilpatrick reported, "Corporate businessmen in expensive suits kneel and weep uncontrollably as they repent of secret sins. Drug addicts and prostitutes fall to the floor on their faces beside them, to lie prostrate before God as they confess Jesus as Lord for the first time in their lives. Reserved elderly women and weary young mothers dance unashamedly before the Lord with joy. They have been forgiven. Young children see incredible visions of Jesus, their faces a picture of divine delight framed by slender arms raised heavenward."

The Holy Spirit's emphasis during the Brownsville outpouring was a deep conviction of sin leading to repentance. There were similar manifestations of the Spirit's presence to the broader Toronto Blessings, but fewer "exotic" or weird reactions. This made the movement much more acceptable to many Christians, who wanted to "rate" or compare the movements for validity. Sometimes we forget who is God—He can do whatever He chooses with people who are available. To judge ANY move of God by outward appearance is very dangerous. There can be many explanations for the differences seen in Brownsville to Toronto—maybe America needed one more than the other, which had a broader, international reach? Although there was an undeniable connection to the Toronto outpouring, the "manifestation" of the Holy Spirit carried a greater emphasis on holiness, and large numbers of people, especially youth, were being saved through their time there.

The Father's Day morning service didn't finish till 4pm, the evening service for over 5 and a half hours. Steve Hill was asked to stay on, and the church began to hold meetings 4 nights a week. Visitors began to flood towards Pensacola, coming from across the nation, and then around the world. Over the next decade, over 150,000 salvations were recorded, and between 3.5—4 million visitors attended the church.

Youth Pastor Richard Crisco was initially skeptical, and concerned that the intense emotional experiences would replace the fundamentals of the faith. He began to see plentiful evidence of the changed lives of his young people, who had a deep hunger for God and began seeking prayer meetings instead of the parties and recreational activities that had previously consumed their church lives.

The Brownsville Revival had a big impact on their home denomination. The Assemblies of God had been in decline, but began to report increases in conversions, baptisms, and missions giving, which reached an all-time high ($117 million).

It has been said "The Holy Spirit is easily quenched by pride, greed, selfish religious agendas, and broken relationships." There were a number of fleshly issues that arose amongst the leadership of the Brownsville Revival, as there has been in every move of God throughout history. Most historians saw a decline from 2000, when Steve Hill moved on, Michael Brown (who headed the Revival School of Ministry) was moved on, and in 2003 John Kilpatrick handed over the leadership of the church to pursue an Apostolic role.

My personal belief is that in all of these movements we see an initial purity, which degrades as the flesh nature creeps in. The Holy Spirit has laid seeds in ALL of these movements, which will come to fruition in the Next Wave/Coming Flood. The maturing process is still ongoing.

A common feature of all of these moves is a belief amongst the leaders that "this is IT. WE are the ones chosen." I believe there is an extent to which that is true at the time, but their hopes and understanding of what that entailed were polluted by ambition, lack of knowledge (Hosea 4:6), and a lack of humility. To be fair, I don't know ANY Christian leader who honestly hasn't had such thoughts at certain times—it's just that most haven't been in a situation where their errant interpretations get publicised around the world.

We need to be really faithful praying for leaders—especially those thrust into the public eye, whether we agree with them or not. More importantly, we need to shut our mouths, especially if we have a public platform. As Isaiah 58 says, we "cover the naked" with our prayers in the closet, not by "the pointing finger and malicious talk."

1996

April, 1996

Heidi Baker visits Toronto - Revival in Mozambique

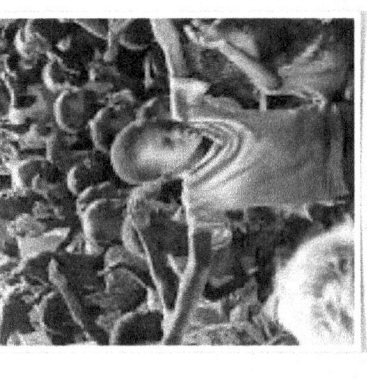

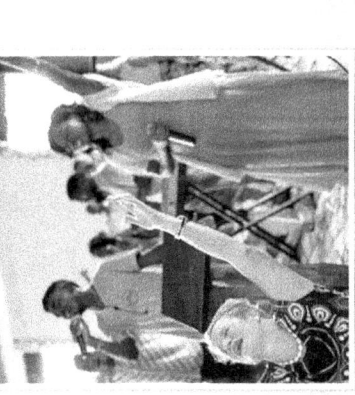

- Heidi and Rolland had been serving the Lord in Mozambique, battling a hostile government, rampant poverty and rescuing orphans.
- Heidi was hospitalised with TB and pneumonia. Burned-out.
- Rolland had just returned from Toronto, and the change in him was evident, so she wanted to go.
- Healed on the first night, and recipient of hours of gentle ministry, often unable to move.
- Jesus appears in a vision, showing her the thousands of needy, and says: "There is Always Enough, because I died.
- Food by the Truckload, pastors adopt orphans
- Food multiplication, villages saved

28

Heidi Baker visits Toronto

In 1995, Missionaries Heidi and Rolland Baker got their long-awaited invitation to Mozambique. They had prayed for God to "send us to the poorest of the poor, to "the least of these," and for several years had been watching war-torn Mozambique, where 26 years of civil war had been replaced by banditry and drought. The illiterate, starving population were totally dependent on international aid—half of the children died before they were 5 years old. The wars, famine and disease had left nearly a million children orphaned. Heidi told of children 9 years old scavenging the rubbish dump or prostituting themselves to keep their baby brothers and sisters alive.

The Bakers had lived by faith for years, trusting God to provide for their small family, and had no idea how they were going to meet the needs that were so apparent every day. But God opened doors, and they began to collect children, often from the rubbish dump. By November they had 160 street children, most of whom had accepted Jesus. They repaired a bakery and began baking hundreds of loaves a day, both to feed the children and for sale. By December 1996 they had 300 children, providing food, medical care, and love for the unwanted of the world.

The town they were in was being renewed, as prayer and deliverance began to rule over the witchcraft and abuse that had prevailed. But the eighteen-hour days and battles with corrupt government officials was wearing Heidi out. She was diagnosed with pneumonia and doctor feared she had tuberculosis as well. She was totally exhausted, and had hear several reports of what God was doing in Toronto, Canada. Several friends were urging her to go there, and Rolland had just returned himself, having been dramatically impacted by the experience. Heidi wrote that he was "full of faith and compassion, which made me want to get there all the more."

When she arrived in California, she was hospitalised again, and could barely breathe or walk. She longed for a simple, non-stressful job, "blue-light specials at K-Mart." She felt that after all her doctoral education she didn't know what to teach anymore.

When she arrived in Toronto, she was healed in the first session, and was able to breathe easily for the first time in weeks. She spent many hours being "soaked" in prayer by the ministry team, stuck to the floor under the heavy weight of the Lord's presence. She said she was carried out at the end of the day loaded into a car, driven to her hotel, dropped on the bed, and then carried back in to the carpet the next day.

One night she was groaning in prayer for the children of Mozambique, seeing the huge need, and crying out "No, Lord, there are too many!" Suddenly she had a clear visitation with Jesus, who told her to feed them from His body, and give them a drink from the blood and water that flowed from his side. He told her, "There is always enough, because I died."

Heidi returned to Africa re-energised and full of faith, and the bottom fell out of their ministry. Within days the communist government revoked privileges, put all sorts of constraints on evangelising the children, and gave them 48 hours to evacuate the premises. They battled to find somewhere to put the children, but ended up with around 100 of the neediest children crammed into their little two-bedroom flat, with no food. A sister knocked at the door with a pot for Heidi and her family, blanched when she saw all the children, and turned to leave. "I need to go home and cook some more."

Heidi told her it was too late, and they'd have to pray. They dished out a full bowl to everyone present, and the Lord kept multiplying the food. Everyone had enough! The ministry grew and flourished, as the children's faith that their God would meet their needs was met time after time. Iris ministries now hosts students from around the world, and sees miracles all the time.

Recently, some personal friends went over to the base there, as they knew Rolland very well. They witnessed multiplication of food after church one morning, when a bigger crowd than expected showed up. They went with a team 10 hours into the bush where they had been invited to minister to a village. They showed the Jesus film, and prayed for the sick. When one of the Chief's wives was totally healed, the whole village lined up to accept Jesus.

No-one can be a pastor in their ministry who isn't willing to adopt orphans, and the blessings continue to flow, because they were faithful to go to the "least of these."

1999

19 September, 1999

24/7 Prayer begins at IHOP-KC

- KCF had practised 3 corporate prayer sessions per day from 1983, when Mike Bickle called the KC Churches to a "Solemn Assembly" of prayer and fasting. A prophetic word came to do "24/7 prayer in the spirit of the Tabernacle of David" - *Harp and Bowl*
- After establishing IHOP-KC on May 7, 1999, a humble and hungry group of young people who would cry out to God 13 hours a day. Four months later, they went 24/7
- When the two first met, Bob Jones told Mike Bickle that the Lord would use him to pastor a young adult movement of singers and musicians who would pray for Israel and have strong ties to Asia.
- Mike has always understood that we don't just decide to do this, God has to give the Grace to meet the demands of such a calling.

29

24/7 Prayer Begins at IHOP-KC

Mike Bickle had been aware of the eventual establishment of "night and day" prayer since his encounter with the Lord in Cairo in 1982. He had been careful over the years at Kansas City Fellowship not to get ahead of the grace God was giving them. Nevertheless, they maintained 3 corporate prayer meetings each day for around 15 years.

One of the things the Lord had taught them over the years was what is now known as the "Harp and Bowl" model, which is taken from Revelation:

"Now when [Jesus] had taken the scroll, the four living creatures and the twenty-four elders fell down before the Lamb, each having a harp, and golden bowls full of incense, which are the prayers of the saints," (Revelation 5:8).

Mike said, "Thank God for the musicians." Corporate prayer meetings can be deathly boring, as nearly every church has experienced at some point. Mike was originally told by the Lord that their prayer would be "in the spirit of the Tabernacle of David." (David had pitched a tent in

Jerusalem, [1 Chron 16:1,2] but it was the 'tabernacle of the tent', the 'Tent of Meeting.' [1Chron 6:32] It is never called the 'Tabernacle of David,' and it was a temporary arrangement until Solomon built the Temple, set up according to Moses' directions. The 'Tabernacle of the Lord' remained in Gibeon [1Chron 16:39; 21:29]).

Most Christians these days have at least some knowledge that David's tabernacle "broke the rules" that Moses had established. There was no veil (mentioned) separating the people from the presence of the Lord (represented by the Ark of the Covenant), but they were 'covered' by continuous prayer and worship. David had teams of musicians and singers who would worship continuously before the Ark. Amos 9:11 says:

> *"In that day I will restore David's fallen tent.*
> *I will repair its broken places, restore its ruins, and build*
> *it as it used to be…"*

In May of 1999, International House of Prayer began in a couple of donated trailers. At first, the team were spending 13 hours a day worshiping and interceding in the presence of the Lord. In September, they were able to go full-time, as people moved to join the team and caught the vision of a sacrificial prayer life.

Over the last 20 years, IHOP-KC has trained over 20,000 people, many of whom have returned to their home churches and started their own intercessory groups. The worship ministry has been very influential—cross-pollinating with Bethel, Morningstar and other ministries. The 24/7 prayer room is now live-streamed over the internet, and people around the world can tune in and participate.

Not only was this a fulfilment of the vision that God had given Mike may years ago, it has spawned an undercurrent of prayer groups around the world, interceding for the body of Christ and seeking to "gaze upon the beauty of the Lord".

From the IHOP-KC website:

"Jesus' infinite beauty is enough to warrant extravagant and continual worship. Upon this reality, the angels, elders, and creatures in the throne room never ceased to worship (Rev. 4, 5). Our 24/7 sanctuary serves to reflect that continual worship on earth as it is in heaven. The concept of the prayer room is also modelled after the tabernacle of David where 4,000 musicians and 288 singers were employed to minister to the Lord night and day (my MTh father points out these numbers specifically refer to the bringing of the Ark to Jerusalem. The actual numbers in the ongoing worship teams are not spelled out in Scripture).

> Here are 5 reasons why IHOPKC is committed to keeping a 24/7 sanctuary:
>
> To minister to God in adoration as response to greater revelation of His beauty.
>
> To sit at His feet like Mary as an offering of love, extravagant worship, and meditation on His Word.
>
> To encounter God to receive greater grace to love and obey Him with all our heart.
>
> To intercede to release God's power to win the lost, revive and strengthen the Church, and impact every sphere of society.
>
> To participate in the Spirit's emphasis on raising up prayer and worship across the nations.

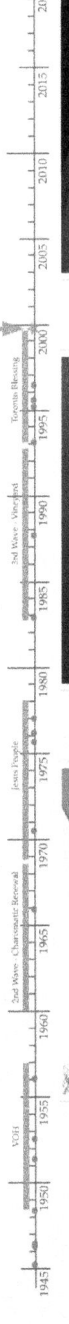

1999

Bethel Church launches Jesus Culture

- In 1994, Bill Johnson visit Toronto - made the promise to God that he would make "the outpouring of the Holy Spirit" the sole purpose of his existence.
- 1995 - Invited to succeed his father as Senior Pastor of Bethel Assembly
- 1999 - Youth Pastor Banning Liebscher organises the first Jesus Culture Youth Conference
- 2005 - Unanimous vote to separate from the AG to create a network and be catalysts for revival

30

Bethel Church and Jesus Culture

In February, 1980, Bob Jones had an angel appear, telling him the Lord was going to visit him on July 3rd. Bob eagerly waited for the date to arrive, but nothing happened. Each year, he would wonder if this was the year. In July 1981, he had a vision of three Eagles' nests with 1000 baby eagles in each one. He was told the Lord would anoint youth in three cities: Reading (California), Albany (Oregon), and Kelowna (Canada), and he would institute a move of God "in the land of the chickadee." Bob was told he was not to accept invitations to these three cities until the Lord gave him permission.

In February, 1984, the same angel appeared to Bob: "This is the year," and told him to get ready. Bob could scarcely wait for July to come around. He worked on a list of questions to ask the Lord, then finally thought, "if I only have limited time with Him, I don't want to waste it. I want to hear what He has to say," and threw the list away.

On the night of July 3rd, Bob had difficulty falling asleep. He finally dropped off, and it seemed like straight away the Lord Jesus walked in the room. "My dear friend. I've been waiting for this for so long."

"**You** have?" Bob thought sarcastically.

The Lord went on: "I want you to pray to me while I'm standing in front of you, and I'm going to tell you what to pray. These are the three most important prayers for the church at this time:"

1. Psalm 12:1 – "**Help Lord. Raise up the Dread Champions, the champions of Righteousness**." The Lord said, "I'm going to touch 35 international Apostles" – Bob saw them come and carry the glory of God on their shoulders. They will restore Godly government to the church.
2. "**Help my Unbelief**". Bob said we need to ask for more faith. The weakest Faith is for finances to do the work of the Kingdom. He was told to pray for 100x what we are currently asking for. The Lord then prophesied a million-dollar offering in one meeting as a sign. That was fulfilled at Kansas City in 1991 (my parents were in the meeting), where Terry Law was asking for help to get 1,000,000 Bibles into Russia after the Iron Curtain came down.
3. "**Give us Kingdom Power**". The angel had told Bob that a double rainbow over his house would be the sign that the Lord was going to visit him. A double rainbow represents individual anointing. 1st rainbow was corporate, the 2nd is for individual covenants with the Father. Jesus told Bob we need to get the mind of Christ on inventions, Real Estate, etc. He said "the sceptre of the wicked is no longer going to reign over the righteous."

On February 28th, 2001, the Lord visited Bob again. He drew three 500-mile circles around the three cities. "You've been avoiding them. Go now. I'm going to start a movement of which the Jesus Movement was just a token." Soon after Bob was invited to Kelowna Canada, to the Dunamis Conference with Wes Campbell.

God had already been working in those three cities in preparation. In 1994, Bill Johnson visited Toronto, to see what the Lord was doing, and Catch the Fire himself. He made the promise to God that he would make "the outpouring of the Holy Spirit" the sole purpose of his existence. The next year, he was invited to succeed his father as the Senior Pastor of Bethel Assembly, in Redding, California. Bill agreed with the stipulation that he would always be preaching about revival and God's empowering presence. The leadership agreed, though nearly 1000 people left the church in the early years.

In 1998, Bill and his associate pastor, Kris Vallotton, began the Bethel School of Supernatural Ministry, to train young people in walking with God throughout their lives. The next year, Youth Pastor Banning Liebscher led the first Jesus Culture Conference for youth, with the purpose of raising a generation to love and serve the Lord by discipling nations. The worship ministry particularly took off, and has become a globally-known youth movement in its own right.

Bill Johnson's leadership and oversight has seen the church grow and flourish, and become the "Eagles Nest" Bob Jones saw so many years before. In 1995, Bethel withdrew from the Assemblies of God denomination, feeling that their respective calls were moving in different directions. Bill is now an internationally recognised Christian Leader, and is regularly invited to speak all over the world.

Jesus Culture has energised young people in worship all over the world, through conferences, albums, and recently a church plant in Sacramento.

Bethel Church have become globally known in recent decades and have become a favourite target for the Internet Pharisees. Their worship music is popular around the globe, and Bill Johnson's sermons have blessed many, though the criticisms of their opponents are very vocal. I recently had a minister tell me: "We will not use any Bethel songs because I disagree with their Church's theology." So, the validity of the worship is now subject to theological interpretations?

One particular accusation leveled at the church was the furore over "grave-sucking" - the name coined for those who would lie on a grave to gain a measure of anointing from the deceased. This apparently occurred at Bethel through a few overzealous students, whom the pastors then moved to correct, but many have been led astray by the accusations of witchcraft practices and the like.

To be clear, anointing ONLY comes from the Lord, through the Holy Spirit. If you need more, go to Him. I do know of ministers who were told by the Lord to visit this place or that grave, because the Lord wanted to teach them or impart something connected with that minister to them. We need to follow the Lord's warning to "be careful how you judge" (Matt 7).

Personally, I have been blessed by many of Bill Johnson's sermons over the years. God has used him to help me through some difficult times, which is sort of the point of the Body of Christ.

2000

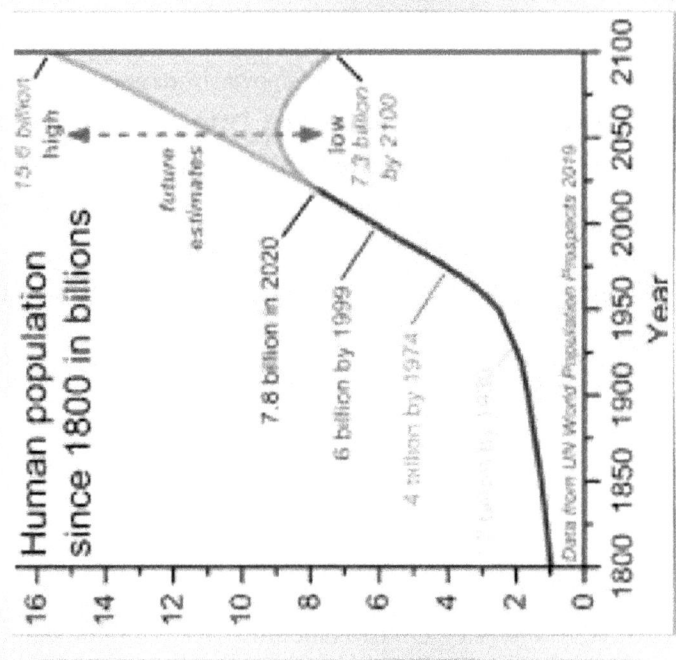

World Population Reaches 6 Billion

- Population reaches 6 Billion just before the Millennium
- Y2K proves fake news
- Death Toll from AIDS reaches 5 million
- Shepherd's Rod - The Lord's priority is YOUTH (GOTR)
- Over half of the world's population are under 18, poor, and in the nations….

31

The Millennium

Just before the Year 2000 Millennium, the world population reached 6 Billion people, as Jesus had told Bob Jones in 1975. The world at the time was consumed with fear over "the Millennium Bug", an hypothesised flaw in Microsoft systems which only used two characters for dates. Since much of the business world ran on Windows software, the fear was that computers all over the globe would crash on January 1st, causing massive chaos to Western society.

The Y2K bug proved to be a massive dud, but emphasised a recent warning from Bob Jones and others that the enemy's strategy was now focused on releasing fear into men's hearts. Since then, we have had a never-ending succession of "panic" news stories, from virus outbreaks, to bush fires, floods, hurricanes, the Twin Towers on 9/11 (September 9, 2001), the Second Gulf War, Afghanistan (again), and Climate Change. The news reports seem to go from extreme to extreme with no gap in between.

Also, at the turn of the Millennium, the death toll from AIDS reached 5 million people, which wasn't big news.

For almost a decade, Bob Jones had been publishing "The Shepherd's Rod"—a prophetic message he and others would receive each year on the Jewish Day of Atonement concerning the next 12 months. Many of these are online and can be ticked off by comparing with the news stories of the day. In 2000, the Lord told Bob his priority was YOUTH.

At the time, over half of the world's population was under 18, poor, and in the nations (NOT the Western world).

2001

May, 2001
The Postman's Letter - Dunamis Conference

- July, 1981 - Bob Jones has vision of three Eagles Nests - not to visit those cities. 1000 baby Eagles in those cities
- Feb 29, 2001 - Lord draws 500-mile circles around Albany, OR, Kelowna, Canada and Redding, CA. "Go now. I'm going to start a movement for which the Jesus movement was just a token."
- Soon after Bob finally accepts Wes Campbell's invitation to Kelowna.
- Jesus tells him to prophesy *The Postman*.
  - Dry bones
  - No Government
  - Colour-blind youth come from everywhere to deliver the messages. They refuse to stop even if they're being killed. Their faith restores (God's Apostolic) Government
  - Lord said: "Youth in the US are looking for something to die for. I'm going to give them something to live for – reveal myself to them. They're going to run with my message, starting within the three circles. This is my priority!"
- Lord is seeking Post Offices (churches) from which the youth can operate
- NB: Mail always has priority (right-of-way) in the US

32

The Postman's Letter

As mentioned before, Bob Jones had been told not to visit the three cities from his 1991 vision until the Lord told him. In February, 1991, the angel appeared to him and told him he was "to prophesy a movie you saw recently," Kevin Costner's *The Postman*, and it was time to start accepting invitations. Not long after Wes Campbell tried again to invite Bob to Kelowna, Canada, to the Dunamis Conference he was planning for mid-year.

Wes and his wife Stacey are the senior pastors of New Life Church in Kelowna, and founders of RevivalNOW! Ministries (www.revivalnow.com) and "Be A Hero" (www.beahero.org). Wes is a gifted teacher and is passionate about teaching people to "pray the bible"—turning the Bible passages into prayer to the Father. The Be A Hero mission organisation is committed to sending 100% of money raised to meet the needs of orphans around the world. Stacey has founded the Shiloh Company, which aims to mentor prophetic people in growing in character as well as gifting.

THE POSTMAN'S LETTER

During the 2001 Conference, Wes interviewed Bob Jones, prompting Bob to share significant revelations the Lord had given him over the years. The message was called *The Postman's Letter*, and is available online. Bob told many of the stories I've mentioned so far, and then spoke about the movie *The Postman*, which the Lord had told him to prophesy, particularly concerning the youth.

The Postman is a post-apocalyptic tale of a broken society. A drifter crawls into a crashed mail van in a storm, and takes the dead man's clothes, as they are better than his own rags. He starts reading the letters strewn over the back of the van, and realises he can benefit from delivering the mail. He approaches the next walled town wearing the uniform, and claiming that a government has been re-established, and the first priority is re-establishing communication through the mail.

The lie takes on a life of its own, but the vision of a government energises the youth, who stream to the Postman to join his new Postal Service. The local warlord starts to kill them as the vision challenges his own claim to authority, but they refuse to be stopped. In one iconic scene, the Postman gallops along the road to snatch a letter from the hand of a small boy, who wanted it delivered. The Postman admits his original lie, in an effort to preserve the young people's lives, but the youth won't be stopped, and in the fullness of time, a new government is formed, to bring the country back into unity.

Bob was told to prophesy this as an image of the re-establishment of God's Apostolic government being set up for the church. There has been much criticism over the use of the word Apostolic over the years, not just from Cessationists who claim that time has passed—even though Eph 4:11 says clearly "...**until** *we all reach unity in the faith and in the knowledge of the son of God.*" Much of the criticism is partially valid—few of those claiming the title have been commissioned by the Lord, though many have been called—they're just not there yet. Premature inheritance can be deadly, as King David knew. True Apostles ARE coming back, we're just not there yet.

Bob spoke about the youth being "colour-blind"—meaning they had no prejudice concerning people's skin colour. They were delivering the messages from the Father. The Lord told Bob, "Youth in the US are looking for something to die for. I'm going to give them something to live for. I will reveal myself to them. They're going to run with My message, starting with the three circles (He'd had Bob draw on the map around the three cities). This is my priority."

Bob said the Lord was looking for Post Offices (churches) from which these young people could operate. Churches who would dedicate themselves to teach young people to hear God for themselves, and disciple them to grow in character and wisdom.

The final scene of the movie is the dedication of a statue of the Postman, by his daughter. The scene of him snatching the letter from the hand of the small boy at full gallop was immortalized in bronze, with the dates of his life etched below.

He was (in the movie) born in 1973—the year Bob always identified as being the release of God's Deliverers!

Bob finished the message sharing a panoramic vision of the end times. He saw the general move of the Holy Spirit over each decade up to 2050. So far, it's been accurate.

2008

April - Oct. 2008

The Florida Healing Outpouring - Lakeland Revival

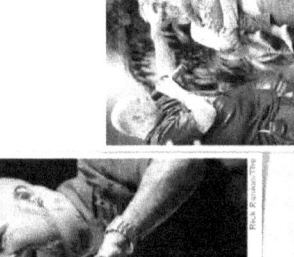

- In May, Todd Bentley of Fresh Fire Ministries began holding meetings to Ignited Church in Lakeland, Fla (the SAME church where RHB had seen a pre-Toronto outbreak). What began as a few days of meetings became four months of twice-daily meetings that were aired around the world by GOD-TV and streamed on the internet as God moved with signs and wonders.
- By May 29, Bentley's ministry estimated that over 140,000 people from over 40 nations had visited, and 1.2 million had watched via the Internet. By June 30, over 400,000 people from over 100 nations had attended.
- In August, Todd "burned out", and everything fell apart - including his marriage, ministry, etc. He then went through an extended restoration with Rick Joyner, who said God told him to: "restore the fallen brother gently…"
- *"To those who were blessed in Lakeland, do not allow the seeds of hope and healing that were sown into you there be uprooted by this leader's mistakes. It was God who touched you and no one can take that away unless you allow it. I am aware that the devil wants to tempt some people to say, 'I told you so.' Do not allow yourself to become his instrument by using the sword of truth without mercy this way. Before you cast a stone, remember that you are not without sin yourself. This is how pride can gain a subtle hold in your heart. What you sow now, you will reap in the future."* (John Arnott)

33

Todd Bentley and The Florida Healing Outpouring

2006 was the Jubilee (50 year) anniversary of William Branham's 1956 prophecy that the Healing Revival was being taken away by the Lord. The Biblical Jubilee year signified a release of captives, restoration and celebration. Many Christians I know began to go through the worst challenges of their lives from around this time, which I believe was the Enemy reacting to what he knows God is about to do. My own life really fell apart from this year.

It was at the end of 2006, after an horrific year of intimidation and bullying, I met Raf Shaw, who I had heard could hear the Lord in an extraordinary way. Not long after, the Lord told Raf to "get up near the Hospital (Flinders Medical Centre in Adelaide) and start healing people." In April, 2007, we started the Ancient Wells Healing Rooms, where anyone could drop in and receive ministry.

I now believe the 50-year Jubilee signified a major re-emphasis of the Holy Spirit on the ministry of Healing. This is not to denigrate the huge impact of the Third Wave, Toronto Blessing and so on in raising the awareness of the church that God still heals, and encouraging them to pursue this, but simply that something changed around that time. We have seen great fruit in Adelaide over the years, but the biggest global event was the Florida Healing Outpouring of 2008.

Todd Bentley was saved from a very dark past, and radically transformed to seek Jesus. He was launched into ministry by several supernatural words, and was soon leading major evangelistic and healing campaigns around the world. In the third world, he would see incredible miracles that rivalled the tales from the 50s, but the conferences in the Western world just didn't see the same results.

We had the opportunity to go to Queensland in 2007 to a conference on the Gold Coast. Raf was with us, ministering in a friend's church at the same time. All week I was wondering at the difference between what we were seeing in the Conference, which was no different to what we saw in Adelaide, and the reports from Africa, India and so on. On the Sunday night we were sitting around at Tumbulgum, NSW, on the hotel balcony, and I mentioned this to Raf.

"Oh I know that," he responded. "The Lord told me this week: *Marketing undermines your spiritual authority—it cuts across the anointing.* From now on we're not selling anything—we'll give it away if we have to." Immediately I had a 'download' of understanding from the Lord. Todd would pay for everything in the Third World, but would campaign around the western Church "flogging the till" (Raf's phrase) to raise money for his next campaign overseas, which was the ministry model he'd been taught and a common feature of the US scene. I knew it was the answer I'd been praying about all week. Pray it through yourself.

In 2008, after Todd's Fresh Fire Ministries had seen over a million souls saved around the world, Todd began a series of meeting in Lakeland,

Florida, where the Holy Spirit began to move again in a dramatic way. What started as a few days of meetings became a four-month-long outbreak of twice-daily meetings. People once again began to stream to Florida from all over the world, and GodTV began to stream the meeting free over the Internet. Every night there were testimonies of healings and some miracles.

It was a time of great excitement, and Todd a figure of great controversy. He was bold, showy, tattooed and confident that God would do what He said He would do. The Internet Pharisees had a field day—criticising the tattoos (what they're going to do when bikers start getting saved, I don't know), the showy style of Todd's stage presence, the teaching they felt was "unscriptural", and of course, the very fact that anyone would **dare** to believe that God still healed people.

Bob Jones and others had previously warned Todd about his workload, and urged him to adopt a more balanced lifestyle. Todd had recently returned from an 18-month sabbatical, where he had been seeking the Lord, and working on his marriage, which had suffered from years of travelling and ministry.

By the end of May, it was estimated that 140,000 people from all over the nations had visited the revival, and 1.2 million had watched via the Internet. Meetings continued every night, with Todd himself ministering each time. By the end of June, estimates were 400,000 people from over 100 nations had been through the huge marquee.

In August, Todd "burned out", having ignored the wise advice of several senior men of God to spread the load. This was soon after a special commissioning service where a number of leaders laid hands on Todd and prophesied "a new supernatural strength will flow through this ministry. A new life force will penetrate this move of God. Government will be established to set things in their proper order. God will pour out a higher level of discernment to distinguish truth from error. New relationships will surface to open the gates to the future." A few weeks later, Todd was exhausted. His marriage fell apart, both parties were tired of trying. The Internet Pharisees rejoiced, feeling vindicated in their criticisms.

There were accusations of adultery, which were untrue, though a heart relationship **had** formed with one of his interns. Todd retreated into depression, stepped away from the ministry, and especially from the attention of the Christian media. God spoke to Rick Joyner, and told him, "Brothers, if someone is caught in a sin, you who are spiritual should restore him gently" (Galatians 6:1). Rick brought Todd and his new wife Tessa to Morningstar, and began a period of restoration, ministering healing, teaching and correcting. They were very open throughout the process, posting regular updates on Todd's progress.

The wider Church was suffering after the revival fell apart, and many hopes and dreams seemed to be shattered. John Arnott, one of the leaders involved in the commissioning of Todd in July, posted:

"To those who were blessed in Lakeland, do not allow the seeds of hope and healing that were sown into you there be uprooted by this leader's mistakes. It was God who touched you and no one can take that away unless you allow it. I am aware that the devil wants to tempt some people to say, 'I told you so.' Do not allow yourself to become his instrument by using the sword of truth without mercy this way. Before you cast a stone, remember that you are not without sin yourself. This is how pride can gain a subtle hold in your heart. What you sow now, you will reap in the future."

Rick and Todd identified several "stumbling blocks" in Todd—many unhealed wounds from his abusive past, or simply lack of understanding about some Bible basics due to the suddenness of his conversion and launch into evangelistic ministry. After many years, Todd was released back into ministry, and has again stepped out into limited evangelistic work.

It is very easy to see error in others, and totally miss the massive faults we ourselves are not dealing with (through repentance and receiving forgiveness and healing). We need to be very careful, again, NOT to indulge in "the pointing finger and malicious talk." There are those who refuse to admit Todd can ever be used by God again, which is cruel, and patently un-Biblical. King David committed both murder and adultery, and God still used him, and kept him as King.

The prophetic words spoken over a person at any time are not nullified by a stumble, or a fall, only by lack of faith. God has a plan for each one of us, and NONE of us are free of sin. **ANY** sin in our hearts can give the devil a "foothold" from which to attack our lives, resulting in sickness (Acts 10:38), oppression and worse. I absolutely believe God will still use Todd Bentley in the future, and for all of us, **God saves the Best till Last** (John 2:10).

2014

14 Feb, 2014   *Charlotte, North Carolina*

Bob Jones Dies on Valentine's Day

- The man who's main message was "have you learned to love?" Passed away on Valentine's Day (lover's day)
- The last 12 hours of his life:
  - Snowing (rare in NC) - everything shuts down, chaos
  - He was prophesying over every visitor, despite dialysis, broken leg, slipping in and out of consciousness
  - 3 am on the 14th, hospital coordinator Don is in his office, exhausted. Hears the keypad on the outside of his door, and Bob runs in shouting in tongues. Don had avoided him because he was a conservative and scared of him.
  - "Don, get behind the desk, take notes."
  - Forgive these people…. You're getting bitter
  - Pages of messages for individuals - about 2 hours
  - Don noticed that Bob had blood on his arm. Was going to wipe blood away, but Bob said "Don't touch me. If you touch me you'll die - I haven't changed yet"
  - Don fell asleep at his desk, hears that Bob passed away at 6:22am. Has the papers on his desk. Went back to read the paper - written in a foreign script, except for a note about "don't touch me to you'll die"
  - Language was Ancient Aramaic - messages about this generation (GOTR) and what we are called to be. Linked to Daniel "seal up the words…."
  - AoC crossing Jordan river vision. Bob asks to help carry it. Jesus says: "No, it's not for your generation."
  - 300 Prophetic ministers invited to Trump White House

34

Bob Jones Dies on Valentine's Day

The attacks against Christians and the spiritual warfare throughout the world intensified over the next few years, as "The Hordes of Hell" began to be released. 2009 saw the election of the first African-American president, Barack Obama, who unfortunately oversaw the release of more wickedness into the earth than any preceding leader. In the eight years he was in office, the US went overboard in pursuing and legalising unrighteousness to an unprecedented degree, and much of what was "legalised" was in direct violation of the US Constitution!

Bob Jones continued to preach about the coming waves of revival Jesus had prophesied to him in 1975. As the West descended into deeper darkness, Bob was expecting God to release the First Wave of the Billion-Soul Harvest any day.

On Valentine's Day, 2014, the man whose main message was "have you learned to love" passed away, and went to be with his beloved Saviour. Bob was by this time widely recognised as a Prophetic Father, and in particular a Seer-prophet. Mike Bickle once said, "He's the most like Ezekiel of anyone we know in the earth." Everything with Bob was weirdly supernatural. Strange prophetic signs, angelic appearances, dreams and visions. Many ministers would tell of having a dream that troubled them, which they knew was from God, but couldn't fathom any understanding. They would call Bob, who'd already "seen it", and could interpret for them.

An Australian friend of ours was ministering in Charlotte a few years before this, and was driven every day past Bob's house to the meetings where he was speaking. Every different driver would point out, "That's Bob Jones' house. That's where the prophet lives." On the final day, he was heading to the airport to fly out, and yet another driver pointed out Bob's house.

"Can you pull over," he asked? "I think I need to go in there."

He sheepishly knocked on the door, and Bonnie Jones answered.

"I'm so sorry," he began. "I don't normally do this, but I think the Lord wants me to come in here."

"What kept you?" was her response. "He's been waiting for you all morning. You're late." Bob then gave our friend a word of encouragement from the Lord.

It needs to be said, again, that Bob was a man like us all. He had his own sin battles to overcome through the years, and he made some horror mistakes. None of us are perfect. We ALL need the saving grace of Jesus to cover our sin by His blood, and we ALL are **growing** to be like Him. **NONE** of us are there yet.

At 3 am on the 14th of February, the hospital coordinator, Don, was in his office, exhausted. He was aware that Bob Jones was in the hospital, but as an orthodox evangelical, Don was steering clear of the Prophet. He had been dealing with crises all day, and had finally fallen asleep on his desk. He suddenly awoke to the sound of the keypad on his office door being pressed. Only Don and his assistant had the code. Bob Jones opened the door and ran into the office shouting in tongues. At the time Bob was lying in a hospital bed with two broken legs.

Bob told Don, "Get behind the desk and start taking notes," and then began to instruct Don with messages for himself and others. "Forgive those people," he told Don, "You're getting bitter."

Don wrote pages of messages for about two hours, overwhelmed by the presence of God in the room. He noticed that Bob had blood on his arm, where the cannula would have been inserted, and went to wipe it away. Bob held up his hands, "Don't touch me. If you touch me, you'll die. I haven't changed yet." (That raises a few questions).

Don fell asleep again on his desk, and woke to find Bob had passed away at 6:22am. The pad on his desk was covered with pages of his handwriting, but in a language Don didn't understand. It was later found to be ancient Aramaic. There were many messages about the Generation of the Righteous and what they are called to be and to do, but they are "sealed for a time", as Daniel was instructed to do. Jeff Jansen has both a photo of Don's notes and is working on having them translated. The Lord led him to a man who recognised the text as an obscure dialect of ancient Aramaic, and it contains messages for a number of people.

Bob once had a vision where he saw the Ark of the Covenant, representing the presence of the Lord, being carried across the Jordan river. Bob asked the Lord, "can I help carry it?" but was told," No, it's not for your generation."

So, the man whose message was "Have you learned to love?" dies on Valentine's Day? With Bob Jones, **everything** was a prophetic sign.

2015

18 Feb, 2015

Place

John Paul Jackson Dies

- Jackson was diagnosed with cancer in May 2014 when doctors found a large growth in his leg that they identified as an aggressive form of cancer. The tumor was described as "nerf football sized" and weighed 12 pounds when it was removed through surgery.
- I wrote to him in 2014
- Nightmares 69 nights in a row - attacks of bees. Came under terror. Angel takes him outside the house - covered in bees. "Blow on it!" Whispering breath. "No, BLOW" - House cleared. The angel looked at me and said, "Never allow the enemy to do that to you again! The Spirit of the Living God will stop it if you will let Him come forth from you. Never stop the breath of God!"

35

John Paul Jackson Dies

In the Kansas City Prophets days, John Paul Jackson was recognised as having an amazing prophetic gift. Paul Cain once prophesied John Paul would "take over" his own leadership role in the prophetic when he eventually went to glory. John Paul ministered throughout the Vineyard network, pastoring a Vineyard fellowship for a while. He eventually was led to start Streams Ministries, teaching the church how to function in the prophetic, and particularly how to understand dreams and visions.

In 1997, I had an opportunity to hear John Paul speak, in the one visit he made to South Australia. I was going through an absolutely horror year, and was very discouraged and confused. A notice appeared in our church newsletter that John Paul would be ministering at another church over the next weekend. I spent that week telling anyone who would listen, "You need to be there."

Personally, I was desperate for a word from the Lord. I was so stressed by my work situation, that I would get worse every time I ran onto the Rugby field—I couldn't do anything right, and it was taking a physical toll as well as the spiritual and mental pressure. I spent the week begging God for something.

On the Friday night, we were in the audience, with a number of students from the Christian school, and a few from our home church. John Paul had planned a message for the night, but it was the evening after Princess Diana's funeral, and the Lord had impacted him with another message about the "Princess of Wails", and how the hearts and hopes of so many people had been broken.

When it came time for him to minister, he called us to stand first. My wife was pregnant with our second baby, and was again having spot bleeding—technically a "threatened miscarriage." My sister had some years before had a pregnancy terminated after the baby was found to have no brain, which can be fatal for the mother. John Paul told my wife of her fears of the same situation, and broke them off. The bleeding stopped that night. He then turned to me:

"…and the husband is a reluctant leader and a frustrated athlete…" The kids from school all snickered—the sight of my battered body limping into Monday morning Chemistry had become a class joke. The words John Paul spoke over me that night encouraged me through that particular time of trial, though also sparked some confusion. Although I determined to "lay down" my pursuit of sporting success, I ended up the Sports Coordinator of that school. Sometimes God's sense of humour is 'wicked'.

So, it was quite a shock to hear in 2014 that John Paul had been diagnosed with a "nerf football sized" tumour in his leg. The aggressive tumour was removed, and found to weigh 12 pounds (about 5.5 kg for those of us in the 'real world'). He shared through his email network some of the struggle he faced, as the cancer had spread. I had by this time been involved with the Healing Rooms for some years, and we had learned a few things. I had been asking the Lord what the root of the cancer was, and was told about a fear issue, which I shared with John Paul via email. He graciously wrote back that he felt I was right.

But it was not the "key" issue, and he died in February, 2015 (there's something about the month of February…).

One story that John Paul shared publicly was a period where he was attacked by the enemy with nightmares. For 69 nights in a row, his sleep was disturbed by visions of attacking bee swarms. He came under terror, afraid of falling asleep. On the 70th night, an angel came to him, and took him (in the spirit) outside the house. He saw that the whole house was covered in bees.

"Blow on it," the angel commanded, and he mustered a whispering breath.

"No, BLOW," the angel repeated, and John Paul sucked in his lungs and let rip, clearing all the bees of his house. The angel looked at him intently and said, "Never let the enemy do that to you again! The Spirit of the living God will stop it if you let Him come forth from you. Never stop the breath of God!"

John Paul understood that he had failed to use the authority God has given us to decree defeat to the enemy. Sometimes we just need to tell him to, "Back off Devil."

2015

Sep 5, 2015

Jeremiah Johnson's dream of the attack on the prophets

Greetings.

On September 5, 2015, I had a prophetic dream about Kim Clement that deeply troubled my spirit. Several days later, I read news online about how he suffered blood on the brain and was in critical condition at the hospital. Because I do not know Kim Clement personally or any of his associates, I reached out to several leaders in the body of Christ and shared what I had seen and heard because I was so disturbed. I have spent more than two months praying in silence for Kim and now after receiving news this week that he has been attacked again. I feel I must share publicly what God showed me several months ago. I want to be clear, my hope and desire in publishing this dream is to release clear strategy to intercessors that pray for Kim and also warn prophets that will face possible similar situations in the future.

The Dream

I walked into a large cave and as I turned the corner, there were four large principalities that were huddled together talking. They all wore different types of armor and did not notice my presence there as I stood behind a rock and watched them from around 100 feet away. As I listened to them, one of the principalities, which I knew was the Middle East, printed on his breast plate, stepped forward and said, "I want Kim Clement dead. He cannot keep prophesying about Iran and the Middle East." The principalities began to laugh and it sent a chill up my spine that I don't have words for immediately, that principally and 2 others left the cave.

There was one demonic principality that remained and it had, "Death" on its breastplate. As I focused my gaze toward it, it turned and looked at the cave wall behind its back. My eyes instantly fell on a list of names on the wall. Many of the names I did not recognize, but it was names of prophets specifically. One name I did recognize was John Paul Jackson. I said to the Lord in this dream, "Did John Paul Jackson die before his time? The Spirit said, "Yes". I then said, "Where is Bob Jones name on the wall?" The Spirit said to me, "Bob Jones did not die before his time."

As the Holy Spirit spoke these words to me, I instantly woke up in my room and it felt as if I was sitting in the presence of Jesus. I sat up in my bed and said, "Lord, are there really demonic principalities assigned to take out prophets?" He said, "Yes". I then received an open vision of John Paul Jackson's book, Needless Casualties of War.

The Spirit said to me, "This book must be read by all intercessors and prophets if they want to stay off the hit list. Kim has engaged in warfare in regards to Iran and the Middle East that I did not legislate and it must be renounced for the curse to be lifted."

Based off of this prophetic dream and vision as I woke up, I believe Kim Clement has been attacked by a demonic principality responsible for Iran and the Middle East and we as intercessors need to renounce any warfare that Kim might have engaged in that was not legislated from Above so that he may fully recover and live.

May God continue to grant us greater understanding into the rules of engagement when it comes to addressing demonic principalities and may his prophets and intercessors of the Most High God fulfill His purposes in their generation. Saints, we must have more informed and strategic prayer in this hour. Praying and standing with Kim.

Jeremiah Johnson

- John Paul Jackson was exposing Jezebel
- Kim Clement was interceding for the Middle East

- Read *"Needless Casualties of War"* - DO NOT War against Principalities unless the Lord authorises it!

37

36

The Attack on the Prophets

Over the last few years Jeremiah Johnson has become known as a prophetic voice. I recently became aware of the following dream he shared from 2015, which gives insight into some of what has been going on with prophetic leaders in the last decade.

> Greetings,
>
> On September 5, 2015, I had a prophetic dream about Kim Clement that deeply troubled my spirit. Several days later, I read news online about how he suffered blood on the brain and was in critical condition at the hospital. Because I do not know Kim Clement personally or any of his associates, I reached out to several leaders in the body of Christ and shared what I had seen and heard because I was so disturbed. I have spent more than two months praying in silence for Kim and now after receiving news this week that he has been attacked again, I feel I must share publicly what God showed me several months ago. I want to be clear, my hope

and desire in publishing this dream is to release clear strategy to intercessors that pray for Kim and also warn prophets that will face possible similar situations in the future.

The Dream

I walked into a large cave and as I turned the corner, there were four large principalities that were huddled together talking. They all wore different types of armour and did not notice my presence there as I stood behind a rock and watched them from around 100 feet away. As I listened to them, one of the principalities, who had "Iran and the Middle East" printed on its breast plate, stepped forward and said, "I want Kim Clement dead. He cannot keep prophesying about Iran and the Middle East." The principalities began to laugh and it sent a chill up my spine that I don't have words for. Immediately, that principality and 2 others left the cave.

There was one demonic principality that remained and it had, "Death" on its breastplate. As I focused my gaze toward it, it turned and looked at the cave wall behind its back. My eyes instantly fell on a list of names on the wall. Many of the names I did not recognise, but it was names of prophets specifically. One name I did recognise was John Paul Jackson. I said to the Lord in the dream, "Did John Paul Jackson die before his time? The Spirit said, "Yes". I then said, "Where is Bob Jones name on the wall?" The Spirit said to me, "Bob Jones did not die before his time."

As the Holy Spirit spoke that to me, I immediately woke up in my room and it felt as if I was sitting in the presence of Jesus. I sat up in my bed and said, "Lord, are there really demonic principalities assigned to take out prophets?" He said, "Yes". I then received an open vision of John Paul Jackson's book, Needless Casualties of War.

The Spirit said to me, "This book must be read by all intercessors and prophets if they want to stay off the hit list. Kim has engaged in warfare in regards to Iran and the Middle East that I did not legislate and it must be renounced for the curse to be lifted."

Based off of this prophetic dream and vision as I woke up, I believe Kim Clement has been attacked by a demonic principality responsible for Iran and the Middle East and we as intercessors need to renounce any warfare that Kim might have engaged in that was not legislated from Above so that he may fully recover and live.

May God continue to release understanding into the rules of engagement when it comes to addressing demonic principalities and may the prophets and intercessors of the Most High God fulfil His purposes in their generation. Saints, we must have more informed and strategic prayer in this hour.

Praying and standing with Kim,
Jeremiah Johnson

I believe the interpretation of this dream is self-evident. It gives some insight into John Paul Jackson's untimely death, and the "voiding" of prophetic words about him that were not fulfilled.

John Paul was told by the Lord to write "Needless Casualties of War." I tell our people it's one of the books they **need** to read. John Paul then wrote another book exposing a particular demonic principality in our society. Join the dots…

2016

23 Nov, 2016 Tulsa, Oklahoma

Kim Clement Dies

- In 2015 Kim suffered bleeding on the brain. Diagnosed with a malignant brain tumour.
- Removed successfully though it had already metastasized. He had a number of surgeries in the last 16 months.
- Hospitalized with pneumonia and complications due to his diseased lungs, and his body was just too weak to combat the illness.

37

Kim Clement Dies

Sadly, it seems that Jeremiah Johnson's warning did not make it through to Kim Clement, and he died soon after. Kim had come from South Africa and was a well-known worship leader, and a very accurate prophet.

In 2015, Kim suffered bleeding on the brain, and was diagnosed with a malignant brain tumour. It was successfully removed though it had already metastasised (spread through the body). He had a number of surgeries over the next few months, and was eventually hospitalised with pneumonia. His lungs were so compromised by the complications he was too weak to fight the disease, and died in November, 2016.

Jeremiah Johnson's revelation indicated that Kim had stepped out in spiritual warfare that God had not authorised. There has been a lot of teaching over the years about spiritual warfare and the authority of the believer that is simply wrong. Various people have put together doctrines from their limited understanding that are getting people killed.

Mike Bickle first talked about this back in the late 80s, and he said they learned a lot from Paul Cain. Paul would regularly be physically attacked in his bedroom by demonic beings, particularly if he spoke against certain issues publicly. He was adamant he would not "lead the church" to attack certain issues unless he had a mature body of praying men supporting him, and the Lord's permission, because the demonic counter attack was too much.

Mike remembered a troubling parable Jesus told of a King sending overtures of peace to his enemy, because he realised he wasn't strong enough to attack him at the time (Luke 14:32). Mike once had a lovely old lady come up to him at a conference to tell him her church was "fasting and praying to break the spirit of freemasonry over their city."

"Mike laughed and replied, "Oh that's wonderful. God is so gracious. He won't allow you to have any impact." The lady was very offended, and Mike had to explain.

"You don't understand. If you even drew the attention of some of those demonic principalities your church would cease to exist in a very short time. We don't have the faithful prayer support or unity to even consider attacking those principalities yet."

At the Healing Rooms we teach, you have authority over any demon that manifests around you, or that you discern is holding someone captive, to set people free. You don't move against demonic principalities over regions, cities or even governments and organisations without the Lord's permission.

Another relevant issue is that contrary to a lot of popular teaching, **every** illness has a demonic component. *"Jesus ... went about doing good and healing all who were oppressed by the devil, for God was with Him."* (Acts 10:38). If you need "healing", you are "oppressed by the devil."

Dis-ease is a lack of peace. Jesus is the Prince of Peace. If you can hear the Lord clearly about what the blockage is, or the sin that needs to be repented, you can set people free. The demonic foothold is broken by the blood of Jesus and the sickness **has** to leave.

What we have observed in the Healing Rooms is that most of us have a lot of "footholds", or "open doors" in our lives, and the devil will always look for another avenue of attack. He then gives the **same** disease, which undermines faith and causes the victim to think, "Oh, it didn't work." You need to keep showing up, and progressively deal with **all** the open doors in your heart, to see lasting freedom.

2019

12 Feb, 2019 *Santa Maria, California*

Paul Cain Dies

- **Paul Cain-Ministries - January 30, 2019**
- DEAR FRIENDS, HAVING SPENT OVER A WEEK IN HOSPITAL WITH DOUBLE PNEUMONIA AND HEART ISSUES I WANT TO EXPRESS MY SINCERE APPRECIATION FOR THE MANY WHO PRAYED FOR ME AND SENT MESSAGES OF ENCOURAGEMENT. GOD WILLING, I SHALL BE HOME TOMORROW. LAYING IN THE HOSPITAL BED WITH OXYGEN AND TUBES ATTACHED, AND FEELING SO DREADFUL, I NEVERTHELESS WAS MINDFUL OF MANY OF THE THINGS THAT GOD HAS REVEALED TO ME IN THE PAST, AND AM RESOLUTELY CONVINCED I WILL SEE THE GOODNESS OF THE LORD.
- FRESH BREATH IS COMING TO THE PROPHETIC MINISTRY, AND HEART ISSUES RESOLVED BECAUSE OF RENEWED VISION OF HARVEST.
- PLEASE JOIN WITH ME IN RISING TO OUR FEET TO RAISE OUR HANDS TO HEAVEN AND ASK GOD FOR THE GREATEST REVIVAL THE NATIONS HAVE EVER SEEN, NOT JUST IN AMERICA AND EUROPE, BUT IN EVERY NATION. LET THE REDEEMED OF THE LORD SAY SO! EVERYTHING IS IN PLACE, GOD IS AT WORK. TRUST HIM - PAPA PAUL
- James Goll: I had just woken from a dream where I saw all of heaven dancing when I heard the news.....

38

Paul Cain Dies

Paul Cain had a difficult time after the collapse of the Vineyard platform. His mother Anner, who Paul always maintained heard the Lord much more clearly than he himself, died at the age of 105. Anner had been Paul's most faithful intercessor, and her loss was painful on both natural and spiritual arenas.

Paul's gift had opened doors to a realm of authority where he was invited to meet with world leaders, and speak to them the word the Lord was giving them. It is public knowledge that he advised several US presidents, and even was invited to meet with Saddam Hussein. Paul was on speed dial from the Oval Office for two Presidencies, and had his own direct number to call the FBI if the Lord showed him something.

There was a particular controversy about Paul's personal life which arose during the 90s, and damaged many relationships between parts of the body of Christ. Like us all, Paul had wounds that had not been healed, and sin that he had to overcome. It is a terrible indictment of the Body of Christ that so few people can hear the Lord clearly enough to help a brother or sister get free of the sins that entangle them. As a young teen, Paul had been molested by an older pastor, and at the time had not been able to get the help he needed. Indeed, this is still true for many in the body of Christ.

He became connected with the Santa Monica Healing Rooms, and spent a lot of time there both receiving ministry and blessing others. Dan Reise, Paul's assistant for his later years, was asked of his most vivid memory of Paul. Dan replied, "He was so kind." Paul was a gentle, kind, father-figure to so many during his last decades, and continued to speak words of encouragement and healing at many conferences.

Paul's health had never been "good" since his silent years, when he had not really looked after himself very well. It seems odd that a man who had seen so many healed struggled himself, but we know from our time in the Healing Rooms that it's not at all unusual. It's just one reason why we need each other.

One of the recurring visions the Lord had given Paul over the years was the well-known Stadium Vision. Paul would see a news anchorman saying:

> **"Well folks. There's no news tonight but good news. It seems like the whole world is turning to Christ. We don't even have any sports news, because the games have been cancelled through lack of interest. Instead, the stadiums are filled with large crowds of people who have spontaneously gathered to worship Jesus Christ. We don't know the people who are leading them, it like they're faceless. Some of them have been there for two or three days without change of raiment of food and they're announcing into the microphone 'We've had a resurrection over here', or 'there's a cripple walking**

here'. Everywhere you look people are falling to their knees proclaiming 'Jesus is Lord'."

Paul often spoke of the nameless, faceless generation that were coming I the last days. Some years ago, Paul was reading through Psalm 14:5, which says: "There were they in great fear: for God is in the generation of the righteous" (Ps 14:5). When he read this, the Lord spoke to him and said, "This is the end-time generation of people who receive the double portion."

"That's wonderful," Paul thought, and the Lord continued, "You don't know what that means. The double portion is the Holy Spirit without any limits. I deliberately limited what was available to the first century church, because 'God saves the best till last'."

As a good Sydney Anglican I was very cautious about that seemingly new doctrine, and began to pray and ask the Lord for confirmation in the scriptures. After some weeks I was reading through Romans 8, and struck verse 23:

"*And not only this, but also we ourselves, having the first fruits of the Spirit, even we ourselves groan within ourselves, waiting eagerly for our adoption as sons, the redemption of our body.*" The Lord said: "There's your answer."

At the beginning of his ministry, Paul proclaimed he was "*not in the least inferior to the 'super-apostles'*" (2 Cor 12:10), and often spoke as if he was expecting the second coming of Jesus 'any day now'. But in Romans, written at the end of his earthly ministry, he is acknowledging that the first century church only received the "first fruits".

Paul Cain's ministry was one of challenge and encouragement. He was a "sovereign vessel" called from the womb, and set apart for God's purposes. He demonstrated a clarity of revelation that we can also attain, if we walk with the Lord in the place where He can speak to us.

From his hospital bed, Paul wrote (he tended to 'shout' when typing): "FRESH BREATH IS COMING TO THE PROPHETIC MINISTRY, AND HEART ISSUES RESOLVED BECAUSE OF RENEWED VISION OF HARVEST. PLEASE JOIN WITH ME IN RISING TO OUR FEET TO RAISE OUR HANDS TO HEAVEN AND ASK GOD FOR THE GREATEST REVIVAL THE NATIONS HAVE EVER SEEN, NOT JUST IN AMERICA AND EUROPE, BUT IN EVERY NATION. LET THE REDEEMED OF THE LORD SAY SO! EVERYTHING IS IN PLACE, GOD IS AT WORK, TRUST HIM—PAPA PAUL

James Goll (another former 'Kansas City Prophet') had just awoken from a dream where he saw all of heaven dancing, when he heard the news of Paul's passing into glory. Paul Cain overcame much and finished well, and his life stands as a lesson and a challenge to us to walk into the purposes of God in our own lives.

Just as Bob Jones' death on Valentine's Day, 2014, was a sign of his core prophetic message, Paul Cain, the Prophet who introduced so many of us to the history of the Voice of Healing and Latter Rain Revivals, died on February 12th, 2019, the Anniversary of the Latter Rain Visitation in Canada.

2019

13 Feb, 2019

Kari Browning's post about PC

- On February 12, 2000, we hosted Shawn Bolz for the first time at a conference entitled "Your Sons and Daughters Shall Prophesy."
- In 2006, Paul Keith Davis called me (at the exact moment that I was talking to Larry Randolph and Steve Shultz about several things that had occurred on February 12 in the past) to ask me if I knew the significance of the date "February 12." When I asked him why he was asking, he told me that Bob Jones had just heard "February 12" audibly.
- In 2007, we hosted Paul Cain for the first time on February 12. (Shawn Bolz was also there.) Paul Cain had been a part of the Latter Rain Revival that began on February 12, 1948. A few days before Paul came, I read that it was on February 12, 1989, that Paul had stood in John Wimber's pulpit the first time and announced that he was the beginning of the "new breed" and that he was there to pass him a torch symbolically.
- On February 12, 2012, we hosted the "Fullness of Time" conference, with Shawn Bolz and others, believing that God was going to restore the power that they had in the Latter Rain Revival that had begun on that date in 1948. God TV broadcasted that conference to the nations.
- Shortly thereafter, I was with Shawn Bolz when he began to receive high level words of knowledge like Paul Cain and others had received during the Latter Rain Revival!
- In January 2012, Kim Clement prophesied: "He (God) spoke to me about the beginning of a seven-year period starting in 2012. Everything begins in February. There will be a death – and everybody will know about it – and then there will be life that will begin to manifest."
- During the Fullness of Time Conference in 2012, Whitney Houston died. As we just came to the end of the seven-year period, Paul Cain died!
- I checked Paul's facebook page shortly after midnight on February 12 and read the announcement that he had just died. I knew his death would be a sign confirming the word.
- Paul died on February 12 of lung and heart issues. Before he died, he had written on his page that "FRESH BREATH IS COMING TO THE PROPHETIC MINISTRY, AND HEART ISSUES RESOLVED BECAUSE OF RENEWED VISION OF HARVEST."
- Let it begin! Fresh breath on the prophetic ministry. Heart issues resolved. A new breed of ministry to arise with purity and power.

39

The Significance of February

On Feb 13th, 2019, after Paul Cain died, Kari Browning of Coeur D'Alene, Idaho, shared the following post about the significance of February. Bob Jones had said for years that "it's always February."

- On February 12, 2000, we hosted Shawn Bolz for the first time at a conference entitled "Your Sons and Daughters Shall Prophesy."
- In 2006, Paul Keith Davis called me (at the exact moment that I was talking to Larry Randolph and Steve Shultz about several things that had occurred on February 12 in the past) to ask me if I knew the significance of the date "February 12." When I asked him why he was asking, he told me that Bob Jones had just heard "February 12" audibly.
- In 2007, we hosted Paul Cain for the first time on February 12. (Shawn Bolz was also there.) Paul Cain had been a part of the Latter Rain Revival that began on February 12, 1948. A few days

before Paul came, I read that it was on February 12, 1989, that Paul had stood in John Wimber's pulpit the first time and announced that he was the beginning of the "new breed" and that he was there to pass him a torch symbolically.

- On February 12, 2012, we hosted the "Fullness of Time" conference, with Shawn Bolz and others, believing that God was going to restore the power that they had in the Latter Rain Revival that had begun on that date in 1948. God TV broadcasted that conference to the nations.
- Shortly thereafter, I was with Shawn Bolz when he began to receive high level words of knowledge like Paul Cain and others had received during the Latter Rain Revival!
- In January 2012, Kim Clement prophesied: "He (God) spoke to me about the beginning of a seven-year period starting in 2012. Everything begins in February. There will be a death – and everybody will know about it – and then there will be life that will begin to manifest."
- During the Fullness of Time Conference in 2012, Whitney Houston died. As we just came to the end of the seven-year period, Paul Cain died!
- I checked Paul's Facebook page shortly after midnight on February 12 and read the announcement that he had just died. I knew his death would be a sign confirming the word.
- Paul died on February 12 of lung and heart issues. Before he died, he had written on his page that "FRESH BREATH IS COMING TO THE PROPHETIC MINISTRY, AND HEART ISSUES RESOLVED BECAUSE OF RENEWED VISION OF HARVEST."

- Let it begin! Fresh breath on the prophetic ministry. Heart issues resolved. A new breed of ministry to arise with purity and power.

Interestingly, Bob Jones, John Paul Jackson and Paul Cain were each buried on February 22nd (2/22), as was Martin Luther, the architect of the Reformation. Three of the most gifted Prophetic ministers in our lifetimes buried on the SAME day! A Biblical principle is that anything repeated three times signifies that thing taken to fulfilment.

Some want to jump in and interpret the significance of the three prophets all being buried on the same day. Lets' just call it interesting, and wait on the Lord for an answer.

Proverbs 25:2 says, "*It is the glory of God to conceal a matter, But the glory of kings is to search out a matter*". He doesn't hide things **from** us—He hides things **for** Us. The Christian Life is a treasure-hunt we're supposed to take with our Heavenly Father, in relationship.

Keep watching February….

2019

1 Sep, 2019

Neville Johnson Dies

Brisbane, Australia

- Neville was born again in Hebron Tabernacle in Sunderland when he was 12 years old and felt a call to ministry at age 14. His family moved to NZ when he was a child, and he worked on the South Pacific Mission Fields in the 60s. He went back to NZ as pastor of Auckland assembly in 1970
- 1983 - Went through a scandal of immorality, repented
- By the 2000s was ministering regularly with Bob Jones and team including Paul Keith Davis, Sadhu Sundar Selvaraj
- Many testified to his Prophetic Gifting and close walk with the Lord in his later years. He had many angelic visitations and revelations
- Around 2014 - angel appeared - translocated to Buckingham Palace in the Queen's Bedroom. "How are you here?" He told her "I am a prophet of God sent by God with a message for you.." Queen responded "What is the word of the Lord?" He told her: "You shall not appoint Prince Charles as the next King…" (video - Sadhu)
- Passed away after a long sickness of several months

40

Neville Johnson Dies

I knew nothing of Neville Johnson until around the turn of the Millennium, when he suddenly appeared ministering at Prophetic Conferences with Bob Jones, Paul Keith Davis, Sadhu Sundar Selvaraj, and Shawn Bolz. I first heard a story about this guy from Perth who'd had the Archangel Michael burst through the ceiling of his room, deliver a message, and take off again. I was able to find out a little bit about this prophetic person who spent years in Australia.

Neville was born in England, and gave his heart to the Lord at age 12 in Hebron Tabernacle in Sunderland. His family moved to New Zealand not long after. He worked on the South Pacific Mission fields in the 1960s, and then returned to New Zealand in 1970 to Pastor the Auckland Assembly.

In 1983, he went through a public scandal of immorality, and spent years working through repentance and restoration. Like Clark Taylor, another friend of our ministry who moved in great power in the 70s, he was cut loose by his home denomination, who refused to have anything to do with him.

Many testified to the prophetic gifting Neville moved in, and his close walk with the Lord in his later years, including many angelic visitations. One in particular stands out, related by his friend Sadhu Sundar Selvaraj, a prophet from India.

Neville was waiting on the Lord around 2014. An angel appeared and translocated him to the Queen's bedroom in Buckingham Palace. The Queen asked in shock, "How are you here?" and was about to call security before the stunned Neville could answer, "I am a prophet of God sent with a message for you."

The Queen responded, "What is the word of the Lord?"

Neville told her she must not appoint Prince Charles as King to follow her, as he had touched the New Age and other unrighteous things. When he had finished, the angel took him back.

Late last year, Neville passed away after a sickness of several months.

2020

Middleton, SA, Australia

Where Are We Now?

- Paul Cain's Stadium Vision - the nameless, faceless generation (Joel's Army, Army of Ezekiel 37, Samuel Generation...)
- Bob Jones' Billion-Soul Harvest - The Next Wave
- Civil War in the Church - purifying move - Don't "demonise" the enemy. No-One with blood on their hands......
- The Battle Rages
  - US Election/SCOTUS Nomination
  - "In the dream, I heard the voice of God say, 'The enemy has intended to strike out Donald Trump at a very critical hour in history. But behold, supernatural help is on the way, for I will slow down the advancement of the enemy and allow him to knock this out of the park. For it is simply a matter of time before the victory.'" Jeremiah Johnson
  - READ *The Final Quest* - we are living it NOW!

41

Where are we now?

In 2020, the world has been attacked once again by an onslaught of great fear—the coronavirus. Whether you agree or disagree with the measures taken by governments, the outcome was the same, the world and its systems were shaken. For many churches, their lack of power and anointing was held up for all to see, as the "churchianity" activities were suddenly exposed as meaningless.

For nearly a decade, all the major leaders of different streams of the Church around the world have acknowledged that we are on the verge of a major move of God. Those of us who have known the prophecies have been eagerly awaiting the Next Wave, the Billion-Soul Harvest, and some have struggled with discouragement when our hopes seemed dashed year after year, and instead we were dealing with marriage breakups, broken kids, and as I previously mentioned, the worst spiritual battles of our lives.

I preached a message some years ago at our ministry base in Middleton called "Road Map to the End Times", going through the major Biblical passages of events still to come in the earth. We are already in the middle of

Ezekiel 37, the Valley of Dry Bones, and are awaiting the breath to enter the bodies, so they stand up, a vast army. At the same time, we are almost done with Jeremiah 50 and 51, the Gulf Wars and the destruction of the "land of the Babylonians." I tried to warn the Christians of Iraq to "flee" as instructed, but they said they felt led to stay. Many died within a year at the hands of ISIS. The next major Biblical marker I believe is Isaiah 17—the destruction of Damascus, which puts us on the road to Armageddon (Ezekiel 37-38).

From the words of the prophets over the years, we are in the first part of the *Final Quest* vision, and we are about to see the Lord's wounded army come back. We are on the verge of the *Civil War in the Church*, which will be nasty, but **must** be won without "demonising the enemy". The Lord said in the *War and Glory* vision, "No-one with his brother's blood on his hands will be used to build My Kingdom."

In the Ancient Wells Healing Rooms, Raf has been teaching us for years, "get into the prayer closet until you can hear the Lord clearly." It is the foundation of how we minister—people come in, we ask the Lord what the key is, tell the subject and lead them to repentance. We have seen many salvations and miracles over the years since 2007. Raf developed his ability to hear the Lord by playing hide and seek with his prayer partner, not only could they find each other, the Lord taught them to "keep listening, because people change their minds." So often we get so excited by a single word we stop paying attention to the Holy Spirit, and then get into a mess.

We are all taught to keep short accounts with the Lord, to forgive quickly, and not to minister publicly if we're battling through stuff in our hearts—we certainly don't want others to get 'slimed'. The Lord is calling us all to walk much closer to Him than most of us have ever managed, and He is saying it's necessary for survival in what is coming on the earth. As Bobby Conner likes to say:

We've become way too familiar with a God we barely know!

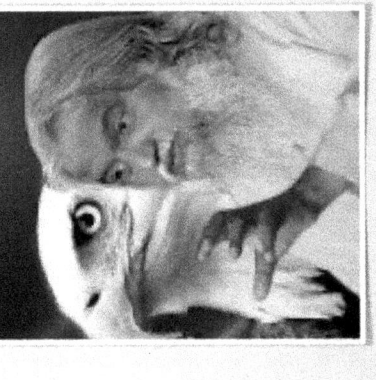

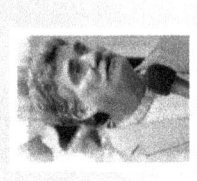

2020

Middleton, SA, Australia

Who is Still Around?

- Rick Joyner, Paul Keith Davis, Bobby Conner, Shawn Bolz, Larry Randolph, Patricia King, Todd Bentley Chuck Pierce, Sadhu Sundar Selvaraj
- Our own Raf Shaw - who rebelliously swears he isn't a prophet yet hears clearer than any of us
- New faces such as Jeremiah Johnson, Lana Vawser, Chris Reed

42

Who is still around?

In the last few years, we have seen all of those I personally considered to be operating in the Ephesians 4 Office Ministry of Prophet die. This is not a judgement of individuals or evaluation of giftings. Most Charismatic/Pentecostal/Renewal ministers understand that there is a difference between operating in the gift, and being commissioned into the Office. Those in the Office are the gift—they're not just gifted individuals. I am not saying that the remaining prophetic ministers are not in the Office, just that so far, I am not seeing it.

John Paul Jackson taught on this some years ago. He said, "I call myself a prophetic minister, because I have seen what's coming in the prophetic, and I am not there yet." I believe many of those claiming Office titles at the moment are premature, allowing for the fact that in speech we often simplify. Just because someone mis-uses a term we should not assume they are considering themselves higher than they ought. It's not our place to judge. They're servants of God.

Some are beginning to emerge who are hearing very clearly. We need to be very careful not to allow a spirit of competitiveness or jealousy into our hearts when God uses someone else powerfully. One of the features of God's army from Joel 2 is: "*...They all march in line, not swerving from their course. They do not jostle each other; each marches straight ahead...* (Joel 2:7-8). There will be no self-promotion or jealousy in God's End-Time Army—we are all going to know our place and be content.

We also need to be diligent in sifting the multitudes of prophetic words that are being publicly shared via the Internet—some are just wrong. At the same time, we need to be gracious to those who "missed it", because we **all** "*... know in part and we prophesy in part...* (1Co 13:9). Only together in unity will we begin to get a complete and accurate picture of what the Lord is saying and where he is leading us.

Prophetic vision is like looking through binoculars with no idea of the magnification factor. In addition, God "*... calls things that* are *not as though they were...*" (Romans 4:17). A person may have a revelation of an event which looks "real soon now" and is actually years away. Patience and faith are always required, and we are rarely ass mature as we like to think. So be gracious with earnest devout people who are genuinely trying to bless you—especially when they miss it.

Rick Joyner is still leading at Morningstar, and one of the few Kansas City connections still alive. Jim Goll is another. Paul Keith Davis, Bobby Conner, Shawn Bolz, Sadhu Sundar Selvaraj, Larry Randolph, Patricia King and Chuck Pierce, are all still active prophetic ministers. There are new faces stepping up, such as Jeremiah Johnson, Lana Vawser (I taught her husband, Kevin, at school), Chris Reed, and many others—we're looking for a whole generation, after all.

Others such as Todd Bentley, Heidi Baker and our own Raf Shaw, are not primarily called as prophetic ministers, yet hear clearly from the Lord on a regular basis.

We need to seek the Lord to hear clearly ourselves, and step forward boldly, but cautiously, judging each word for fruit. The Holy Spirit has flowed from movement to movement in the Western Church, and has done even more in the nations over the last 20 years than we can hope to cover here, even in outline. I am hearing wonderful reports of revival amongst the Orthodox Church in Russia, of entire villages of Muslims having the same dream of "the man in white" overnight, and waking up followers of Jesus. God is not limited in **any** way, and He is working to bring to maturity the nameless, faceless Generation of the Righteous, who will become the "glorious bride, without spot or wrinkle," and manifest His kingdom on earth.

At any moment the Holy Spirit Tidal Wave could come, and our chaotic, confusing coronavirus-lockdown of a year will vanish into history as we struggle to deal with the vast numbers of people being "swept into the Kingdom." Our current structures are not going to cope—we need to start preparing.

As we have been praying for years:

"*Let Your kingdom come, on earth, as it is in heaven.*"

43

There are Not Enough Lifeboats

I wrote the following prophetic article years ago, before 9/11, Iraq, GFC and Covid-19. I believe it is still valid today, and we, as the Church, are NOT READY for what God is about to do. As John Wimber discovered in May, 1980, having the Holy Spirit grow a church from 400-1700 in three months is an incredibly difficult process. As Jesus told Bob Jones, we are about to see a "**billion** souls swept into the Kingdom in three great waves." How will your church cope? Do you even allow the Holy Spirit in, or is He "stand(ing) at the door," knocking to be allowed into His church? I don't believe we have a lot of time to get this right—ALL of the senior Prophetic Fathers believed that it was imminent.

Recently I have felt the Holy Spirit stirring me about Revelation 3:17-18, which I believe is the scariest verse in the Bible:

> *"You say, 'I am rich; I have acquired wealth and do not need a thing.' But **you do not realize** that you are wretched, pitiful, poor, blind and naked. I counsel you to buy from me gold refined in the fire, so you can become rich; and white*

> *clothes to wear, so you can cover your shameful nakedness; and*
> *salve to put on your eyes, so you can see."*

It is scary to think we may miss out on our divine purpose, and be "spat out of His mouth", because we didn't accurately discern the time of our visitation (Luke 19:44). We need to be diligent and pray, make sure we do NOT despise prophecy (1 Thessalonians 5:20), and ensure we DO pray Psalms 139:23-24 **often**:

> *Search **me**, O God, and know **my** heart;*
> *test **me** and know **my** anxious thoughts.*
> *See if there is any offensive way in me,*
> *and lead me in the way everlasting.*

In the next chapter I will give some insight into how we can prepare our hearts for the Billion-Soul Harvest.

****

*The following Revelation was received by Paul Davies on 27th Sept., 1998. As with all prophetic words, these must be weighed and tested with a spirit of humility and repentance. Where Bible passages are referred to, the interpretations given are not intended to be seen as **the** interpretation of the passage, but as God speaking to his people's current situation by giving **an** interpretation.*

In Job 33:14 the Bible says: "*For God does speak—now one way, now another—**though man may not perceive it**.*" (emphasis mine).

While listening to a sermon in church, the Lord began speaking to me about the film of the year—Titanic, and what it meant to the Church at large. The Spirit drew together things He had been saying to me for many months, and gave me understanding of the bigger picture, with the clear word:

"There are not enough lifeboats!"

The Lord is about to sink (by increasing the water of His Spirit) the worldly structures we have taken as a base of security, in the world and in the Church. The problem is that the church doesn't have enough lifeboats in place, and our losses will be great if this situation continues.

The Lord gave me to understand that the lifeboats were structures put in place before a disaster to enable people to survive. The disaster will be the Revival that many of us are seeking so earnestly. The increase of the Spirit that accompanies Revival will accomplish wonders, but we will lose many opportunities if we have not trained our people to be ready, and provided a framework in our congregations that will cope with rapid growth. In our churches, the lifeboats are reorganised structures and policies that will allow the people of God to overcome the disaster. We must put aside our pride in our heritage, and our preferences for certain ways of doing things, and especially seek the Lord for His ways and not assume that we already know what He wants us to do.

Introduction

God often speaks through events in the world, and significant events often have a spiritual significance beyond what we see with our earthly eyes. The movie *Titanic* has broken many records in the last year, and has captured the minds of the Western world with the tale of the fateful voyage. Documentaries abound on TV about the search for the wreck, and the continuing exploration, as well as the many unanswered questions people have about the disaster.

In the spiritual, the warnings of the Titanic disaster are just as relevant today as they were in 1912, and we have apparently learned little. It is therefore, important that we understand what the Titanic represented.

The Titanic and the Church

The Titanic and the events surrounding its fateful voyage are a type of the church today. Consider the following:

*   **The Titanic was the largest liner, a floating palace of luxury with the latest technology, and was claimed to be unsinkable.**

The church today is the largest it has been throughout history, the richest and most well-resourced of any period in history, and is so large worldwide that many Christians find it unthinkable that any real threat to Christianity exists.

*   **Captain Smith was more interested in getting the speed record for an ocean crossing of the Atlantic than in the safety of his vessel, because of his arrogant assumption that the ship was unsinkable.**

The church is full of self-promoting ministries more concerned with their ability to keep ministering than with the real needs of those they are ministering to. This leads to a competitive spirit between ministries rather than a willingness to listen to the Spirit of God and respond to changing circumstances.

* **The ship was filled with a cross-section of the rich and famous, and on the surface, was the grandest thing afloat. Yet this was only for First-Class passengers. The vast majority of those aboard were kept below decks, and forbidden to participate in the activities on the Upper Decks. When the ship began to sink, these were even locked below, so that the more important people could get to the lifeboats first.**

The ministry of the church is supposed to be the ministry of the whole body, not just the paid Pastors. But few who have not "jumped through the hoops" of acceptance into ministry get a chance to minister. How often have you heard a non-ordained but anointed person from your own fellowship preaching on Sunday? It may not be their full-time role, but in larger churches especially there are sure to be many who the Lord has anointed, but who are not Pastors, so they are never considered. It is the utmost arrogance to insist that only those trained in seminaries will be able to preach effectively. Similarly, in many churches it is the Pastors and the Ministry Team who are the only ones allowed to participate in praying for the sick, or giving prophetic words publicly, or getting revelation on what the Lord wants to do next. Few ever ask if anyone in the pews has a Word from God (though it is slowly starting to happen in some places). Far more significant is the exclusion of most of the congregation from prayer ministry (discussed in detail below), as this is a direct violation of the Lord's instructions to the Apostles in Matt 10:7,8 and Matt 28:20, and robs most of the church from participating in doing the works of the Kingdom. Truly, the "lower classes" are locked below decks.

* **The Titanic ignored the warnings of icebergs ahead and continued to sail full steam into the danger zone.**

The church has been ignoring Prophetic warnings for over 20 years, and still prefers to argue whether something is God or not rather than take steps to prepare for the future.

* **The Titanic lookouts were not supplied with binoculars to increase their ability to see ahead. If they had been, the ship would have been able to turn aside in time.**

The church has mostly silenced Prophetic ministries and found excuses not to listen to them, rather than sift through the Words (and the errors) for what the Lord was saying. They have denied their Watchmen the ability to give effective warning.

* **The rudder was too small to turn a ship of that size in the time required.**

The church is unable to respond quickly to anything, since most congregations are run, or heavily influenced by several committees with differing political or theological views. Also, we have hampered ourselves with our particular "policies" that do not allow us to easily make exceptions to suit new situations.

* **Instead of taking the hit head-on, when it was clearly too late to turn away, the Titanic turned, and ripped open its sides. Engineers claim that the ship would have survived a head-on impact at full-speed.**

The church has a problem in accepting responsibility for its actions, and its mistakes. When we finally realise God is serious about our sins, that is, when His judgment has begun (1 Peter 4:17), we try to turn aside, rather than repent and face the music. This causes more damage to our credibility and makes the restoration process that much harder (e.g. Priests being exposed as molesters/adulterers). Consider the difference in attitudes to sin expressed by 1. Jimmy Swaggart and 2. Jimmy Bakker. Both were publicly shamed, and exposed in sexual sin, but their repentance responses were very different. (Bakker wrote a book called "I was Wrong" confessing his sin and detailing his path to restoration.)

* **Finally, after the impact, it was realised that there were not enough lifeboats.** Due to cost-cutting and the arrogance of the builders, and their desire to keep messy-looking lifeboats off the First-Class decks, there were only enough boat seats for under half of the total complement of the ship.

Jesus told us to count the cost. Sometimes, this means taking unpopular decisions and going out on a limb when there seems no reason to do so, other than the Lord seems to demand it. The Word the Lord gave me very clearly was: **there are not enough lifeboats**, for what He is about to do.

The End of an Era

There is a theory, debated hotly by Theologians, that the first 3 chapters of the book of Revelation, where Jesus speaks to the seven churches, equate to seven major periods of Church history. Although exceptions can be found to almost every rule in the History of the Church, I believe the general spirit of each time period is outlined in these passages. Many preachers in the last 20 years have seen increasing parallels between the Laodicean Church and our own.

What concerns us here is the last two passages, concerning the church in Philadelphia (Rev 3:7-13), and the Church in Laodicea (Rev 3:14-22). The Philadelphian Church is the Evangelistic Church, representing the time period from about 1650—1900 A.D. The church exploded around the world in an unprecedented period of evangelistic fervour ("I have placed before you an open door that no one can shut" Rev 3:8), which resulted in conversions in nearly all countries around the world. Great deeds and sacrifices were accomplished in the Name of Christ, and missionary heroes from that era have been role models for every succeeding generation.

The biggest single contributor to this outreach was England, through the worldwide reach of the British Empire, as they worked out the God-given favour to take the gospel to the nations. However, by 1900, the pride and arrogance that accompanied the spread of Empire had begun to destroy much of that which had been sown, and the Lord was about to take His blessing off England and give it elsewhere. The Titanic sinking was the symbol in the natural of the collapse of the British anointing, and, in the natural, it has been downhill ever since.

The Titanic was the greatest ship built, unsinkable, built as a floating palace with incredible luxury and speed. Yet all the trimmings were on the surface—the bulk of the passengers (providing the bulk of the money to run the ship) travelled in crowded accommodations below decks, denied the luxury and privilege of the First-Class upper crust. The pride in the ship was shown to be just as shallow, and the confidence placed in man's knowledge and ability, stated in the famous remark "not even God Himself could sink this ship", reflected the shallowness of the "civilisation" through-out the Empire. The sheer stupidity of not providing enough lifeboats, not providing binoculars for lookouts, having too small a rudder, etcetera, etcetera, can only be wondered at, and the tragic loss mourned. It really did signify the end of an era, and it is plain to see that the lead in Christian

Evangelism in the 20th century passed to America, just as the survivors of the Titanic did.

Yet the message to the church is the same today. We have learned little from the disaster, and if we don't take urgent steps to rectify the problems, we will find that WE don't have enough lifeboats, and our losses will be tragic.

The Legacy of all

The Laodicean church is the Materialistic church, who are "lukewarm", and about to be "spit … out of my (Jesus') mouth" (Rev 3:16). The tragedy of the Laodicean age is that we have for too long thought that it was wealth that made us Laodicean. In reality, the key is in Rev 3: 17: "You do not realise…". It is our lack of understanding that makes us lukewarm. We have not understood that the last church carries the legacy of all the preceding churches, and we will have to overcome all of the hang-ups they had, by overcoming our own pride which prevents us from seeing ourselves as we really are. Like the lack of binoculars for the lookouts on the Titanic, which would have given time to miss the iceberg, we have not given place and care to the Prophetic Ministry, and the Lord cautions us in Rev 3:18 to buy a "salve for your eyes so you can see".

Many today are given to a confidence in the World which simply cannot be relied upon—the 1987 stock market crash gave clear warning of this, as does the recent financial crisis in Asia, yet many are confidently explaining that 1929, and 1987, cannot happen again. The church, however, seems to have no answers in preparing for the financial crises which many Prophetic voices are predicting—most are so concerned with meeting their monthly budgets, they have no resources left over to put away for a crisis. Businesses are not heeding the warnings about the "Year 2000 bug", which could potentially destroy Western society, the Banks are increasing fees and charges almost daily, yet more and more people are getting further and further into debt.

Churches are being rent apart by controlling "Jezebel Spirits" (Rev 2:20—Thyatira), by compromise with the World (Rev 2:14-15—Pergamum), by persecution (Rev 2:10—Smyrna), and by Death (Rev 3:1), yet even the recent moves of the Spirit around the World during the 80's and 90's have made little impact. In fact, many of us have "lost" the lessons of the 80's in the thrills of the move of the 90's. We are not, in Western countries, seeing large-scale revival (though there are pockets), and the level of power operating in our churches and ministries is less than it was years ago.

Into this scenario comes the movie Titanic, with the warnings it brings, and we must be careful not to let our Laodicean assumptions, or our Philadelphian pride, prevent us from hearing the warnings and acting accordingly.

The Lessons of the Third Wave

I find it very hard to recognise that most of those who were in Renewal in the 80's have not continued in the basic principles that were taught at that time, and have replaced them with other methods, that are not as effective, and do not have the same priority goals. The Third Wave movement in the 80's and early 90's, spearheaded by the ministry of John Wimber, was primarily about one thing—teaching the average Christian to "do the stuff". This was the ministry they were commanded to do by Jesus when they went out (Luke 9, Matthew 10). Preach the gospel, heal the sick, drive out demons. He commanded the Apostles to "teach them to obey everything I commanded you" (Matthew 28:18). This means quite clearly that every Christian is to be taught to do the basic ministry—praying for others. When Wimber taught this to his church in 1984, they grew by 100 people in three months, as the people had the faith and experience to offer to pray for people's needs, and many were converted as the Lord answered prayer. The average Christian is like the average soldier—the real work is done by privates.

I find it disturbing that so many Churches have discarded this model for a specialised "ministry team", which excludes the rest of the body from growing in faith by exercising the gifts regularly. This has been popularised by the actions taken at the Toronto Airport Church to deal with the huge number of unknowns they were hosting, and unfortunately, many churches have copied their practice (the right response to a unique situation), and made it a part of their congregational practice. It is justified as preventing damage being done to people by immature or deliberately malicious, but is basically an attempt to control the situation, rather than allow the Lord to control, and "pastor" (shepherd, counsel or discipline) mistakes as they arise. Immature people make messes, but they will never learn if they aren't allowed to make messes (Prov 14:4), and God does permit ungodly people to minister (e.g. Judas).

In situations where I have had personal experience of witches trying to pray for people in our meetings, they were quickly identified and reported and dealt with by the leaders. Satan has got the church so scared of his ability to interfere with God's people that we have no faith that the Lord will protect and guide His people. This is not to say that we have an "anything goes" mentality, but the responsibility of Pastors and Teachers is to allow the people to have a go, and then deal gently and with wisdom with mistakes as they arise, not to stifle and control the opportunities so that nothing bad can happen. Part of the difficulty is that we read the Bible through Western eyes—in the Eastern world teaching is a process of instruction, modelling, assisting students to have a go, and then letting them do it and dealing with errors as they arise. This is clearly how the Lord trained the Disciples in His years on Earth. We, however, tend to think that a sermon or two is enough, and the rest can happen in home groups, but this is rarely enough. If it is enough, why are our churches not effectively out in the streets doing the work of the kingdom in power?

The defences for a specialised group doing the praying are many, but they all come down to one thing—the body as a whole is not being empowered, and they are therefore not taking the ministry out of the doors onto the streets. We are not providing a safe environment for Christians to have a go, and as a result, they don't, and we cannot therefore claim to be adequately preparing them for ministry.

If revival is going to come, it has to leave the doors of the church. It does seem a little silly to make such a fuss about preparing for Revival, growing in holiness for revival, praying for revival and so on, when many of our people lack the basic teaching in the fundamentals of gospel ministry, and are prevented from gaining personal experience in their home congregations.

Taking back what he Stole—building lifeboats!

In essence, we have allowed Satan to convince us to disarm ourselves. All he had to do was send a few crazies into our congregations, maybe a few witches, and we react to the fear of pollution by trying to protect and control the situation so that this cannot happen. Thus, we react to Fear spirits by allowing Control spirits a doorway into our churches, and remove the weapons from the hands of our soldiers.

Many have compared Faith to a muscle—it needs to be exercised regularly. If we don't provide our soldiers with the chance to exercise their faith by involving them in ministry in church, they will never suddenly develop this skill when it is needed outside the church building. Soldiers learn to shoot before they go into battle. If they don't know how to use the weapon they won't—they will hide, and avoid the conflict.

Satan has also deceived us about Spiritual Warfare, by many teachings that lead us to fight from our prayer rooms, yelling at spiritual beings in the heavenlies, instead of actually accomplishing anything by doing the work of the Kingdom (which we can't because we never get to practice). Whilst there is a measure of success in these techniques, they are inherently unbiblical—they are inferred from dubious interpretations of passages and not directly mentioned in Scripture. That they have any effect is possibly more to do with God's Grace than any affirmation of the technique. We are told that what we bind on earth will be bound in heaven (Matt 16:19, 18:18). We don't bind in heaven. Like any soldiers, we fight the enemy in the territory he is disputing. We do Spiritual Warfare by doing damage to the effects of Satan's power on earth.

How did Jesus model this? By proclaiming "the Kingdom of heaven is here", and by doing the work of His Father (i.e. the work of the Kingdom)—healing the sick, cleansing lepers, raising the dead and casting out demons. He then commanded this to be taught to all Christians. If Satan has hurt people by disease, hurt, etc., we take that back by ministering healing and compassion. When the unsaved see this—they will have a reason to listen to our preaching—Wimber called it Power Evangelism.

If we are not teaching this to all those under our pastoral care, we are in great danger of ignoring a basic command of the Son, and that will have serious consequences. We must carefully examine our practices, our hearts and our assumptions in the light of the ministry of Jesus revealed in the Gospels, which Paul did not specifically mention as most of his letters were written in response to specific situations that had arisen. we are supposed to be ministering as Jesus did, and doing "greater works than these", but we have modelled too much of our church life, and our reading of the Gospels, on assumptions we have made about Paul's teachings, rather than viewing his works from the revelation in the Gospels—we have it backwards!

Finally, and most importantly, we must seek the Lord for specific revelation concerning His plans for our churches, to determine which changes should be made immediately, and which brought in slowly. Most important is timing, as I believe strongly that we have little time to prepare before the Next Wave hits the Church. We cannot ignore the warning of the Titanic any longer.

44

Abiding in Him

I do not believe ANY of us are ready for the Harvest, though some have been diligent in preparing as they are able. I really think we will ALL get a shock at the magnitude of the Lord's work.

As we have seen throughout this book, the Holy Spirit has been weaving His plan over decades, moving through diverse servants and different denominational groups, revealing truths and building on them elsewhere.

As Captain Malcolm Reynolds said in the movie *Serenity:* "If I start fighting a War, you're going to see something new." How much more will the Holy Spirit "offend our minds to reveal our hearts" in this Next Wave. Throughout history, the main opponents of each new move of God have been the leadership of the previous move—we saw this in the Voice of Healing Revival, the Charismatic Renewal, and especially the Third Wave and Toronto. Even now, IHOP-KC, Morningstar and Bethel are subjects of intense public criticism, with no acknowledgement of the positive influences they have. I wonder how many of us will have "eyes to see" when the Next Wave breaks?

The key to survival for us all is making Jesus our "magnificent obsession." He is, after all, worthy. Few of us are close to him, fewer still in a place where He can rest in us. As the Lord told Paul Cain when he was complaining of not getting enough rest, "What about me? I haven't been able to rest in you since 1952," which was when the purity of the Voice of Healing Revival was lost, according to Paul.

We need to "hear His voice." The Christian walk is supposed to be a relationship of Hearing and Obeying (as opposed to reading and presuming). Few of us can hear clearly, and fewer still know how to develop that skill, yet the answer is amazingly simple.

Spend time in His presence, waiting on Him!

John 15:7-8 says:

> "If you abide in Me, and My words abide in you, ask whatever you wish, and it will be done for you. My Father is glorified by this, that you bear much fruit, and so **prove (yourselves) to be My disciples**" (emphasis mine).

Many claim the title of Disciple, without fulfilling the Biblical criteria—**getting your prayers answered**. Few have the evidence that they are abiding in Him.

So many testified of the leading Evangelists of the Voice of Healing Revival that they spent long periods alone with the Lord. Paul Cain told of waiting on the Lord for hours to get clear understanding of the evening ahead. "I was full of revelation," he said of his younger self, "but didn't have much wisdom." There was a definite difference between the Holy Spirit's ministry through men like Branham, Paul Cain, A.A. Allen and Jack Coe, and the healings witnessed by many other evangelists of the day. Very few maintained a personal anointing that enabled them to continue in the supernatural after the general anointing lifted, and there was a lot of valid criticism of miraculous claims in the 60s and 70s that were simply not true. Unfortunately, this caused people to discount the ones that were valid.

NONE of us are yet where we need to be!

In the Healing Rooms in Adelaide, we operate by revelation. We ask the Lord what the problem is, and he usually always gives us an answer, and we see a measure of healing. There are some occasions where He will not speak, and we have to seek Him further for understanding. Sometimes the subject is simply NOT going to repent of whatever the issue is, or cannot get the faith they need to overcome in time. Sometimes it's us—we go through our battles like everyone else, and it does affect our effectiveness. Generally, however, the Lord gives us insight into the "foothold" the enemy is using to attack the person.

In the other cases, it's back to the prayer closet, where our war is fought. Many Christians know their Bibles by heart, few can apply the Word to their lives effectively. The Pharisees knew the Old Testament by rote, yet were criticised by the Messiah for missing the point (e.g. Luke 11:52). We've been told the Word of God is a Book (the Bible), and we all need to know it better.

The Word of God is a PERSON—the man Christ Jesus.

> *In the beginning was the Word, and the Word was with God, and the Word was God.* ***He*** *was with God in the beginning. Through* ***him*** *all things were made; without* ***him*** *nothing was made that has been made. In* ***him*** *was life, and that life was the light of men. The light shines in the darkness, but the darkness has not understood it.* (Jn 1:1-5)

The Book (the Bible), is that **part** of the Word that was written down as a benchmark, against which all revelation (whether hearing, reading, dreams, vision or "I was there") must be tested. Scripture doesn't tell us as individuals where we should evangelise, how to speak to a particular person, where we need to move to fulfil God's call on our lives, or who to marry. We need to get that from Jesus—direct, by hearing His voice.

> *"My sheep hear My voice, and I know them, and they follow Me"* (Jn 10:27).

Again: **We are way too familiar with a God we barely know!**

The challenge for all of us is to spend more time with the Master—to get into the prayer closet until we can hear Him. Then, to carefully and submissively test what we hear, usually under the guidance of trusted shepherds, so that we grow in confidence. You WILL make mistakes—we ALL do, as you learn to discern Jesus' voice from the loud thumping of your own fleshly desires.

The Fast Track

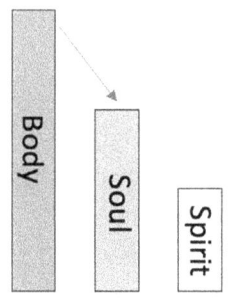

Most Christians are still controlled by their flesh-nature. Their renewed spirit is NOT in charge of their passions.

The most effective way to put the flesh down is fasting—give up SOMETHING for the Lord for a time: your time, your sleep, food, whatever. Discipline yourself to seek the Lord. As 1 Cor 14:4, says: *"He who speaks in a tongue edifies himself..."* An edifice is a building! Praying in the Spirit builds you up on the inside.

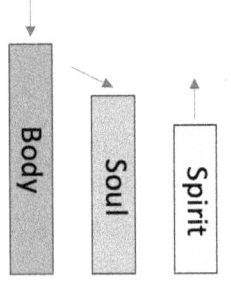

As you put your flesh to death by fasting, and build your spirit up by praying in tongues (1 Cor 14:4), your inner man begins to grow. Your flesh has less of a hold on you.

Praying in Tongues is the only spiritual gift you can turn on at will, and every word you speak is set aside by the Father to build you up. If you haven't been activated in tongues, don't worry. Even in the Old Testament, it says:

*"Make a joyful **noise** unto the LORD..."* (Ps 100:1)

If you have to, go with "La, la, la...." Just keep doing it to the Lord. He will anoint it.

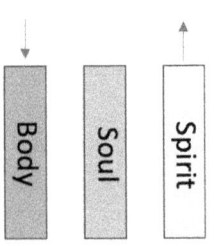

If you continue, you will reach an impasse, where your spirit and flesh are level. This is where all Hell will break loose to try and cause you to give up. This is the Battle Zone.

Keep going. Most of us have a LOT of flesh to overcome. Don't stop.

The Battle phase is where so many Christians break, and give up. Surround yourself with other believers who will encourage you and pray with you. Jesus promised:

> *"You will seek me and find me when you seek me with all your heart"* (Je 29:13).

Eventually you will come to a place where your spirit starts to overtake your flesh, and the Holy Spirit begins to lead and direct your thoughts and actions. This is the place where your prayers start to get answered, because you are beginning to abide in Him.

> *"…because those who are led by the Spirit of God are sons of God"* (Ro 8:14).

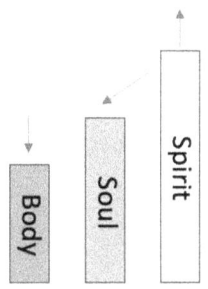

Break through! When your renewed spirit comes into the ascendency, you will find your prayers start coming in answered, because your soul is being led by the Holy Spirit.

We call this the Fast Track! There is no faster way to grow in God, and develop your capacity to carry more of the anointing/presence of the Holy Spirit. Some think they can receive an impartation of the Holy Spirit from another minister, **and they can!** However, most of us cannot hold what we have received, and need another "boost" every few weeks, which has led to the 'conference junkie' phenomenon in recent decades, where believers race from conference to conference to get the latest 'impartation' from a visiting speaker\ We need to develop our capacity to keep what we receive—there are no shortcuts.

And wouldn't you rather get it from Jesus yourself, anyway? So, get yourself ready.

> *Therefore, prepare your minds for action; be self-controlled; set your hope fully on the grace to be given you when Jesus Christ is revealed. As obedient children, do not conform to the evil desires you had when you lived in ignorance. But just as he who called you is holy, so be holy in all you do; for it is written: 'Be holy, because I am holy.'* (1Pe 1:13-16)

Our Lord is returning for a glorious bride, *"without stain or wrinkle or any other blemish, but holy and blameless"* (Ep 5:27).

We can look backwards to the successes of the men who went before us. They set a level in the Spirit that our generation hasn't yet seen. Yet we are called to go even further, and "bear much fruit."

The Lord has warned us of the coming Harvest, the Generation of the Righteous, or the Next Wave of the Holy Spirit.

Will YOU be ready?

45

Prophets and Prophecy

There is a lot of confusion and misunderstanding about prophecy, Prophets and the prophetic in the modern church. Much is being taught by people with no experience of the prophetic, based on their limited understanding of a few Old Testament passages. Some of the better books on the subject are Larry Randolph's *User Friendly Prophecy*, and Mike Bickle's *Growing in the Prophetic*—the latter written from the perspective of a pastor who did not believe in prophecy and ended up with a church full of prophetic ministers.

Just a few points for you to consider…

Several passages list some of the different ways God speaks to people:

> *For God does speak -now one way, now another -*
> *though man may not perceive it.*
> *In a <u>dream</u>, in a <u>vision</u> of the night,*
> *when deep sleep falls on men*
> *as they slumber in their beds,*

> *he may <u>speak</u> in their ears*
> *and terrify them with warnings...* (Job 33:14-16)

> *"If there is a prophet among you,*
> *I, the LORD, shall make Myself known to him in a <u>vision</u>.*
> *I shall speak with him in a <u>dream</u>.*
> *Not so, with My servant Moses,*
> *He is faithful in all My household;*
> *With him I speak <u>mouth to mouth</u>,*
> *Even openly, and <u>not in dark sayings</u>,*
> *And he <u>beholds the form of the LORD</u>."* (Nu 12:6-8)

From these passages we can note: **Dreams** (always symbolic, needing interpretation), **Visions** (a literal observance of an event), **Darkspeech** (Godly puns), **Face-to-face visitation** (angel or theophany), and **Translocation** ('I was there' with Him). Of course, God also (and most commonly) speaks through the revealed word of **Scripture**, which the Holy Spirit can 'quicken' to a man as relevant to their situation.

Old versus New Covenant

Old Testament Prophets and Seers were servants, not sons, operating in the Office of Prophet. Little is known of the "company of the prophets" (1 Sam 19:20) or the "sons of the prophets" (1 Kings 20:35) mentioned in the Bible, except they were not held in the same esteem as the recognised Prophets such as Samuel, Elijah and so on. The Holy Spirit came upon them, and they had a revelatory experience. <u>Their responsibility was to accurately convey that message and its interpretation</u>, and they were revealed as false if what they said in the name of the Lord did not happen.

> *"I will raise up a prophet from among their countrymen like you, and I will put **My words in his mouth**, and he shall speak to them all that I command him. It shall come about that whoever will not listen to My words which he shall speak in My name, I Myself will require it of him. But the prophet who speaks a word **presumptuously** in My name which I have not commanded him to speak, or which he speaks in the name of other gods, that prophet shall die. You may say in your heart, 'How will we know the word which the LORD has not spoken?' When a prophet speaks in the name of the LORD, if the thing <u>does not come about or come true</u>, that is the thing which the LORD has not spoken. The prophet has spoken it presumptuously; you shall not be afraid of him,"* (Dt 18:18-22).

Old Testament Prophets were rare—there was usually only very few on the earth ay any one time. They were sovereign vessels, chosen by God, and appear to have had little choice about accepting or refusing God's call. Old Testament Prophets spoke with the authority of the very words of God. Their "Thus saith the Lord" was not open to question—it was either wrong or right.

Mike Bickle writes: "Because Old Testament prophets received <u>direct and unmistakable revelation</u>, they were 100% accurate… The only way they missed it was because they blatantly changed what God had said or deliberately made up a false prophecy." Therefore, the consequences for such falsification were dire.

Under the New Covenant Jesus brought about, we are adopted as sons of the Father (Romans 8; 2 Corinthians 6:18; Galatians 3:26, 4:5; Ephesians 1:5; Hebrews 12:5,7-8), and Christ is the firstborn (Revelation

1:5). We receive the Holy Spirit indwelling us (John 14:26; Acts 2:17-18), and we need to learn how to hear His voice clearly (John 10:27), and move in the gifts of the Spirit, as He leads.

The gift of prophecy in the New Testament is general—distributed throughout the body of Christ. New Testament prophetic ministers are NOT writing Scripture, and as sons, bear a relational responsibility to the Father, and to their 'siblings' in the words they bring. They are not separated to the Lord living apart, but are part of the Body, involved in the local church, and under authority of leaders.

New Testament revelatory experiences are also different. As sons we are connected by relationship to the Lord in a way that Old Testament prophets were not. "Direct revelation" is rare—most often the Lord speaks through lesser means, which need to be judged, interpreted and correctly applied. The general principle is:

The higher the level of revelation, the greater the consequence for error or disobedience. John Paul Jackson said he would rather have symbolic dreams than literal visions, as he had more grace for not quite "getting it right" if he made a mistake. If an angel, or the Lord Himself shows up, be careful to do **exactly** what you're told. We all want to hear God clearly, but we may not want the consequences our immaturity may bring. Be happy with the simple stuff, and be faithful with what you have. God will grow you as He sees fit. But

"... *eagerly desire the greater gifts*" (1Co 12:31).

In the New Testament, leaders are instructed to "let two or three prophets speak, and let the others judge" (1 Cor 14:29). Paul also tells the Thessalonians: "*Do not quench the Spirit. Do not despise prophecies. Test all things. Hold fast to what is good*" (1 Thessalonians 5:19-21). There is a clear implication that the Old Testament standard has changed—New Testament prophecies **must** be judged, for mixture as well as error.

Not only that, but the Bible is clear that, after Pentecost, all Christians can prophesy:

> *In the last days, God says,*
> *I will pour out my Spirit on **all people.***
> *Your sons and daughters will <u>prophesy</u>,*
> *your young men will see <u>visions</u>,*
> *your old men will dream <u>dreams</u>.*
> *Even on my servants, both men and women,*
> *I will pour out my Spirit in those days,*
> *and they will prophesy.* (Ac 2:17-18)

It seems ridiculous to speak of "stoning" sons and daughters for inaccurate or immature prophetic words. We "*know <u>in part</u> and prophesy <u>in part</u>*" (1 Cor 13:9), **which means there is ALWAYS mixture**. None of us have the full revelation we need—God made us to be a mutually dependent Body. We need others to "test" our words, and assist us to grow in accuracy, maturing in our hearing the voice of the Master. In the same way we grow in the "gifts of the Spirit", as well as the "fruits of the Spirit."

Gift or Office

It is also in the New Testament that we first hear of the **gift** of prophesy (1 Cor 12 and 14), as distinct from the **Office** of Prophet (Eph 4:11). All believers can operate in the gifts, but a person in the Office **is** the gift to the body. Ephesians 2:20 says the church is "built on the foundation of the Apostles and Prophets." There is a <u>foundational</u> aspect to the Office ministries that sets them apart from the gifts that any Christian can access.

There is a lot of misunderstanding about the Corinthians passage on Spiritual gifts. The key word used is "manifestation" of the Spirit. A manifestation is NOT a lasting event. It is a brief, short-term operation of the person in that gift. We can all move in all of the gifts—you did NOT receive **part** of the Holy Spirit, but **all** of Him. This does not mean we should always expect Him to manifest through us in the same way each time we try and minister (though we all do). It's not about us. A person who often operates in a particular gifting may have a ministry in that area. Don't be hasty to claim a title—premature inheritance can be deadly.

Paul Cain spoke of his call to be a "sovereign vessel"—a term the Lord used in a face-to-face encounter. He was called from the womb and set apart by the Lord from an early age. He had no choice about the gifts that manifested in his life—they just happened (and he bitterly resented being different from other children). He told his assistant, Dan Reise, that it was actually very unusual for himself and William Branham to be on the earth together as their gifts were very similar.

Most of us have not had angelic experiences from a young age, or regular prophetic encounters and dreams. We struggle to hear the Lord's voice clearly, and many of us have been taught that spiritual experiences are "demonic deception". We need to spend time with our Lord, waiting on him, and listening for any word He may speak to us.

Dark Speech

God often speaks through "dark sayings"—Holy Ghost puns, coincidences and the like which mean little to others, but give us encouragement or direction. As these are hard to interpret, there are less consequences for mistakes or misunderstanding, but they are usually very personal and help build our intimate walk with our Father.

For example, I was pondering how to introduce the subject of **"threes"**. I told of Paul Cain understanding the Word to the Vineyard from the "555" on the clock (five being the number of Grace—therefore Grace, Grace, Grace).

Three is an important number throughout the Bible, representing the Triune nature of God. Many events in Scripture lasted three days. Jonah was in the belly of the whale for three days, Jesus in the tomb…, Peter's denial and restoration. Raf says in most cases three days of fasting will break off most problems.

Some of the prophets pay attention to hotel room numbers and the like, and the Lord speaks to them through this. I only know a few, such as 7—the number of God (who rested on the 7th day), and 6—the number of Man (created on the 6th day). Another which turns up a lot is "341", which represents the Trinity—"three for one", and it just happened to be the time on the clock when the Lord woke me up this morning! He spoke to my heart today to get onto it.

Anything repeated three times in Scripture is symbolic of that thing being fully completed. It was actually very offensive to a first-century Jew to repeat a question which had been answered. To ask a third time would be a deadly insult. This is why Peter's denial of Jesus (three times) represented a full and complete denunciation. When Jesus restored Peter, he asked him three times, "Simon, do you love me?" The third time Peter was "hurt"—he didn't realise Jesus was undoing each of the denials he had made.

This also gives some insight into the "number of the beast" from Revelation. Six is the number of Man, so 666 represents the worship of a man as god taken to its fullest expression in the end times.

Many years ago Bob Jones prophesied that the Kansas City Chiefs would win the Super Bowl again, and it would be a sign that the Revival was imminent. This happened on 02/02/2020 (a palindrome). It was the coach's 222nd win! It was also the 50th year (Jubilee!) since the Chiefs had made it to the Super Bowl. The number 2 signifies Unity in the Bible, which is a big issue the Lord is highlighting to the church at the moment.

Assumptions

We all tend to make assumptions about how the prophetic works, and what Prophets do or don't know. I heard the stories about Bob Jones seeing the dreams others were having, and thought for a while that was general to all prophets. I have learned that God works differently with them all. Bob was a Seer—all visions, dreams, weird signs and so on. Paul Cain was a Prophet—he would see the amber glory of God rest on a person, and as he looked at it, revelatory "words of knowledge" would come to him.

We don't have a lot of Biblical understanding of the range of revelatory people—we know more about the writing prophets than others such as David's Seer Nathan, simply because there is so much more material. Yet in most cases, they use the phrases "the word of the Lord came to me", or "as I looked…" and we have to try and guess the mechanics of how that gift operated. Reading books by a number of different prophetic people can be helpful, simply to get more of an idea how different they all are.

I take the position that I always expect them to know more than I think, and am often surprised to find out when they don't. I do know, and teach:

A Prophet is known on earth by what they SAY—they are known in heaven by what they DON'T.

It's a good lesson. Just because God shows you something doesn't mean you should tell anyone else. Sometimes he tells us things just for US.

Also, Prophetic people are called to certain places, people and tasks. They don't have authority outside those God-given limits, and need to be careful not to stray in presumption.

Growing Ourselves

We need "eyes to see and ears to hear" the things that God is always speaking to us, whether we are His "sheep", operating in the "gift" of prophecy, or called to a ministry in the prophetic. We need to make time to "wait on the Lord", not just praying, worshiping or reading scripture, but also waiting quietly to listen.

We also need a safe place to practice sharing what we believe we have heard. Find a church or home group who you can journey with, and who can provide a safe place to "have a go". This is both to receive encouragement when we get it right, and be protected when we make a mistake. Let me finish by quoting again the key passage of the Adelaide Healing Rooms:

"If you abide in Me, and My words abide in you, ask whatever you wish, and it will be done for you. My Father is glorified by this, that you bear much fruit, and so prove to be My disciples" (Jn 15:7-8).

Let's aim for that!

46

Further Reading and Sources

Books *(1950s)*
William Branham—A Man Sent From God by Gordon Lindsay
Supernatural: The Life of William Branham (1-6) by Owen Jorgensen
Footprints in the Sands of Time vol 1 & 2 by William Branham
God's Generals by Roberts Liardon
The Price of God's Miracle Working Power by A. A. Allen

(1960s)
Nine O'Clock in the Morning by Dennis Bennett
All Things Are Possible by David Edwin Harrell, Jr

(1970s)
Angels on Assignment by Charles and Frances Hunter
The Man Who Talks With Angels by Sharon White

(1980s)
Power Evangelism by John Wimber

Some Said it Thundered by David Pytches
A Prophetic History by Rick Joyner
Surprised By the Power of The Spirit by Jack Deere
The Happiest People on Earth by Demos Shakarian

(1990s)
Catch the Fire: The Toronto Blessing by Guy Chevreau
There Is Always Enough by Heidi Baker
The Final Quest by Rick Joyner
The Harvest by Rick Joyner
The Nameless and Faceless Generation by Robert Towery
Needless Casualties of War by John Paul Jackson
A. A. Allen and Miracle Valley by Steven Phipps

Magazines/Journals
The Voice of Healing Magazine
Miracle Magazine
The Morningstar Prophetic Journal
The Morningstar Prophetic Bulletin

Taped Messages—Audio
Interview with Bob Jones—Mike Bickle and Bob Jones
The Postman's Letter—Bob Jones and Wes Campbell
Joel's Army, Now in Training—Paul Cain
Naturally Supernatural—John Paul Jackson
The Ministry of William Branham—Paul Keith Davis and Steve Shelley
The Coming Flood—Larry Randolph
Messages from the Ranch—Brent Rue

Video

Interview With Paul Cain—Mike Bickle and Paul Cain

John Wimber—Personal Testimony

Prophetic Experiences & Visions of the End-Time Harvest—Wes Campbell and Bob Jones

Web

Numerous YouTube interviews and sermons on all the major people named. Many links are in the "Prophetic History" and "Voice of Healing Revival" sections of the Ancient Wells website (www.AncientWells.org.au).

Miracle Valley Archives—www.miraclevalleyarchives.org

Voice of God Recordings—www.branham.org—all surviving recordings and transcripts of William Branham's sermons

Afterword

My prayer is that this book will open your eyes to what the Lord has **already** done, so that you can have faith for what He is **about to do**, in which YOU are called to **play a part**. Please continue to research these events and these people God used, separate the "precious from the vile", and ask the Lord to show you which is which.

Our walk as Christians is following our Master—hearing His voice and obeying what we hear. We need to practise our hearing in a "safe" group, and encourage each other to love and good works. You **will** make mistakes, get ahead of God, step out in hope rather than faith….—we **all** do. Don't give up!

Finally, test **everything**, as Paul instructed us to do. I would advise my students never to blindly accept a scientific Paper as accurate, unless they themselves had verified the results. So many mistakes, misprints and outright fabrications are in the public arena, that it is difficult even for professionals in a field to know whom to trust. Fortunately, we have the Spirit of truth living inside us—if we keep seeking Him, we will get there in the end.

Our website for the Ancient Wells Healing Rooms in Adelaide is: www.AncientWells.org.au. If you need help, we'd love to pray with you, and do what we can to assist you grow in faith.

PaulD

www.ingramcontent.com/pod-product-compliance
Lightning Source LLC
Chambersburg PA
CBHW070554100426
42744CB00006B/274